T5-BYU-639

AFC Programmer's
Guide

Université du Québec à Hull
RETIRÉ DE LA
COLLECTION · UQO
2 5 NOV. 1998
Bibliothèque

Stephen R. Davis

Microsoft Press

AFC Class Model

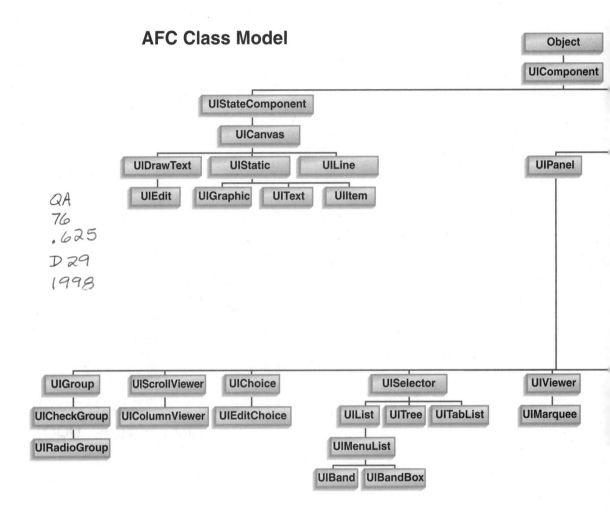

QA
76
.625
D 29
1998

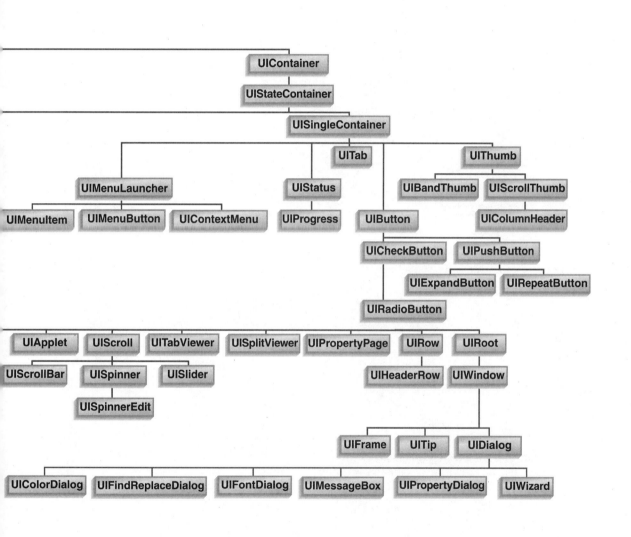

AFC Programmer's Guide

Published by **Microsoft Press**
A Division of Microsoft Corporation
One Microsoft Way
Redmond, Washington 98052-6399

Copyright © 1998 by Stephen R. Davis

All rights reserved. No part of the contents of this book may be reproduced or
transmitted in any form or by any means without the written permission of the publisher.

Library of Congress Cataloging-in-Publication Data
Davis, Stephen R., 1956-
     AFC Programmer's Guide / Stephen R. Davis.
        p.   cm..
     Includes index.
     ISBN 1-57231-732-9
     1. Internet programming. 2. Java (Computer program language)
   3. Microsoft Visual J++. 4. User interfaces (Computer systems)
   5. Application software--Development.   I. Title.
   QA76.625.D38   1998
   005.13'3--dc21   97-44443
                                                         CIP
Printed and bound in the United States of America.

1 2 3 4 5 6 7 8 9   WCWC   3 2 1 0 9 8

Distributed to the book trade in Canada by Macmillan of Canada, a division of Canada Pub-
lishing Corporation.

A CIP catalogue record for this book is available from the British Library.

Microsoft Press books are available through booksellers and distributors worldwide. For further
information about international editions, contact your local Microsoft Corporation office. Or
contact Microsoft Press International directly at fax (425) 936-7329. Visit our Web site at
mspress.microsoft.com.

Macintosh is a registered trademark of Apple Computer, Inc. Microsoft, Microsoft Press,
Visual C++, Windows, and Windows NT are registered trademarks and Visual J++ is a
trademark of Microsoft Corporation. Other product and company names mentioned herein
may be the trademarks of their respective owners.

Companies, names, and/or data used in screens and sample output are fictitious unless otherwise noted.

Acquisitions Editor: Eric Stroo
Project Editor: Victoria Thulman
Manuscript Editor: Jennifer Harris
Technical Editor: Jean Ross

To my son, Kinsey,
and my wife, Jenny.

Table of CONTENTS

Acknowledgments

Even though only a single name appears on the cover, the creation of a book such as this is truly a team effort. This book could not have appeared without the aid of Jennifer Harris, Victoria Thulman, Jean Ross, and Roger LeBlanc, who tirelessly edited my clumsy prose. I would like to thank Derick Jamison and Ford McKinstry for their technical support. Of course, no book would ever be commissioned without the close cooperation of the acquisitions editor and the agent, in my case Eric Stroo and Claudette Moore.

Finally, I would like to thank my fellow members of the Greenville Area Social Pedalists (GASP) bicycle club for their patience during all those rides I didn't join because I was working on the manuscript.

INTRODUCTION

As its name implies, *AFC Programmer's Guide* is a guide to using Microsoft's Application Foundation Classes for Java—or as we in the know prefer to call it, Microsoft AFC.

WHAT IS AFC?

AFC is a set of classes designed by Microsoft to extend the capabilities of Java beyond those provided by the Abstract Windowing Toolkit (AWT), the windowing toolkit built into the standard Java library. AFC adds significant features to the AWT, including tabbed windows, tree lists, splitter windows, three-section windows (such as those used by Microsoft Windows Explorer), repeating buttons, and progress bars—to name just a few.

Despite what you may have heard, AFC is not specific to Microsoft Visual J++, to Microsoft Windows, or to Microsoft Internet Explorer. AFC supports any reasonable implementation of Java on any machine using any operating system (assuming that those machines support Java, of course). In other words, AFC is "100% pure Java."

WHO ARE YOU?

You should be a programmer who wants to get more powerful Java applet–based graphics on the Web in less time and with less effort. You should already be familiar with Java programming at some level. You do not need to be an expert with the AWT. You may even be a total klutz at developing applet windows. Don't worry. This book can help.

What This Book Is Not

This book is not an introduction to Java or Visual J++, but with even a passing knowledge of the syntax of Java, you should be able to understand the information presented.

This book is also not a tutorial in the use of the Visual J++ Integrated Development Environment (IDE). I find the IDE to be largely self-explanatory. However, if you have questions about the IDE, you can always refer to the Visual J++ documentation.

This book is also not an extended press release for AFC. Usually, I try to not let my opinions cloud the message I am trying to convey; however, if I feel strongly about something, I will say so. So if I think some feature of AFC is particularly good, or if I think some feature really stinks, you'll know.

Organization of This Book

AFC Programmer's Guide is divided into three parts:

- **Part One: AFC and Its Roots**—Describes the basis of AFC. This part presents an overview of the components that make up the AWT, including an explanation of the bridging mechanism between AFC and the underlying AWT substratum.

- **Part Two: Modern Componentry**—Describes the components that make up AFC. This part is organized as a reference work with examples. Classes are grouped by function. For example, one chapter concentrates on the subclasses of *UIButton* (*UIPushButton*, *UIRadioButton*, and so on); another examines different types of lists. For each of the major groups of classes, I have provided an example to demonstrate its use.

- **Appendixes**—Parts One and Two are followed by appendixes. Appendix A, "Signing Applets," describes the building and signing of a trusted applet. Appendix B, "Utility Classes Used in This Book," describes a series of versatile non-AFC classes that are used throughout this book to simplify the code examples.

Conventions Used in This Book

Adopting a clear and consistent coding style makes programs easier to write, debug, and understand. If your coding style is the same as everyone else's, so much the better. The Java community seems to have adopted the coding standard shown in the following table. Who am I to change it?

Coding Convention	Example
Identifiers tend to consist of multiple words merged into a single term, with each word retaining an initial capital letter (as opposed to using underscores to separate the individual words).	`class ThisIsAClass {…}`
Static final members appear in all capital letters. This is an exception to the above rule. The first part of the name indicates the role of the member; the second part indicates the value. An underscore divides the two parts.	`public static final int NAVDIR_UP = 1;` `public static final int NAVDIR_DOWN = 2;`
Classes start with a capital letter (other than *I*).	`public class UIButton {…}`
Interfaces start with a capital *I*. (This is a Microsoft-only standard, but I really like it; however, since it is a Microsoft standard, interfaces that originate from the AWT will not follow this rule.)	`public interface IUIAccessible {…}`

Primitive variables start with a single lowercase letter that indicates their type. (This convention does not apply to *static final* members—it appears to be a Microsoft-only standard, based on Hungarian notation, and even then it isn't applied universally.)	`boolean bFlag;`
	`byte yField;`
	`char cOneChar;`
	`int nValue;`
	`long lValue;`
	`float fValue;`
	`double dValue;`

Function names start with a lowercase letter; this letter does not indicate the return type.	`int someFunc() {…}`

Braces are used to indicate a block of code, even if that block is only one line. The braces are aligned with the preceding control structure.	`if (nSomeValue < 0)`
	`{`
	`    nSomeValue = -nSomeValue;`
	`}`

The following table shows the typographical conventions used in this book.

Typographic Convention	Description
monospace	All code examples appear in a monospace font.
italics	Identifier names, defined terms, values, and embedded code strings are shown in italics when they appear within text.

LET'S GET STARTED

This book is full of examples. Practically every class in AFC has an example program dedicated to it. However, you learn better by actually doing. Go over the example programs in detail—study and modify them. Once you feel comfortable with the examples, write a few applets of your own. Only when you dig in can you really master AFC. So let's get started.

Using the Companion CD

The Sample Files

The CD included with this book contains all the sample programs discussed in the book. The samples are in the Samples folder:

- Samples for Part One, Chapters 1 through 4, are in the App_PartI subfolder.
- Samples for Part Two are in subfolders named for book topics that relate to the samples.

Installing the Sample Files

You can view the samples from the CD, or you can install them onto your hard disk and use them to create your own AFC applets.

 NOTE

If you're unable to browse the files in the Samples folder, you might have an older CD driver that doesn't support long filenames. If this is the case, to browse the files, you must install the sample files on your hard disk by running the setup program.

Installing the sample files requires approximately 10 MB of disk space. To install the sample files, insert the CD into your CD-ROM drive and run Setup.exe. If you have trouble running any of the sample files, refer to the Readme.txt file in the root directory of the CD.

You can uninstall the files by selecting Add/Remove Programs from the Control Panel, selecting AFC Programmer's Guide, and clicking the Add/Remove button.

MICROSOFT VISUAL J++ VERSION 1.1 TRIAL EDITION

Another folder you'll find on the CD is VJTrial, which contains the files for installing Microsoft Visual J++ version 1.1 Trial Edition. If you do not have Visual J++, you can install this trial version and use it to work with the sample files. You'll find all the information regarding Visual J++ Trial Edition in the Readme files contained in the VJTrial folder.

MICROSOFT SDK FOR JAVA VERSION 2.0

Also included on the CD is the Microsoft SDK for Java version 2.0. To install the SDK on your hard disk, run SDKSetup from the JSDK folder. For information on the SDK, visit the Microsoft Web site at www.microsoft.com/java.

NOTE

Install the Visual J++ Trial Edition before you install the SDK.

SUPPORT

For troubleshooting help and support information, see the Readme.txt file in the root directory of the CD.

Part One reviews the concepts that make up the Abstract Windowing Toolkit (AWT) and then examines some recent additions to the AWT, such as the delegation model for event processing. Part One concludes with an introduction to the concepts behind Microsoft Application Foundation Classes (AFC).

Part One sets the stage for Part Two, which guides you through the different classes that make up the AFC and provides you with numerous examples that show how to use these classes in your applications and applets.

PART
ONE

AFC AND ITS ROOTS

Is the Abstract Windowing Toolkit for Real?

I find it's always helpful to begin with a little background before jumping into the primary topic—in this case, Microsoft Application Foundation Classes (AFC). This chapter starts by examining a few of the design considerations behind the Abstract Windowing Toolkit (AWT), the precursor to AFC. Then it discusses the limitations of the AWT contained in Java 1.0 before examining how the AWT in Java 1.1 addresses a few—but only a few—of these problems. The chapter concludes with an overview of AFC, including a discussion of how AFC addresses most of the problems inherent in the AWT.

THE JAVA GUI: A STICKY PROBLEM

From its inception, the Java language was designed as a platform-independent, World Wide Web–oriented language. This Web orientation puts several constraints on a programming language. It means that the executables should be as small as possible to allow for quick downloads. And it forces the language to somehow support multiple CPUs and operating systems with a single executable. In addition, it creates the need to enforce strict security so that malicious applets cannot destroy the hard disk of an unsuspecting person browsing the Web. (The Web is a dangerous enough place to play without people threatening to trash your hard-earned but not backed up disk files.)

Add to this an even greater problem: supporting multiple types of graphical user interfaces (GUIs). Programs aren't worth very much if they can't display output to the user. In fact, these days the snazzier the output, the better. Computer users insist on their GUIs. Be it Microsoft Windows on PCs, Motif in the UNIX world, or Finder among die-hard Apple Macintosh hangers-on, "It don't mean hooey if it ain't got a GUI."

The developers of Java were very much aware of this fact of computer linguistic life. If Java was going to be accepted, it had to support the same type of windowed environment that users were accustomed to seeing in their dedicated applications. But Java's Web preference imposed special requirements.

Although similar, the three main GUI standards (Windows, Motif, and Macintosh) are sufficiently different that users can immediately tell them apart. Java couldn't simply adopt one of these existing standards without alienating the adherents of the other two standards. Suppose Java did pick one of the existing interface standards—say, Motif—for its user interface. While this choice would be ideal for UNIX-based platforms, it would greatly complicate the job of porting Java to Windows-based and Macintosh-based platforms.

Another complicating factor is that Java was designed to execute within a Web browser (for the reasons outlined earlier). The appearance of the windows differs from one browser to the next. Because browser windows can be resized, the applet cannot even be certain of the size or orientation of the window in which it will be executing.

For all of these reasons, the developers of Java created the AWT.

THE ABSTRACT WINDOWING TOOLKIT

The AWT is the windowing package of the Java language, in much the same way that the Microsoft Foundation Classes (MFC) constitute a windowing package for the Visual C++ language. Thus, the AWT is not actually part of the language itself. Just as it's possible to write Windows-based programs in C++ without relying on MFC, it's possible to write Java applets that don't use the AWT; however, there are good reasons not to try it.

Is the Abstract Windowing Toolkit for Real?   CHAPTER

1

Java puts great stock in being portable. In large part, it is the AWT that gives Java much of that machine independence. Using the AWT, the programmer can generate a single sophisticated display that will execute under browsers on numerous different machines.

Structure of the AWT

The AWT consists of two groups of classes: one set I describe as the *direct draw classes* and a second set as the *component classes.* The direct draw classes, such as *Graphics*, give the developer the ability to write directly to the browser display. The developer can draw lines, arcs, and various other shapes in different colors. She can even draw images in the form of GIF or JPEG files to an applet window.

The component classes allow the programmer to create a component, such as a button or a text field, and attach it along with other components to a container. A container might be a window or a dialog box. For example, in Chapter 2, "The Components of the AWT," we will create the applet window shown in Figure 1-1 by attaching Button, TextField, and Label components to a window Frame container.

FIGURE 1-1   *A simple window frame created using the AWT.*

Creating such GUI windows by using the component classes is much easier than creating them "by hand." Component objects handle the details of displaying themselves in today's best finery, including full-color 3-D shadowing. Further, once the programmer has created components and added them to the proper containers, he no longer has to deal with the individual components. An operation performed on the container applies to all components within that container.

Problems with the AWT 1.0

The AWT was initially released with version 1.0 of the Java Development Kit (JDK). While the AWT provided numerous benefits, it also suffered from a number of limitations. Some of these shortcomings are discussed in the following sections.

The AWT lacks detailed control

The programmer doesn't have as much control of the GUI's appearance by using the AWT 1.0 as she would by using a more conventional library such as MFC. For example, the developer does not control the direct placement of objects within a window frame.

The level of control that the AWT programmer has is similar to that provided by the HTML language itself. In the case of HTML, the Web page developer can bracket a piece of text within an H1 element to indicate that the text should be displayed in a large "header 1" font, but he cannot specify the exact font to use, nor can he even specify the size of that font. Instead, the browser grants the developer's request as best it can from the fonts it has available on the current machine.

So it is with the AWT controls. The Java programmer can suggest the positioning of these objects—for example, by indicating that this object should be to the left of that one and this one over here below that one over there. The exact placement, however, is left up to the browser. Perhaps this problem is unavoidable in a language designed to be portable across multiple platforms. Unfortunately, this inability to control precise placement means that the AWT does not generate the same results on all platforms, which complicates the job of generating a machine-independent applet.

The AWT does not provide object-oriented event handling

Not only does the AWT know to handle the output of simple components to the display, but it can also handle input from the user to these components. When the user clicks a button created from an AWT object, for example, an event is fired that eventually makes its way back to the applet for processing.

Unfortunately, the event handling mechanism in AWT 1.0 places the event handling code for all components into a single method of the applet, which means that the method must know about all of the components of all the windows within the applet. The single event handling method turns into a large *switch* statement with cases for each input component. Even the beginning

Is the Abstract Windowing Toolkit for Real?   CHAPTER

1

student of object-oriented programming will recognize that this approach is not object-oriented. Working with this mechanism revealed that it was in need of improvement.

The AWT 1.0 is a low-level tool

Most of the features of the AWT are relatively low level. Components exist for basic concepts such as buttons, text fields, and the like, but more sophisticated features such as band boxes and tabbed windows, to name a few, are missing. Even the relatively simple job of scrolling a window requires the programmer to write a considerable amount of code. Other fairly standard operations are missing completely. For example, the AWT includes no capabilities to support printing or cut-and-paste. Programmers require more from their code libraries these days than what the AWT offers.

The AWT is not optimized for Windows

Although multiplatform capability is a desirable property, the majority of browsers are executing under some form of Windows. Unfortunately, the AWT 1.0 was not optimized for Windows. This limitation means that AWT-based applets generate nonoptimal performance on the majority of browsers in use.

The base size of a component object is roughly 120 bytes. For conventional disk-based programming languages such as C++, this size might not sound like much, even when a single window consists of dozens of components. However, for Web applets, this size is significant—the sizes of the components themselves can add materially to the download time of the applet.

An Incremental Improvement—AWT 1.1

During the early part of 1997, Sun Microsystems released version 1.1 of the JDK. Included as part of the JDK 1.1 were several enhancements to the AWT.

The AWT 1.1 adds several features completely lacking from the AWT 1.0. The two most important are a cut-and-paste capability, which the AWT calls data transfer, and a set of classes that allow applets to print to the printer.

The AWT 1.1 also adds a new event handling mechanism called event delegation. The AWT 1.1 continues to support the existing AWT 1.0 event handling mechanism to remain backward compatible, but it discourages the programmer from using the older scheme because of the problems mentioned earlier. The

AWT 1.1 does not support both event models within the same applet. I will talk about event delegation in more detail in Chapter 3, "Delegation Model Event Processing."

The AWT 1.1 includes a series of relatively minor additions such as *ScrollPane*—a class that creates a scrollable window—and an extended math package. The math package includes features such as a class capable of performing accurate calculations on numbers with an essentially unlimited number of digits.

Last, the AWT 1.1 was rewritten to achieve better performance under Windows.

The AWT 1.1 left untouched many of the problems inherent in the AWT 1.0, however. The AWT 1.1 classes provide no greater level of control than version 1.0 of the AWT. Very few new component types were added to the AWT in version 1.1. The choices of display options remain just as limited. The AWT 1.1 classes are just as big as those of the AWT 1.0. And finally, despite improvements, the AWT 1.1 is not optimized for Windows performance.

ENTER THE APPLICATION FOUNDATION CLASSES

Microsoft's AFC addresses many of the limitations of the AWT. The AFC look and feel has been updated to more closely resemble that of modern GUIs—in particular, Windows. AFC includes support for selection trees, drop-down lists, band boxes, tabbed windows, and other features that Windows users have grown accustomed to.

Like the AWT 1.1, AFC supports event delegation; however, AFC allows both 1.1-style and 1.0-style event handling in the same applet, which increases the flexibility for the programmer. In addition, supporting both models simultaneously makes the transition from 1.0-style to 1.1-style event handling easier because new components using 1.1-style event handling can be added to an existing applet without the need to completely rewrite the event handling for existing components that use the older 1.0 style.

AFC is optimized for Windows to a greater degree than the AWT, resulting in both better appearance and superior performance on Windows-based PCs. Furthermore, AFC is written completely in Java and is portable across platforms in the same way that the AWT is.

Is the Abstract Windowing Toolkit for Real?   CHAPTER

1

Microsoft has also decreased the size of the applet by basing AFC components not on a common base class, as was the case with the AWT, but on a common base interface. This restructuring reduces the theoretical smallest size for a component to zero. Although most components are larger than that, they are smaller than the AWT components.

WHAT'S NEXT

So far, the discussion has been pretty theoretical. Any Java programmer, and even any AFC programmer, needs to understand how the AWT works. In the remaining chapters of Part One, I'll delve into the AWT in more detail. This close examination will provide the foundation you'll need for the remainder of this book, when we'll turn our attention to AFC itself.

The Components
of the AWT

Any programmer who wants to use AFC needs a firm grounding in the care and feeding of the Abstract Windowing Toolkit (AWT). If you feel like you are grounded enough in the AWT, feel free to just skim this chapter on your way to Chapter 3, "Delegation Model Event Processing." Most programmers will want to at least look over the examples in this chapter, however.

Overview of the **AWT**

The AWT consists of a series of classes divided among four Java packages:

- **java.awt**—The java.awt package contains the majority of the AWT. The classes that are not part of java.awt are contained in one of the following three packages.

- **java.applet**—The java.applet package consists of the single class *Applet*. The *Applet* class is the base class for all applets. This class defines methods such as *start*, *stop*, *init*, and *destroy*, which are used to interface with the browser.
- **java.awt.image**—The java.awt.image package contains the classes designed to perform image manipulation such as clipping and filtering.
- **java.awt.peer**—The java.awt.peer package consists of *peer classes*. Peer classes are those classes that are specific to the current machine. These classes interface the generic Java classes that you as a mere mortal Java programmer use with the underlying browser and operating system.

The classes that make up the AWT fall into two broad categories:

- component classes
- direct draw classes

In this chapter, I will quickly go over the AWT component classes. The AWT direct draw classes will be discussed in Part Two, along with the AFC direct draw classes.

CLIPPING AND FILTERING IMAGES

Images start out as GIF or JPEG files on disk. These files are read into an object of class *Image*, which is actually part of the java.awt package. *Clipping* is the act of creating a subset of an image. The clipping functions take one *Image* object and produce another containing the data from some rectangular subset of the original. *Filtering* transforms the original image. For example, Filtering can create a new *Image* object in which all of the red pixels are replaced by green pixels.

AWT Basics

As mentioned in Chapter 1, "Is the Abstract Windowing Toolkit for Real?" the component classes represent common objects that appear in most application windows. There are component classes for buttons, text fields, list boxes, and so on. Each of these classes extends the base class *Component*.

A separate set of component classes represents several of the most basic window types. These classes are called *containers* because they extend the class *Container* (and because they contain components). For example, *Panel*, *Window*, and *Dialog* are all subclasses of *Container*.

To construct user interfaces, the programmer arranges graphical components such as buttons and text fields within containers such as a window frame. Unlike most windowing libraries, the AWT does not allow the developer to control the direct placement of objects within the window frame. But the developer can influence the placement of components both in the order in which they are added to the container and through a special set of classes called *layout managers*. (All layout manager classes implement the interface *LayoutManager.*)

AWT Example

The following simple example highlights how AWT components work together. This applet opens a dialog box containing a labeled, empty text field. When the user clicks the OK button, the applet reads the text field and displays it in the applet window. (Of course, a real applet would do something more worthwhile than simply display the text, but you get the idea.)

NOTE

> The examples in this chapter build on one another. In most cases, only the code that differs from the previous example will be shown. You can view all the code for each project from the companion CD.

The HTML page for this applet is shown here:

```
<html>
<head>
<title>App2_1</title>
</head>
<body>
<hr>
<applet
    code=App2_1.class
    name=App2_1
    width=200
    height=200 >
</applet>
<hr>
<a href="App2_1.java">The source.</a>
</body>
</html>
```

Notice that the App2_1 applet appears between the two <hr> elements just as an image or a table might. To the HTML page, the applet is nothing more than a window producer in the same way that a reference to an image file is.

The applet source JAVA file is shown here:

```java
// App2_1 - Displays a simple dialog box contained within
//          a resizable frame
import java.applet.*;
import java.awt.*;

public class App2_1 extends Applet
{
    // Name entered in dialog box
    String sName = null;

    // Component container
    MyFrame frame = new MyFrame(this, "Important Input");

    // init - Set the dialog box's frame size and show the frame.
    public void init()
    {
        resize(200, 200);

        // Make the frame resizable and
        // set its initial size.
        frame.setResizable(true);
        frame.resize(100, 100);

        // Now make the whole thing visible.
        frame.show();
    }

    // paint - Display the name entered.
    public void paint(Graphics g)
    {
        // If the name has not been updated,...
        if (sName == null)
        {
            // ...just output the message; otherwise,...
            g.drawString("Nothing entered yet.", 20, 20);
            return;
        }

        // ...output the name entered.
        g.drawString("Entered " + sName, 20, 20);
    }

    // setName - Update the name field and repaint the applet
    //           in order to redisplay the name.
```

```java
    public void setName(String sName)
    {
        this.sName = sName;
        repaint();
    }
}


// MyFrame - Creates a frame with three components
class MyFrame extends Frame
{
    // Parent applet
    App2_1 applet = null;

    // Components within the dialog box
    TextField txtfld = new TextField(25);
    Label     label  = new Label("Enter name:");
    Button    button = new Button("OK");

    MyFrame(App2_1 applet, String sTitle)
    {
        // Pass the frame title to the
        // Frame(String) constructor.
        super(sTitle);

        // Now save the applet - we'll need this information
        // to call setName when the user clicks OK.
        this.applet = applet;

        // Use the simplest layout manager - FlowLayout.
        setLayout(new FlowLayout());

        // Add label, text field, and OK button.
        add(label);
        add(txtfld);
        add(button);
    }

    // handleEvent - This method is called whenever
    //               anything happens within the dialog box.
    public boolean handleEvent(Event evt)
    {
        // Retrieve the target object from the
        // event.
        Object oTarget = evt.target;
```

>>

>>

```
        // If this is the OK button,...
        if (oTarget == button)
        {
            // ...save the contents of
            // the text field...
            String sName = txtfld.getText();

            // ...and pass them to the applet.
            applet.setName(sName);
            return true;
        }
        return false;
    }
}
```

The *App2_1* class begins by defining a string that will be used to contain the name entered by the user. It then defines a *Frame* object that will contain the dialog box. The frame is initialized to an object of class *MyFrame*; its title is set to *Important Input.*

NOTE

I could have used one of the other containers, such as *Window, Panel,* or even *Dialog,* to contain the dialog box components; however, *Frame* provides a basic window with all the standard Microsoft Windows–like window dressings such as Close buttons.

The *App2_1* class implements only two of the *Applet* class methods. The *init* method is invoked when the applet is first loaded into the browser. This method sets the initial size of the frame, makes it resizable, and then makes it visible. The *paint* method is invoked whenever the window needs to be refreshed. This method displays the name last entered in the dialog box. If the user has yet to enter anything, *paint* displays the message "Nothing entered yet." The *App2_1* class also implements a method, *setName*, that is not a method of the *Applet* class. The *setName* method enables *MyFrame* to report the name entered in the dialog box text field to the applet.

The *MyFrame* class provides a particular type of dialog box by extending the *Frame* class. The particular dialog box that *MyFrame* generates has a fixed label (*label*), a text field in which the user enters his name (*txtfld*), and an OK button (*button*). Each of these objects is created when the *MyFrame* object is created.

NOTE

> The only difference between the *MyFrame* and *Frame* classes is the addition of the new *handleEvent* method. This method handles the user's clicking of the OK button. In Chapter 3, "Delegation Model Event Processing," I will explain in greater detail the handling of user events, and I will demonstrate how to use the event delegation event handling model present in AWT 1.1.

The constructor for *MyFrame* invokes the *Frame* constructor, explicitly passing it the frame's title, by calling the *super* method.

 NOTE

> Invoking the *super* method on the first line of the constructor has the effect of passing arguments to the base class constructor—in this case, *Frame*.

The *MyFrame* constructor then attaches the label, text field, and button to the frame using the *add* method. This last step is the essence of the AWT's component/container model. The *Frame* class is one form of container. The *Label*, *TextField*, and *Button* classes are various forms of components. Adding these components to the container essentially makes the container responsible for the components' well-being.

The initial results of this layout are shown in Figure 2-1.

FIGURE 2-1   *The initial dialog box displayed by the App2_1 applet.*

 NOTE

> Notice the Minimize, Maximize, and Close buttons, which come standard with the *Frame* class.

This dialog box looks OK, but the name of the frame has been severely truncated because it won't fit in the space allocated and the OK button is a bit chopped off. If the frame is sized too small, you might even see the status bar partially hidden beneath the OK button as shown in Figure 2-1. So let's make the dialog box bigger. Figure 2-2 shows the dialog box after you've grabbed the lower right corner and dragged it down and to the right.

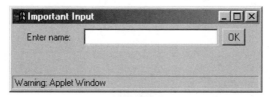

FIGURE 2-2   *The result of resizing the App2_1 dialog box frame.*

Now there's plenty of room for the dialog box title and the OK button is not cropped. But wait a minute. The entire appearance of the dialog box has changed. The label now appears to the left of the text box instead of above it, and the OK button is off to the right instead of at the bottom.

Before you start complaining, think about it. Why did the dialog box take on the initial appearance shown in Figure 2-1? There was nothing in the code to indicate that the components should be arranged one on top of another. The browser chose that arrangement on its own based on the size of the dialog box frame. It shouldn't be too surprising then that resizing the dialog box frame results in a different configuration of components on the display.

Go back and take a closer look at the App2_1 applet. The amount of code dedicated to creating and displaying the dialog box frame is actually quite small. The component/container model embodied in the AWT simplifies the task of creating intricate, high-performance windows within HTML pages. Nevertheless, is there nothing we can do to affect the appearance of our dialog box?

Controlling Appearance Using Layout Managers

Layout managers are used to control the presentation of components within a container. The App2_1 applet used the layout manager *FlowLayout*, the simplest of the layout managers. In *FlowLayout*, the container arranges components in a general left-to-right fashion until there is no more room in the window, at which point it drops the components down to the next line and starts again at the far left.

Using *BorderLayout*

Several other layout managers are available in addition to *FlowLayout*, including *BorderLayout*, *GridLayout*, and *GridBagLayout*. The default layout manager for the *Frame* class is *BorderLayout*. *BorderLayout* gives the programmer somewhat more control than *FlowLayout* by allowing her to place components in one of five regions in the window.

The parts of the window are named for the compass directions rather than top, bottom, left, and right. The programmer can attach components to each of these four parts of the window plus the center. Each time the window is resized, the AWT first allocates the components on the top (*North*) and bottom (*South*) of the window. That done, the AWT then allocates space along the left (*West*) and right (*East*) sides of the window. Any remaining space is allocated to the center (*Center*) component. This allocation scheme is shown in Figure 2-3.

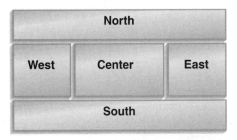

FIGURE 2-3   *The five regions of the window as allocated by the AWT.*

The App2_2 applet is essentially the same as App2_1, but App2_2 uses *BorderLayout.*

```
// MyFrame - Creates a frame with three components
class MyFrame extends Frame
{
    // Parent applet
    App2_2 applet = null;

    // Components within the dialog box
    TextField txtfld = new TextField(25);
    Label     label  = new Label("Enter name:");
    Button    button = new Button("OK");

    MyFrame(App2_2 applet, String sTitle)
    {
        // Pass the frame title to the
        // Frame(String) constructor.
        super(sTitle);
```

>>

>>

```
        // Now save the applet - we'll need this information
        // to call setName when the user clicks OK.
        this.applet = applet;

        // Use BorderLayout - note that this layout manager is
        // actually the default for the Frame class.
        setLayout(new BorderLayout());

        // Add label, text field, and OK button.
        add("North",  label);
        add("Center", txtfld);
        add("South",  button);
    }

    // handleEvent - This method is called whenever
    //               anything happens within the dialog box.
    public boolean handleEvent(Event evt)
    {
        // Retrieve the target object from the
        // event.
        Object oTarget = evt.target;

        // If this is the OK button,...
        if (oTarget == button)
        {
            // ...save the contents of
            // the text field...
            String sName = txtfld.getText();

            // ...and pass them to the applet.
            applet.setName(sName);
            return true;
        }
        return false;
    }
}
```

This code fragment selects an object of class *BorderLayout* to be the layout manager. It then attaches the label along the top of the dialog frame (*North*), the button along the bottom of the frame (*South*), and the text field in the middle (*Center*), between the two. The method *add(String, Component)* is reserved for use with containers that use *BorderLayout*.

Figure 2-4 shows the initial result of running App2_2.

FIGURE 2-4   *Initial display from the App2_2 applet.*

So far, this dialog box doesn't look much different from the App2_1 dialog box created using *FlowLayout*. The differences between the two become apparent, however, when the window is expanded, as shown in Figure 2-5.

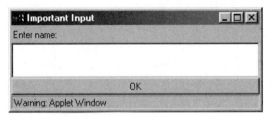

FIGURE 2-5   *Expanded display from the App2_2 applet.*

As you can see, the label hugs the top of the window and the OK button stays along the bottom as the window expands. Both keep their original vertical height, but they expand in the horizontal direction to take up any available space. The text field in the center expands in both directions to fill any left-over space.

This is not quite the effect I was looking for. The label is fine. The OK button extending all the way across the window is a bit nonstandard but not objectionable. However, the text field is misleading. Vertical expansion gives the user the impression that he can enter multiple lines of data; however, because this is just a simple *TextField*, only one line of data can be entered. We would like to somehow keep the text field from expanding vertically.

This problem can be solved—still using the *BorderLayout* layout manager—by recognizing that the *Container* class is a subclass of *Component*. This means that one *Container* class can be added to another *Container* class. Thus, rather than add the text field to the center of the dialog box frame, I can take a two-step approach. This technique is shown in the next code snippet, which is taken from App2_3.

```
// MyFrame - Creates a frame with three components
class MyFrame extends Frame
{
    // Parent applet
    App2_3 applet = null;

    // Components within the dialog box
    TextField txtfld = new TextField(25);
    Label     label  = new Label("Enter name:");
    Button    button = new Button("OK");

    MyFrame(App2_3 applet, String sTitle)
    {
        // Pass the frame title to the
        // Frame(String) constructor.
        super(sTitle);

        // Now save the applet - we'll need this information
        // to call setName when the user clicks OK.
        this.applet = applet;

        // Use BorderLayout  note that this layout manager is
        // actually the default for the Frame class.
        setLayout(new BorderLayout());

        // Add label, text field, and OK button.
        add("North",  label);
        add("South",  button);

        Panel center = new Panel();
        center.setLayout(new BorderLayout());
        center.add("North", txtfld);
        center.add("Center", new Label());
        add("Center", center);

    }

    // handleEvent - This method is called whenever
    //                 anything happens within the dialog box.
    public boolean handleEvent(Event evt)
    {
        // Retrieve the target object from the
        // event.
        Object oTarget = evt.target;

        // If this is the OK button,...
        if (oTarget == button)
```

```
        {
            // ...save the contents of
            // the text field...
            String sName = txtfld.getText();

            // ...and pass them to the applet.
            applet.setName(sName);
            return true;
        }
        return false;
    }
}
```

In this code, the label and button are attached to the north and south edges of the dialog box frame, respectively, just as before. Instead of attaching the text field directly to the center of the frame, however, this applet first creates a dummy panel named *center*. The text field is attached to the top of this dummy panel, and an empty label is attached to the center of the panel. The dummy panel will expand to take up any remaining space as the dialog box frame expands. Rather than vertically expanding the text field, however, Java expands the invisible label in the center of the dummy panel. Once the panel has been constructed, it is added to the center of the dialog box frame.

 NOTE

Adding a container, such as a *Panel* object, to another container is allowed because the *Container* class extends the *Component* class and, therefore, a container is a component. However, you cannot add a *Frame* class to another *Container* class (even though *Frame* is a component) because *Frame* has window dressing.

The resulting expanded dialog box, which is shown in Figure 2-6, is much more to my liking.

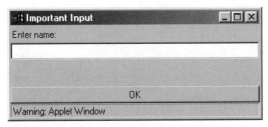

FIGURE 2-6   *Superior results from* BorderLayout *by using containers within containers.*

Using *GridBagLayout*

By using a combination of components and containers, it is generally possible to get close to the results we want using the *BorderLayout* layout manager. The *GridBagLayout* layout manager, however, allows the programmer to get even closer to the desired result—but at the cost of a considerable increase in complexity, as the applet in this section demonstrates.

Again, only the *MyFrame* class differentiates the App2_4 applet from its predecessors. This version of *MyFrame* shows the use of *GridBagLayout*:

```
// MyFrame - Creates a frame with three components
class MyFrame extends Frame
{
    // Parent applet
    App2_4 applet = null;

    // Components within the dialog box
    TextField txtfld = new TextField(25);
    Label     label  = new Label("Enter name:");
    Button    button = new Button("OK");

    MyFrame(App2_4 applet, String sTitle)
    {
        // Pass the frame title to the
        // Frame(String) constructor.
        super(sTitle);

        // Now save the applet - we'll need this information
        // to call setName when the user clicks OK.
        this.applet = applet;

        // Use GridBagLayout.
        GridBagLayout layout = new GridBagLayout();
        setLayout(layout);

        // For GridBagLayout, we will need another
        // object, named GridBagConstraints.
        GridBagConstraints c = new GridBagConstraints();

        // Position the label to the left of the first line.
        c.weightx   = 1.0;
        c.weighty   = 0.0;
        c.gridwidth = GridBagConstraints.REMAINDER;
        c.anchor    = GridBagConstraints.WEST;
        layout.setConstraints(label, c);
        add(label);
```

```
        // Now position the text field in the center of the second
        // line, but don't let it fill the available space.
        c.weightx   = 1.0;
        c.weighty   = 0.0;
        c.gridwidth = GridBagConstraints.REMAINDER;
        c.anchor    = GridBagConstraints.NORTH;
        layout.setConstraints(txtfld, c);
        add(txtfld);

        // Center the OK button on the last line.
        c.weightx   = 0.0;
        c.weighty   = 1.0;
        c.gridwidth = GridBagConstraints.REMAINDER;
        c.gridheight= GridBagConstraints.REMAINDER;
        c.anchor    = GridBagConstraints.SOUTH;
        layout.setConstraints(button, c);
        add(button);
    }

    // handleEvent - This method is called whenever
    //                anything happens within the dialog box.
    public boolean handleEvent(Event evt)
    {
        // Retrieve the target object from the
        // event.
        Object oTarget = evt.target;

        // If this is the OK button,...
        if (oTarget == button)
        {
            // ...save the contents of
            // the text field...
            String sName = txtfld.getText();

            // ...and pass them to the applet.
            applet.setName(sName);
            return true;
        }
        return false;
    }
}
```

The first thing you'll notice about the *GridBagLayout* layout manager is the additional structure known as *GridBagConstraints*. The *GridBagConstraints* object is used to hold extra positioning information about each component before it is attached to the container. *GridBagConstraints* provides both the flexibility and the complexity of *GridBagLayout*. The programmer sets the desired display properties in *GridBagConstraints* before calling *setConstraints*. The *setConstraints* method creates a copy of the *GridBagConstraints* object and attaches it to the component for use during the layout phase. This code shows just a subset of the different properties that can be set using *GridBagConstraints*. Nevertheless, you can see from this example the level of control available.

Here objects are laid out in a left-to-right, top-to-bottom order. Unlike with the *FlowLayout* layout manager, however, the programmer determines how the components are laid out along the rows and how the rows are laid out within the window. The *weightx* property is used to specify to what extent a component will be expanded in the *x*-direction in the event that the dialog box is larger than the sum of the component widths in that row. The *weighty* property serves a similar purpose in the *y*-direction. Setting either property to *0* indicates that the component is not to be resized in that direction when the window is enlarged.

The *gridwidth* property specifies the width of the component. Setting *gridwidth* to *REMAINDER* tells *GridBagLayout* that this component is the last object in the row. The *anchor* property is similar but not identical to the directional parameters used in the *BorderLayout* layout manager.

In App2_4, I have placed the label on the first line. I have specified that the label can be expanded horizontally but not vertically as the user expands the dialog box. I have used *gridwidth* to indicate that the label is on the row by itself and *anchor* to indicate that the label should be left-justified (WEST). Similarly, the text field can be resized horizontally but not vertically and is centered on the row. Last, the OK button appears at the bottom of a vertically expandable row. The button is not resizable horizontally.

The expanded dialog box for the App2_4 applet is shown in Figure 2-7. This dialog box appears to be just what we're looking for. As the user expands the window vertically, both the label and the text field stay together, unexpanded, at the top of the window. The OK button stays at the bottom of the window. The OK button retains the appearance of a button—it does not expand horizontally across the entire window. Allowing the button to expand vertically does not actually make the button any larger. Rather, it allows the button component to take up the remainder of the vertical space between the text field and the bottom of the window.

Even though this version of the *MyFrame* class is considerably longer and more complicated than its predecessors, *GridBagLayout* allows the programmer to specify more accurately his display preferences than was possible with the simpler *BorderLayout* and *FlowLayout* layout managers.

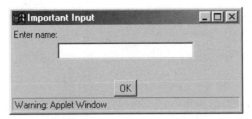

FIGURE 2-7   *Ideal output from the* GridBagLayout *layout manager using the proper constraints.*

OTHER COMPONENTS

You can only do so much with a label, a text field, and an OK button. What other component arrows are in the AWT quiver? The next applet, App2_5, demonstrates the use of the *Choice*, *Checkbox*, and *List* objects. Before we get into the App2_5 applet code, however, let's take a look at the output from it, shown in Figure 2-8.

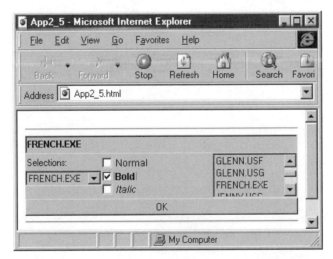

FIGURE 2-8   *A simple file selection applet window using the* Choice, Checkbox, *and* List *components.*

This applet represents a simple file selection applet window. Along the left is a *Choice* component. Clicking the down arrow causes a drop-down list to open showing the contents of a disk directory. When the user selects one of the items from this drop-down list, the applet displays the selection in the read-only text field along the top of the dialog box. This display can be in normal, boldface, or italics, depending on which of the mutually exclusive check boxes has been checked. The list box on the right shows the contents of the same directory.

The list box is ignored in this applet—it appears just to show you what one looks like. The interface to a *List* object is about the same as the interface to a *Choice* object.

CAUTION

> Because this applet accesses the file system, it must be trusted, meaning that either the applet must be executed on the user's machine from the Visual J++ IDE or the applet must be signed with a valid certificate. (The third option, disabling security for Microsoft Internet Explorer, is strongly discouraged.) See Appendix A for instructions on how to sign an applet to make it trustworthy.

The code for the App2_5 applet is shown here:

```
// App2_5 - Demonstrates the use of the Choice (select box),
//           List, and Checkbox objects
import java.applet.*;
import java.awt.*;
// The class from the AppCommon directory is used to
// populate the directory listing
import FileDescr;

public class App2_5 extends Applet
{
    Button      button = new Button("OK");
    Choice      choice = new Choice();
    List        list   = new List(10, true);

    Panel          checks = new Panel();
    CheckboxGroup  grp    = new CheckboxGroup();
    FontCheckbox   bold   = new FontCheckbox("Bold",   Font.BOLD);
    FontCheckbox   italic = new FontCheckbox("Italic", Font.ITALIC);
    FontCheckbox   normal = new FontCheckbox("Normal", Font.PLAIN);

    TextField txtfld = new TextField();

    String[] items   = null;

    public void init()
    {
        // Use BorderLayout.
        setLayout(new BorderLayout());

        // Create an item list consisting of the names
        // of the files in the C:\ directory.
        updateChoiceList();
```

```java
// Update the Choice component with the item list,
// and position it on the left.
for (int i = 0; i < items.length; i++)
{
    choice.add(items[i]);
}
Panel choiceWin = new Panel();
choiceWin.setLayout(new BorderLayout());
Label label = new Label("Selections:");
choiceWin.add("North", label);
choiceWin.add("Center", choice);
add("West", choiceWin);

// Do the same thing for a list on the right.
// (We won't do anything with this list -
// it's just an example.)
for (int i = 0; i < items.length; i++)
{
    list.add(items[i]);
}
add("East", list);

// Position the OK button at the bottom.
add("South", button);

// Create a window in the middle with the three
// check boxes in it.
checks.setLayout(new BorderLayout());
checks.add("North", normal);
checks.add("Center", bold);
checks.add("South", italic);
add("Center", checks);

// Adding the check boxes to the group will ensure
// that only one of them is set at a time.
// (Start out with normal set to true.)
bold.setCheckBoxGroup(grp);
italic.setCheckBoxGroup(grp);
normal.setCheckBoxGroup(grp);
normal.setState(true);

// Now add a text field at the top to display
// the selected entry.
txtfld.setEditable(false);
txtfld.setFont(normal.getFont());
add("North", txtfld);
```

>>

```
            // Now that we've finished, make the whole thing visible.
            setVisible(true);
        }

        // updateChoiceList - Update items with listing
        //                    of a specific directory.
        public void updateChoiceList()
        {
            // Create a file description object on the target
            // directory.
            FileDescr dir = new FileDescr("c:");

            // Allocate space for the number of files found there.
            int nCount = dir.getChildCount();
            items = new String[nCount];

            // Now populate items with the names of the files.
            for (int i = 0; i < nCount; i++)
            {
                items[i] = dir.getChild(i);
            }
        }

        // action - If one of our hot items is selected,
        //          invoke the proper procedure to process it.
        public boolean action(Event e, Object o)
        {
            if (e.target == choice)
            {
                processChoice();
                return true;
            }

            if (e.target instanceof Checkbox)
            {
                processCheckbox();
                return true;
            }

            if (e.target == button)
            {
                processOK();
                return true;
            }
            return false;
        }
```

```
// processChoice - Read the current selection from the
//                 list box and display it in the text field.
public void processChoice()
{
    String s = choice.getSelectedItem();
    txtfld.setText(s);
}

// processCheckbox - Get the font from the currently
//                   selected check box and set the
//                   text field to be displayed with it.
public void processCheckbox()
{
    FontCheckbox selected = (FontCheckBox)grp.getCurrent();
    Font font = selected.getFont();
    txtfld.setFont(font);
    repaint();
}

// processOK - Hide the applet display.
public void processOK()
{
    setVisible(false);
}
}

// FontCheckbox - A check box with an associated Font
//                (could be any property)
class FontCheckbox extends Checkbox
{
    Font font;

    FontCheckbox(String label, int nFontType)
    {
        super(label);
        font = new Font("Arial", nFontType, 12);
    }

    public Font getFont()
    {
        return font;
    }
}
```

App2_5 starts by defining the basic components, *button*, *choice*, and *list*, in addition to three check boxes, *bold*, *italic*, and *normal*. I'll explain the purpose of the *Panel* and *CheckboxGroup* objects later. (Some things are better left until the end.) I'll also return shortly to the fact that our buttons are of type *FontCheckbox*, a local subclass of *Checkbox*, rather than *Checkbox* itself.

Since this applet attaches the components directly to the applet window, there is no need to create a new window, so *init* immediately sets about the task of attaching and displaying components. First it establishes a *BorderLayout* layout manager for itself.

Next *init* needs a list of files to display in the *choice* component. The local function *updateChoiceList* performs a directory search of the directory C:\. Of course, this function could be changed to search any directory on the hard disk that you like. Under different circumstances, the directory might be entered by the user as a string value. The class *FileDescr* is constructed using the name of the directory. The call to *FileDescr.getChildCount* returns the number of files in the directory. The call to *FileDescr.getChild(i)* returns a *String* object containing the i'th filename in that directory. (The class *FileDescr* is one of the classes located in the AppCommon directory on the companion CD; these classes are described in Appendix B.)

The selection box *choice* object is empty when the applet is first constructed. Once *updateChoiceList* has finished creating the list of filenames in *items*, *init* adds the members of *items* to the *choice* object in the *for* loop. That completed, the applet adds *choice* to the center of a dummy panel with a label at the top. The dummy panel is then attached to the left side of the applet window.

The elements in the *items* array are also added to the list that is attached directly to the right side of the applet window. Unlike the *choice* object, this list allows multiple selections. (Remember, in this applet this list is provided for appearance only. I don't do anything with its contents.)

The applet attaches an OK button along the bottom and a read-only text field along the top of the applet window. The *txtfld.setEditable(false)* method ensures that the text field is read-only.

The *normal*, *bold*, and *italic* check boxes are placed inside the *checks* panel, which is then added to the center of the applet window. Placing the check boxes in a common panel is a good way of keeping them together.

Notice that once the check boxes have been added to the panel, they are then added to a *CheckboxGroup* named *grp* using the *Checkbox.setCheckboxGroup* method. Adding check boxes to a check box group has the effect of making the check boxes mutually exclusive, like radio buttons. When the user checks a check box, the check box group deselects the check box that is currently active. The call to *normal.setState(true)* causes the *normal* check box to be selected by default.

Once all of the components have been added to the window, the applet window is made visible by calling the *setVisible* method. This call is left to the end so that the user does not see the components appear one by one as they are attached.

NOTE

The Java Development Kit (JDK) 1.1 method *setVisible(true)* replaces the *show* method of JDK 1.0, and *setVisible(false)* replaces *hide*. The older functions are kept around in the Java 1.1 library, but they are now marked as deprecated. Marking a method as *deprecated* means that compiling any function that calls that method will generate a compiler message warning the programmer not to use that method because it might go away in future versions. This renaming of functions in JDK 1.1 was done to provide a more consistent set of method names.

The *action* method is called when the user activates any of the components in the applet window. The arguments to *action* include an *Event* object that describes the user action. The *Event.target* object references the component that was activated. Thus, the applet looks through all of the components it knows anything about. For example, if the user activates the *choice* component—the user selects a filename from the drop-down list—*action* passes control to the *processChoice* function. Likewise, *processCheckbox* handles the activation of any of the three check boxes, and *processOK* handles clicks on the OK button. If the *Event* object does not refer to any of these three conditions, *action* returns *false*, meaning that it did not process the event.

The three process functions are simple. The *processChoice* function reads the filename selected by the user through the *choice.getSelectedItem* method and stores it in the text field for display. The *processOK* function hides the applet window, giving the user the impression that the applet is complete.

The *processCheckbox* function changes the font used to display the file selection in the text field to either normal, boldface, or italic, depending on which check box was checked. Of the many ways this formatting could have been accomplished, the most straightforward approach might look something like the following:

```
// processCheckbox - A less elegant approach to processCheckbox
//                   using multiple if statements
public void processCheckbox(Checkbox cb)
{
    Font font;
    if (cb == normal)
    {
        font = new Font("Arial", Font.NORMAL, 12);
    }
    if (cb == italic)
    {
        font = new Font("Arial", Font.ITALIC, 12);
    }
    if (cb == bold)
    {
        font = new Font("Arial", Font.BOLD, 12);
    }
    txtfld.setFont(font);
    repaint();
}
```

While this is a common approach, in my opinion it is not the best solution. This technique makes it difficult to add new fonts because the programmer must look into the application code to find all the places where the application checks to see which check box is being selected.

The more object-oriented solution is to make the font a property of the check box. For this reason, I introduced the *FontCheckbox* class. If you examine the *FontCheckbox* class, you'll see that it is nothing more than a *Checkbox* object with an associated *Font* property. When the applet creates the check box, it automatically associates the font. From then on, it's left up to the check box to keep track of its font. All the applet has to do is ask *FontCheckbox* for its font and assign whatever value it gets to *txtfld*.

Now to add additional fonts all I would have to do is define a new instance of *FontCheckbox* and add it to the *checks* panel. No changes to *action* or any other internal method of the applet would be necessary. (I realize that *action* is the only method requiring change in this simplistic applet, but remember that "real world" applets tend to be a lot larger and more complex than the applets appearing in books. The places requiring change using the first approach might not be nearly so obvious in a larger applet.)

NOTE

> In "object-oriented speak," this property of being able to add components without changing the internal code is called *extensibility*. We say that the first approach is not extensible, while the second is. Note that the second approach works equally well for other properties, including active properties. You'll see this approach demonstrated again at the end of this chapter.

OTHER CONTAINERS

As I demonstrated in the first four applet examples in this chapter, the applet window is not the only type of container available to the AWT programmer. The most common container (other than *Applet*) is *Frame*. A *Frame* object is a window with all the window dressings we have come to expect.

Creating our file window in a separate *Frame* is reasonably straightforward, except for one thing: a *Frame* object is independent of *Applet*. The most important implication of this independence is that actions generated by clicking on a component in *Frame* don't propagate up to *Applet*'s *action* method. Instead, *Frame* must have its own *action* method, which means there must be a separate communication path back to *Applet* through which *Frame* can communicate the user's selections.

You can see this drama played out in the App2_6 applet:

```
// App2_6 - Includes the components from App2_5 in
//          a separate window of class Frame
import java.applet.*;
import java.awt.*;
import FileDescr;

// ISetSelection - Provides the setSelection method,
//                 which allows other classes to
//                 report back user selection(s)
interface ISetSelection
{
    public void setSelection(Object[] selection);
}
```

>>

```
>>    public class App2_6 extends Applet implements ISetSelection
      {
          Frame   frame      = new MyFrame("Select a file", this);
          String selection = "No selection";

          // init - Add a single button that opens MyFrame.
          public void init()
          {
              setLayout(new BorderLayout());
              add("South", new Button("Make Selection"));
              setVisible(true);
          }

          // paint - Display previous selection.
          public void paint(Graphics g)
          {
              g.drawString(selection, 10, 20);
          }

          // action - When the user clicks the Make Selection
          //          button, show the selection window.
          public boolean action(Event e, Object o)
          {
              if (e.target instanceof Button)
              {
                  frame.setVisible(true);
                  return true;
              }
              return false;
          }

          // setSelection - MyFrame calls this method to inform
          //                the applet of the user's selection
          //                when the user clicks OK.
          public void setSelection(Object[] selections)
          {
              // Hide the selection window.
              frame.setVisible(false);

              // If there is a selection...
              if (selections.length >= 1)
              {
                  // ...and if it's a String object,...
                  Object o = selections[0];
```

```
            if (o instanceof String)
            {
                // ...update selection and display it.
                selection = (String)o;
                repaint();
            }
        }
    }
}

// MyFrame - This selection window is just like the applet in
//           App2_5 except that it's a separate window.
class MyFrame extends Frame
{
    ISetSelection parent = null;

    Button    button = new Button("OK");

    Choice    choice = new Choice();
    List      list   = new List(10, true);

    Panel     checks = new Panel();
    CheckboxGroup grp= new CheckboxGroup();
    FontCheckbox  bold   = new FontCheckbox("Bold",   Font.BOLD);
    FontCheckbox  italic = new FontCheckbox("Italic", Font.ITALIC);
    FontCheckbox  normal = new FontCheckbox("Normal", Font.PLAIN);

    TextField txtfld = new TextField();

    String[] items = null;

    MyFrame(String title, ISetSelection parent)
    {
        // Create the Frame object with given title.
        super(title);

        // Record the parent applet.
        this.parent = parent;

        // Set the size, and then fix it.
        setSize(350, 150);
        setResizable(false);

        // Use BorderLayout.
        setLayout(new BorderLayout());
```

>>

```
// Create an item list consisting of the names
// of the files in the directory C:\.
updateChoiceList();

// Update the Choice component with the item list,
// and position it on the left.
for (int i = 0; i < items.length; i++)
{
    choice.add(items[i]);
}
Panel choiceWin = new Panel();
choiceWin.setLayout(new BorderLayout());
Label label = new Label("Selections:");
choiceWin.add("North", label);
choiceWin.add("Center", choice);
add("West", choiceWin);

// Do the same thing for the list on the right.
// (We won't do anything with this list -
// it's just an example.)
for (int i = 0; i < items.length; i++)
{
    list.add(items[i]);
}
add("East", list);

// Position the OK button at the bottom.
add("South", button);

// Create a window in the middle with the three
// check boxes in it.
checks.setLayout(new BorderLayout());
checks.add("North", normal);
checks.add("Center", bold);
checks.add("South", italic);
add("Center", checks);

// Adding the check boxes to the group will ensure
// that only one of them is set at a time.
// (Start with normal set to true.)
bold.setCheckboxGroup(grp);
italic.setCheckboxGroup(grp);
normal.setCheckboxGroup(grp);
normal.setState(true);
```

```
        // Now add a text field at the top to display
        // the selected entry.
        txtfld.setEditable(false);
        txtfld.setFont(normal.getFont());
        add("North", txtfld);
    }


    // updateChoiceList - Update items with a listing
    //                    of a specific directory.
    void updateChoiceList()
    {
        // Create a file description object on the target
        // directory.
        FileDescr dir = new FileDescr("c:");

        // Allocate space for the number of files found there.
        int nCount = dir.getChildCount();
        items = new String[nCount];

        // Now populate items with the names of the files.
        for (int i = 0; i < nCount; i++)
        {
            items[i] = dir.getChild(i);
        }
    }


    // action - If one of our hot items is selected,
    //          invoke the proper procedure to process it.
    public boolean action(Event e, Object o)
    {
        if (e.target == choice)
        {
            processChoice();
            return true;
        }

        if (e.target instanceof Checkbox)
        {
            processCheckbox();
            return true;
        }

        if (e.target == button)
        {
            processOK();
            return true;
        }
        return false;
    }
```

>>

```
    // processChoice - Read the current selection from the
    //                  list box, and display it in the text field.
    public void processChoice()
    {
        String s = choice.getSelectedItem();
        txtfld.setText(s);
    }

    // processCheckbox - Get the font from the currently
    //                    selected check box, and set the
    //                    text field to be displayed with it.
    public void processCheckbox()
    {
        FontCheckbox selected =
                    (FontCheckbox)grp.getSelectedCheckbox();
        Font font = selected.getFont();
        txtfld.setFont(font);
    }

    // processOK - Report the selected field to the parent.
    public void processOK()
    {
        String txt = txtfld.getText();

        Object[] selection = new Object[1];
        selection[0] = txt;
        parent.setSelection(selection);
    }
}

// FontCheckbox - A check box with an associated Font
//                (this could be any property); this
//                approach is more extensible than the alternative
//                approach of leaving the font in the applet.
class FontCheckbox extends Checkbox
{
    Font font;

    FontCheckbox(String label, int nFontType)
    {
        super(label);
        font = new Font("Arial", nFontType, 12);
    }

    public Font getFont()
    {
        return font;
    }
}
```

The *init* method of the App2_6 applet creates a single Make Selection button before making itself visible and departing. The *paint* method displays the name of the file last selected in the file selection frame. This name is stored in the data member *selection*, which is initialized to *No Selection*.

When the user checks the Make Selection button, control is passed to the applet's *action* method. Because all the real work is done in the file selection frame, this method does nothing more than unhide *frame* and then exit.

The *setSelection* method is provided to give the file selection frame a means of reporting the user's selection to the applet. The *setSelection* method expects the file selection frame to return an array containing a single *String* object. This string is stored in the *selection* data member for display to the user by the *paint* method.

The *MyFrame* class implements the file selection frame. The constructor for *MyFrame* looks suspiciously like the *init* method from App2_5. In fact, the entire remainder of the applet looks almost the same as App2_5 except for the *processOK* method. This similarity is hardly surprising because *MyFrame* in App2_6 plays the role of the applet window in App2_5. The only reason *processOK* changes is because the selected filename must be reported to the applet through the *ISetSelection* interface.

What's with This *ISetSelection* Interface?

Why mess with the *ISetSelection* interface anyway? And why goof around with an array of objects when there will be only one selection and it will always be a *String* object?

I could have defined App2_6 along the following lines:

```
public class App2_6
{
    // Everything else the same...
    public void setSelection(String selectedFileName)
    {
        selection = selectedFileName;
    }
}
class MyFrame extends Frame
{
    App2_6  parent;
```

>>

```
MyFrame(String title, App2_6 parent)
{
    // Everything else the same...
}
// All the same here too until we get to processOK()...
void processOK()
{
    parent.setSelection(txt);
}
}
```

This version of App2_6 makes no pretense of generality. *MyFrame* is designed to handle one and only one parent, an object of class *App2_6*.

By introducing the *ISetSelection* interface to the original App2_6 applet, however, I wanted to demonstrate how a class like *MyFrame* can be built a bit more generally. *MyFrame* does not require anything from its parent other than the ability to report its results through the *setSelection* method. While forcing the parent to be of class *App2_6* is acceptable for this particular problem, it seems overly restrictive. Thus, as long as its parent implements the interface *ISetSelection*, *MyFrame* is happy.

So why make *setSelection* handle an array? Because the *List* object allows multiple selections. When queried, the *List* class reports an array of strings containing all of the items selected from the list.

Can We Have a *Dialog* About This?

You may think it odd that a file selection dialog box is contained in an object of class *Frame*. Why not class *Dialog*?

There are good reasons why you might want your dialog box in a *Frame* class. For one thing, frames are resizable and can be minimized. Frames can be scrolled. Frames are nonmodal. Dialog boxes created with the *Dialog* object do not have window dressings, so they can't be minimized, they are not resizable, and they cannot be scrolled. Dialog boxes may or may not be modal.

NOTE

A *nonmodal* window does not preclude the user from interacting with other windows. By contrast, a *modal* window captures all user input until the window is hidden or destroyed. Attempts to select another window when a modal window is displayed usually result in an annoying beep.

The part about being resizable and scrollable is simple enough, but how do I know whether I need a modal dialog box? The answer depends largely on the application. Does it make sense to allow the user to do something else before she has answered the questions posed by the dialog box? If not, the dialog box should be modal.

My tendency is to make dialog boxes nonmodal whenever possible. If the user opens a modal dialog box only to find that he has forgotten some data needed for input, he will have to cancel out of the dialog box to find the missing information and then reopen the dialog box. As a user, I am irritated by this.

On the other hand, if your dialog box is not modal your parent applet needs some way of knowing when the user has finished entering data. In App2_6, I used the *setSelection* interface method. The file selection dialog box did not call the method until the user clicked OK.

Nonmodal dialogs can also complicate debugging by introducing numerous extra, perhaps illogical paths as the user opens a dialog box and then proceeds down some other, unrelated path without closing the dialog box. To keep the number of debugging paths to a minimum, nonmodal dialog boxes should never report partial results. A nonmodal dialog box should keep all information to itself until the user clicks OK (or Cancel). Only then should the dialog box report back to the parent.

Placing a dialog box inside an object of class *Dialog* is accomplished easily enough. App2_7 shows the same example applet as App2_6, this time in a *Dialog* object.

```
// App2_7 - Uses a Dialog container to hold the
//          dialog box from App2_6. It's a little
//          more work to create, but this dialog box can be modal.
import java.applet.*;
import java.awt.*;
import FileDescr;


// ISetSelection - Provides the setSelection method,
//                 which allows other classes to report
//                 user selection(s)
interface ISetSelection
{
    public void setSelection(Object[] selection);
}
```

>>

```
public class App2_7 extends Applet implements ISetSelection
{
    // Same as before...
}


// MyFrame - To convert this to a Dialog object is a simple
//           modification.
class MyFrame extends Frame
{
    Dialog dialog = null;

    // MyFrame - Create a subordinate dialog box with
    //           this frame as its parent.
    MyFrame(String label, ISetSelection parent)
    {
        dialog = new MyDialog(label, parent, this);
    }

    // setVisible - Leave the current frame invisible,
    //              but show/hide the subordinate dialog box.
    public void setVisible(boolean b)
    {
        dialog.setVisible(b);
    }
}

// MyDialog - The Dialog class equivalent of MyFrame in App2_6.
class MyDialog extends Dialog
{
    // This class is the same as MyFrame in App2_6
    // except for the following change to the constructor.
    MyDialog(String title, ISetSelection applet, Frame parent)
    {
        // Create a modal dialog box with given title.
        // (Setting the third argument to false would make the
        // dialog nonmodal.)
        super(parent, title, true);

        // Record the parent applet.
        this.parent = applet;

        // Set the size. (Dialog boxes are not resizable.)
        setSize(350, 150);

        // Create an item list consisting of the names
        // of the files in the directory C:\.
        updateChoiceList();

        // The rest of the constructor is the same...
    }
}
```

The *MyDialog* class has been added to handle the chores that were handled by *MyFrame* in the earlier applet. The *MyFrame* class is still required because the constructor for *Dialog* requires a parent *Frame* object in which to open the dialog box. Notice that the third argument in the call to the *Dialog* constructor specifies whether the dialog box is modal or nonmodal. Setting this argument to *true* makes the dialog box modal.

Cheating—The *FileDialog* Class?

As it happens, Java provides a class, *FileDialog*, that performs the same operations as our applets (only much better). The *FileDialog* class is shown in App2_8:

```
// App2_8 - Uses the FileDialog class to do all the work
//          instead of doing it manually (like we've
//          done up to now)
import java.applet.*;
import java.awt.*;
import java.io.File;

public class App2_8 extends Applet
{
    MyFrame frame     = new MyFrame("Select a file");
    String  selection = null;

    // init - Add a single button.
    public void init()
    {
        setLayout(new BorderLayout());
        add("South", new Button("Make Selection"));
        setVisible(true);
    }

    // paint - Display previous selection.
    public void paint(Graphics g)
    {
        if (selection == null)
        {
            g.drawString("No selection", 10, 20);
            return;
        }
        g.drawString(selection, 10, 20);
    }

    // action - When the user clicks the Make Selection
    //          button, show the file selection dialog box,
    //          read it, and then close it.
```

>>

```
>>            public boolean action(Event e, Object o)
              {
                  if (e.target instanceof Button)
                  {
                      selection = frame.readFileDialog();
                      repaint();
                      return true;
                  }
                  return false;
              }
        }

        // MyFrame - This frame lets a FileDialog object do all the work;
        //           it relies on the fact that FileDialog dialog boxes are
        //           modal.
        class MyFrame extends Frame
        {
            FileDialog dialog = null;

            // MyFrame - Create a subordinate dialog box with
            //           this frame as its parent.
            MyFrame(String label)
            {
                dialog = new FileDialog(this, label, FileDialog.LOAD);
                dialog.setDirectory("c:");
            }

            // readFileDialog - Show the file dialog box, read the file
            //                  entered, and then close the dialog box.
            public String readFileDialog()
            {
                // Open the dialog box on top of everything else.
                setVisible(true);
                toFront();
                dialog.setVisible(true);

                // Note: We don't get here until the user clicks OK
                // because the dialog box is modal.
                String s = dialog.getFile();
                dialog.setVisible(false);
                setVisible(false);
                return s;
            }
        }
```

The *init* method of App2_8 looks much the same as its predecessors, as does the *paint* method. The *action* event invokes *frame.readFileDialog* when the user clicks the Make Selection button.

The constructor for *MyFrame* simply creates the *FileDialog* object and starts it off in the root directory C:\. The *frame.readFileDialog* method makes the *File-Dialog* object visible. Because the *FileDialog* object is by definition modal, control will not return from this call until the user has clicked either the OK or the Cancel button. *MyFrame* reads the file selection using the *dialog.getFile* method. (This method returns *NULL* in the event the user selects Cancel instead of OK.)

NOTE

This technique would not work if *FileDialog* were nonmodal because the call to *getFile* would occur before the user had a chance to select a file. It's only because *FileDialog* is modal that this type of approach is allowed.

WHAT'S ON THE MENU?

The other major group of component objects we have not yet covered are those associated with menus. App2_9 demonstrates a simple applet that creates a *Frame* object adorned with a menu across the top:

```
// App2_9 - Example menu applet
import java.applet.*;
import java.awt.*;
import java.io.File;

public class App2_9 extends Applet
{
    MyFrame frame = new MyFrame("Command Frame", this);

    // init - Add a single button.
    public void init()
    {
        setLayout(new BorderLayout());
        add("South", new Button("Open Frame"));
        setVisible(true);
    }
```

>>

>>

```
// action - When the user clicks the Open Frame
//          button, show the file selection dialog box,
//          read it, and then close it.
public boolean action(Event e, Object o)
{
    if (e.target instanceof Button)
    {
        frame.setVisible(true);
        return true;
    }
    return false;
}
}


// MyFrame - Attach a unique menu bar (MyMenuBar) to the
//           frame; when the user selects one of the menu
//           items, invoke the associated process method.
class MyFrame extends Frame
{
    Applet parent = null;

    // Menu members
    MenuBar mb = new MyMenuBar();

    // MyFrame - Create an empty frame with a menu bar.
    MyFrame(String label, Applet parent)
    {
        super(label);
        this.parent = parent;

        // Set the size of the frame.
        setSize(300, 100);

        // Attach a menu bar across the top.
        setMenuBar(mb);
    }

    // action - When the user selects one of the menu items,
    //          take the associated action.
    public boolean action(Event e, Object o)
    {
        if (e.target instanceof MyMenuItem)
        {
            MyMenuItem mmiTarget = (MyMenuItem)e.target;
            mmiTarget.process(parent, this);
            return true;
        }
```

```
            return false;
        }
    }


    // MyMenuBar - A user-defined menu bar
    class MyMenuBar extends MenuBar
    {
        Menu mFile = new Menu("File");
        MenuItem miFileOpen = new MyMenuItem("Open");
        MenuItem miFileClose= new MyMenuItem("Close");
        MenuItem miSeperator= new MyMenuItem("-");
        MenuItem miFileExit = new MyExitMenuItem("Exit");

        Menu mEdit = new Menu("Edit");
        MenuItem miEditCopy = new MyMenuItem("Copy");
        MenuItem miEditCut  = new MyMenuItem("Cut");
        MenuItem miEditPaste= new MyMenuItem("Paste");

        Menu mAbout= new Menu("About");

        MyMenuBar()
        {
            mFile.add(miFileOpen);
            mFile.add(miFileClose);
            mFile.add(miSeperator);
            mFile.add(miFileExit);
            add(mFile);

            mEdit.add(miEditCopy);
            mEdit.add(miEditCut);
            mEdit.add(miEditPaste);
            add(mEdit);

            add(mAbout);
        }
    }


    // MyMenuItem - A MenuItem with an additional process
    //              method, which is invoked when the menu item
    //              is selected; the default process method
    //              does nothing more than display the name of the
    //              menu item in the applet status bar.
    //              Note: This approach is much more extensible than
    //              checking for particular menu items in the
    //              parent frame.
```

>>

>>

```
class MyMenuItem extends MenuItem
{
    MyMenuItem(String label)
    {
        super(label);
    }

    void process(Applet applet, Frame frame)
    {
        applet.showStatus(getLabel());
    }
}


// MyExitMenuItem - This particular menu item has a different
//                  process method; presumably, a different
//                  subclass of MyMenuItem would be needed for
//                  each type of menu action.
class MyExitMenuItem extends MyMenuItem
{
    MyExitMenuItem(String label)
    {
        super(label);
    }

    void process(Applet applet, Frame frame)
    {
        super.process(applet, frame);
        frame.setVisible(false);
    }
}
```

In this applet, the *MyFrame* class creates a customized menu of class *MyMenuBar* and attaches it to the top of the frame using the *setMenuBar* method.

NOTE

Only a *Frame* object can have a menu bar.

MyMenuBar creates three *Menu* objects, labeled *File*, *Edit*, and *About*. In addition, *MyMenuBar* creates menu items for the File and Edit menus. The constructor for *MyMenuBar* adds these subordinate menu items to the *Menu* objects before adding the *Menu* objects to the menu bar, as demonstrated in Figure 2-9.

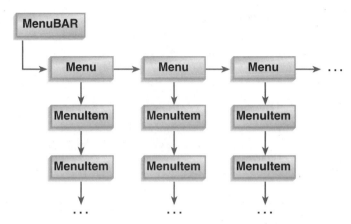

FIGURE 2-9   *The relationship between the* Menu, MenuBar, *and* MenuItem *objects.*

Figure 2-10 shows the resulting applet with the File menu visible.

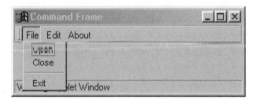

FIGURE 2-10   *The App2_9 applet executing with the File menu open.*

Taking Action on Menu Selections

Displaying menu options is the easy part. Taking action when the user selects a menu item is the next step. Because the menu bar is attached to the *MyFrame* object, this is where the action events from selecting menu items are forwarded. *MyFrame.action* looks for targets of class *MyMenuItem*. All other events are passed on for default processing.

When *MyFrame.action* detects a *MyMenuItem* object, it simply asks the object to process itself by calling the class's *process* method. The *process* method is the only reason for the existence of the *MyMenuItem* class—*MyMenuItem* is simply a *MenuItem* class plus the *process* method.

MyMenuItem.process does nothing more than display the menu item label in the applet's status bar (the area at the bottom of the browser window frame). To complete this applet, the programmer would create a new subclass for each menu item, each with its own *process* method. To demonstrate how this works, I created one example, *MyExitMenuItem*.

Take a look back at the definition of *MyMenuBar*. Notice that the Exit menu item on the File menu is an object of the *MyExitMenuItem* class. Thus, the *MyExit-MenuItem.process* function is invoked when the user selects Exit. This method calls *MyMenuItem.process* before hiding the frame.

NOTE

This approach is very similar to that taken in App2_5. In that applet, I created a new *FontCheckbox* class, which was a *Checkbox* class with a *Font* property added. Adding this class allowed me to associate the *Font* property with the check box in a way that was more extensible than the alternative technique of using a list of *if* statements, one for each *Checkbox* object.

Here I have done the same thing with an active property. I have added a *process* method to *MenuItem* to create the *MyMenuItem* class. By subclassing *MyMenuItem*, I can add new menu items to App2_9 without the need to modify such internal functions as *MyFrame.action*.

WHAT'S NEXT

In this chapter, you've seen most of the classes that make up the AWT in action. You've seen applets, windows, frames, and dialog boxes. You've worked with buttons, text fields, labels, select boxes, and menus. In addition, you've seen how to process events from those objects in an object-oriented, extensible fashion.

In Chapter 3, "Delegation Model Event Processing," we'll expand on this knowledge by examining some of the new features of AWT 1.1, including a streamlined approach to event processing that takes advantage of the listener interface. We'll also look at how inner classes contribute to more efficient, simpler event delegation.

Delegation Model
Event Processing

Even if you are an old hand at the AWT and skipped right over Chapter 2 with nary a glance, there are several additions to the recently released Java 1.1 that you need to know about. One of these features, which has also been adopted by AFC, is *event delegation.* Input into a Java applet almost always involves some type of event processing. The applet presents a series of components in a frame or in the applet window itself. Every action that the user takes triggers an event of some type. If the applet wants to respond to this user input, it must field and process the event. The error-prone event processing model provided by the AWT 1.0 has been replaced by a more streamlined approach in version 1.1 of the AWT.

THE PROBLEM

The event processing model included in the original AWT was based on the *action* method of the container. The following snippets, adapted from the App2_9 applet discussed in Chapter 2, "The Components of the AWT," demonstrate the most common event processing approaches.

Suppose that I had three menu options from which the user could select. My *Frame* class might look like the following code (which shows only the event processing portions of the class):

```
class MyFrame extends Frame
{
    MenuItem miFileOpen  = new MenuItem("Open");
    MenuItem miFileClose = new MenuItem("Close");
    MenuItem miFileExit  = new MenuItem("Exit");

    public boolean action(Event e, Object o)
    {
        // Check to see whether one of our menu items has been
        // selected.
        if (e.target == miFileOpen)
        {
            // Process File Open here.
            return true;
        }

        if (e.target == miFileClose)
        {
            // Process File Close here.
            return true;
        }

        if (e.target == miFileExit)
        {
            // Process File Exit here.
            return true;
        }
        return false;
    }
}
```

The problem with this approach becomes obvious when you consider that most programs with menus offer many more than three options. This approach can result in an *action* method that is too large to be easily maintainable. Dividing the processing into different functions makes the problem a bit more tractable by minimizing the size and complexity of *action*:

```
class MyFrame extends Frame
{
    MenuItem miFileOpen  = new MenuItem("Open");
    MenuItem miFileClose = new MenuItem("Close");
    MenuItem miFileExit  = new MenuItem("Exit");
```

```
public boolean action(Event e, Object o)
{
    // Check to see whether one of our menu items has been
    // selected.
    if (e.target == miFileOpen)
    {
        processFileOpen();
        return true;
    }

    if (e.target == miFileClose)
    {
        processFileClose();
        return true;
    }

    if (e.target == miFileExit)
    {
        processFileExit()
        return true;
    ]
    return false;
    }
}
```

While better, this approach is still not extensible. To add another menu option or set of menu options, you have to go into the *action* method and add new *if* statements.

ONE SOLUTION

App2_9 avoided the problems presented by a single "do it all" *action* method by creating a new subclass of *MenuItem* for each menu option, each with its own *process* method. Armed with these new classes, the *action* method is reduced to the following:

```
class MyFrame extends Frame
{
    // FileOpenMenuItem, FileCloseMenuItem, and
    // FileExitMenuItem are all subclasses of MyMenuItem.
    MyMenuItem miFileOpen  = new FileOpenMenuItem();
    MyMenuItem miFileClose = new FileCloseMenuItem();
    MyMenuItem miFileExit  = new FileExitMenuItem();
```

>>

```
>>        public boolean action(Event e, Object o)
          {
              if (e.target instanceof MyMenuItem)
              {
                  MyMenuItem mmiTarget = (MyMenuItem)e.target;
                  mmiTarget.process();
                  return true;
              }
              return false;
          }
      }


// MyMenuItem - Adds the process method to the MenuItem class
class MyMenuItem extends MenuItem
{
    // Invoked by the action method when the menu item is selected
    void process()
    {
        // Take some default action.
    }
}

class FileOpenMenuItem extends MyMenuItem
{
    void process()
    {
        // Process the File Open command.
    }
}
```

This approach has several advantages. First, it's extensible. There is an axiom of object-oriented programming: "If you touch it, you break it." The implication here is that if you change an existing working function, you must retest it because you might have added a bug of some sort. With this technique, adding new menu options does not involve making any changes to the *action* method. Once the main program has been debugged and is working properly, you can leave it alone.

Second, this approach keeps things packaged in neat little subclasses of *MyMenuItem*. For example, the class *FileOpenMenuItem* would include all of the code necessary to display and process the File Open menu command. This ability to find things easily is a boon come debug time.

One problem remains with this solution, however. The *action* method no longer reflects every object that receives events, but it must reflect every different *type* of object. Consider, for example, what our code snippet would look like if the applet received events destined for components in addition to menu options:

```
public boolean action(Event e, Object o)
{
    if (e.target instanceof MyMenuItem)
    {
        MyMenuItem mmiTarget = (MyMenuItem)e.target;
        mmiTarget.process();
        return true;
    }

    if (e.target instanceof MyButton)
    {
        MyButton buttonTarget = (MyButton)e.target;
        buttonTarget.process();
        return true;
    }

    if (e.target instanceof MyCheckbox)
    {
        MyCheckbox cbTarget = (MyCheckbox)e.target;
        cbTarget.process();
        return true;
    }

    // And so on for each different type of object...
    return false;
}
```

This code doesn't seem too bad, but by cleverly using interfaces, we can remove even this objection.

A Better Solution—Interface Style

The solution demonstrated in the preceding code could also have been implemented using an interface definition, as shown here:

```
// IActionProcess - Object that can be invoked from an
//                  action method in response to an action
//                  event
interface IActionProcess
{
    void process(Event e);
}
```

>>

```
class MyFrame extends Frame
{
    // All the following MenuItems implement the
    // IActionProcess interface.
    MenuItem miFileOpen  = new FileOpenMenuItem();
    MenuItem miFileClose = new FileCloseMenuItem();
    MenuItem miFileExit  = new FileExitMenuItem();


    public boolean action(Event e, Object o)
    {
        if (e.target instanceof IActionProcess)
        {
            IActionProcess actiontarget = (IActionProcess)e.target;
            actiontarget.process();
            return true;
        }
        return false;
    }
}


// FileOpenMenuItem    Now inherits directly from MenuItem
//                     but implements IActionProcess
class FileOpenMenuItem extends MenuItem
                    implements IActionProcess
{
    void process()
    {
        // Process the File Open command.
    }
}
```

The programmer still must implement a separate class for each menu option, but now rather than base these new classes on a user-defined base class, she can use a newly defined interface.

An added advantage of this approach is that this version of *action* is capable of processing all types of components as long as the components implement the *IActionProcess* interface. Thus, a new button could be added as follows:

```
class CancelButton extends Button implements IActionProcess
{
    void process()
    {
        // Invoked when the user clicks the Cancel button
    }

    // Other stuff necessary for button...
}
```

By virtue of the fact that *CancelButton* implements the *IActionProcess* interface, the existing *action* method automatically knows how to handle the event.

AN EVEN BETTER SOLUTION—EVENT DELEGATION

As we saw above, the same *action* method can handle any number of classes as long as they
implement the *IActionProcess* interface. The event handling solution adopted
in the AWT 1.1 takes this interface-based solution one step further, as demonstrated in the following example:

```
// App3_1 - The App2_5 applet converted to use delegation
//          event handling
import java.applet.*;
import java.awt.*;
import java.awt.event.*;
import FileDescr;

interface IParentApplet
{
    TextField      getTextField();
    void           setVisible(boolean b);
    void           repaint();
}

public class App3_1 extends Applet implements IParentApplet
{
    Button      button = new Button("OK");
    Choice      choice = new Choice();
    Panel       checks = new Panel();
    CheckboxGroup grp = new CheckboxGroup();
    FontCheckbox  bold   = new FontCheckbox("Bold",   Font.BOLD);
    FontCheckbox  italic = new FontCheckbox("Italic", Font.ITALIC);
    FontCheckbox  normal = new FontCheckbox("Normal", Font.PLAIN);

    TextField txtfld = new TextField();

    // Implement the interface access functions.
    public TextField getTextField()
    {
        return txtfld;
    }
```

>>

```
// init - Set up the components in the applet window.
public void init()
{
    // Use BorderLayout.
    setLayout(new BorderLayout());

    // Create an item list consisting of the names
    // of the files in the C:\ directory.
    updateChoiceList();

    // Update the Choice component with the item list
    // and position it on the left.
    Panel choiceWin = new Panel();
    choiceWin.setLayout(new BorderLayout());
    Label label = new Label("Selections:");
    choiceWin.add("North", label);
    choiceWin.add("Center", choice);
    add("West", choiceWin);

    // Add an event handler.
    choice.addItemListener(new ChoiceHandler(this, choice));

    // Position the OK button at the bottom.
    add("South", button);
    button.addActionListener(new OKButtonHandler(this));

    // Create a window in the middle with the three
    // check boxes in it.
    checks.setLayout(new BorderLayout());
    checks.add("North", normal);
    normal.addItemListener(new CheckboxHandler(this, normal));

    checks.add("Center", bold);
    bold.addItemListener(new CheckboxHandler(this, bold));

    checks.add("South", italic);
    italic.addItemListener(new CheckboxHandler(this, italic));

    add("Center", checks);

    // Adding the check boxes to the group will ensure
    // that only one of them is selected at a time.
    // (Start with Normal set to true.)
    bold.setCheckboxGroup(grp);
    italic.setCheckboxGroup(grp);
    normal.setCheckboxGroup(grp);
    normal.setState(true);
```

```
        // Now add a text field at the top to display
        // the selected entry.
        txtfld.setEditable(false);
        txtfld.setFont(normal.getFont());
        add("North", txtfld);

        // Now that we've finished, make the whole thing visible.
        setVisible(true);
    }


    // updateChoiceList - Update items with a listing
    //                    of a specific directory.
    public void updateChoiceList()
    {
        // Create a file description object on the target
        // directory.
        FileDescr dir = new FileDescr ("c:");

        // Allocate space for the number of files found there.
        int nCount = dir.getChildCount();
        String[] items = new String [nCount];

        // Now populate items with the names of the files.
        for (int i = 0; i < items.length; i++)
        {
            items[i] = dir.getChild(i);
        }

        // Add this list of filenames to the choice list.
        for (int i = 0; i < items.length; i++)
        {
            choice.add(items[i]);
        }
    }
}


// OKButtonHandler - Hide the parent applet's window
//                   when the OK button is clicked.
class OKButtonHandler implements ActionListener
{
    IParentApplet parent;
```

>>

>>

```
    OKButtonHandler(IParentApplet parent)
    {
        this.parent = parent;
    }

    // actionPerformed - Hide the applet display.
    public void actionPerformed(ActionEvent e)
    {
        parent.setVisible(false);
    }
}

// ChoiceHandler - Place selected text in the parent's text field.
class ChoiceHandler implements ItemListener
{
    IParentApplet parent;
    Choice        choice;

    ChoiceHandler(IParentApplet parent, Choice choice)
    {
        this.parent = parent;
        this.choicc - choice;
    }

    // itemStateChanged - Read the current selection from
    //                    the list box and display it in
    //                    the parent's text field.
    public void itemStateChanged(ItemEvent e)
    {
        if (e.getStateChange() == ItemEvent.SELECTED)
        {
            String s = choice.getSelectedItem();
            TextField tfTarget = parent.getTextField();
            tfTarget.setText(s);
        }
    }
}

// FontCheckbox - A check box with an associated Font.
//               (This could be any property.)
class FontCheckbox extends Checkbox
{
    Font    font;
```

```
        FontCheckbox(String label, int nFontType)
        {
            super(label);
            font = new Font("Arial", nFontType, 12);
        }

        public Font getFont()
        {
            return font;
        }
    }

    class CheckboxHandler implements ItemListener
    {
        IParentApplet parent;
        Checkbox cb;

        CheckboxHandler(IParentApplet parent, Checkbox cb)
        {
            this.parent = parent;
            this.cb = cb;
        }

        // itemStateChanged - Set the parent applet's text
        //                    field to our font.
        public void itemStateChanged(ItemEvent e)
        {
            if (e.getStateChange() == ItemEvent.SELECTED)
            {
                TextField txtfld = parent.getTextField();
                txtfld.setFont(cb.getFont());
                parent.repaint();
            }
        }

    }
```

When this applet is executed, the output appears identical to that of App2_5
(beginning on page 30). Many parts of this applet's code are identical to App2_5.
However, the way that this applet processes events is completely new. This
applet uses the *event delegation model* of event handling. In this example, the
event delegation model is implemented as follows.

This example includes three classes in addition to those in App2_5, from which this example was built: *OKButtonHandler*, *ChoiceHandler*, and *Checkbox-Handler*. *OKButtonHandler* implements the *ActionListener* interface, and *ChoiceHandler* and *CheckboxHandler* implement the *ItemListener* interface. If you look at the documentation for these interfaces, you'll see that both the *ActionListener* and *ItemListener* interfaces implement the *EventListener* interface. The *import java.awt.event.** statement at the beginning of the applet grants the applet access to this newly introduced group of interfaces.

The calls to *addItemListener* and *addActionListener* in the applet's *init* method associate a listener object with a component. The add listener methods are also newly introduced in version 1.1 of the AWT. Each component in the AWT 1.1 has an add listener method of some type that allows the programmer to associate a listener object with the component.

Each of the listener classes contains a single *action* method in addition to a constructor. These *action* methods are invoked when the user selects the associated component. The contents of these *action* methods are virtually identical to the *process* methods we implemented on our own earlier. For example, the following statement creates a new *addItemListener* object of class *Checkbox-Handler* and associates it with the *bold* check box object:

```
bold.addItemListener(new CheckboxHandler(this, bold));
```

When the user selects the *Bold* check box, the AWT invokes the *Checkbox-Handler.itemStateChanged* method to process the action.

From an object-oriented, extensibility standpoint, this solution is ideal. Listener objects can be created and added to other components without modifying the core of the applet. This solution is even more flexible than the solution I implemented earlier using the AWT 1.0 features. For one thing, multiple listener objects can be added to the same component. When the component is activated, all of the listener objects are invoked (but in no particular order). In addition, listener objects can be added, removed, and replaced at any time during processing. This flexibility allows the applet to easily enable, disable, or redefine the function of a button or menu item.

The only problem with this solution is fairly obvious when you stand back and examine the App3_1 code: it requires the creation of a large number of fairly trivial classes. This problem wouldn't be too bad except that in order to perform their process function, these classes generally need access to the internals of the parent class. In this example, I created the interface *IParentApplet*, which the listener classes can use, but this solution still means the addition of constructors, the passing of *this* pointers, and other such nuisances.

A Version That's a Little Less Classy!

The entire process would be much easier if the listener classes could somehow be made a part of the applet class itself. In order to encourage the use of event delegation, this capability, known as *inner classes*, was added to the Java syntax along with the introduction of the AWT 1.1. Using inner classes, the following syntax is now allowed:

```
class OuterClass
{
    int nSomeMember;

    class InnerClass
    {
        int nSomeOtherMember;

        void innerMethod()
        {
            // This function has access to both nSomeMember
            // and nSomeOtherMember.
        }
    }

    void outerMethod()
    {
        // This function has access to nSomeMember but not
        // nSomeOtherMember.
    }
}
```

Here the *InnerClass* class is defined as an inner class to the class *OuterClass*. (What else?) The methods of *InnerClass* have access to the members of both *InnerClass* and *OuterClass*; however, the methods of *OuterClass* have direct access only to the members of *OuterClass*.

The App3_2 applet is App3_1 implemented using inner classes:

```java
// App3_2 - The App3_1 applet implemented using inner classes to
//          reduce the number of extra classes and their complexity.
import java.applet.*;
import java.awt.*;
import java.awt.event.*;
import FileDescr;

public class App3_2 extends Applet
{
    // Define a button and its handler.
    Button      button = new Button("OK");
    class OKButtonHandler implements ActionListener
    {
        // actionPerformed - Hide the applet display.
        public void actionPerformed(ActionEvent e)
        {
            setVisible(false);
        }
    }

    // Now define the Choice object and its handler.
    Choice      choice = new Choice();
    class ChoiceHandler implements ItemListener
    {
        // itemStateChanged - Read the current selection
        //                    from the list box and display
        //                    it in the parent's text
        //                    field.
        public void itemStateChanged(ItemEvent e)
        {
            if (e.getStateChange() == ItemEvent.SELECTED)
            {
                String s = choice.getSelectedItem();
                txtfld.setText(s);
            }
        }
    }
```

```java
// Finally, define the check boxes.
Panel       checks = new Panel();
CheckboxGroup grp = new CheckboxGroup();
FontCheckbox  bold   = new FontCheckbox("Bold",   Font.BOLD);
FontCheckbox  italic = new FontCheckbox("Italic", Font.ITALIC);
FontCheckbox  normal = new FontCheckbox("Normal", Font.PLAIN);

// (The FontCheckbox class includes its
// handler class internally.)
class FontCheckbox extends Checkbox
{
    Font    font;

    class CheckboxHandler implements ItemListener
    {
        // actionPerformed - Set the parent applet's
        //                   text field to our font.
        public void itemStateChanged(ItemEvent e)
        {
            if (e.getStateChange() == ItemEvent.SELECTED)
            {
                txtfld.setFont(getFont());
                repaint();
            }
        }

    }

    FontCheckbox(String label, int nFontType)
    {
        super(label);
        font = new Font("Arial", nFontType, 12);

        addItemListener(new CheckboxHandler());
    }

    public Font getFont()
    {
        return font;
    }
}
```

>>

```
// The text field has no handler class.
TextField txtfld = new TextField();

// init - Set up the components in the applet window.
public void init()
{
    // Use BorderLayout.
    setLayout(new BorderLayout());

    // Create an item list consisting of the names
    // of the files in the C:\ directory.
    updateChoiceList();

    // Update the Choice component with the item list
    // and position it on the left.
    Panel choiceWin = new Panel();
    choiceWin.setLayout(new BorderLayout());
    Label label = new Label("Selections:");
    choiceWin.add("North",  label);
    choiceWin.add("Center", choice);
    add("West", choiceWin);

    // Add an event handler.
    choice.addItemListener(new ChoiceHandler());

    // Position the OK button at the bottom.
    add("South", button);
    button.addActionListener(new OKButtonHandler());

    // Create a window in the middle with the three
    // check boxes in it.
    checks.setLayout(new BorderLayout());
    checks.add("North",  normal);
    checks.add("Center", bold);
    checks.add("South",  italic);
    add("Center", checks);

    // Adding the check boxes to the group will ensure
    // that only one of them is selected at a time.
    // (Start with normal set to true.)
    bold.setCheckboxGroup(grp);
    italic.setCheckboxGroup(grp);
```

```
        normal.setCheckboxGroup(grp);
        normal.setState(true);

        // Now add a text field at the top to display
        // the selected entry.
        txtfld.setEditable(false);
        txtfld.setFont(normal.getFont());
        add("North", txtfld);

        // Now that we've finished, make the whole thing visible.
        setVisible(true);
    }


    // updateChoiceList - Update items with a listing
    //                    of a specific directory.
    public void updateChoiceList()
    {
        // Unchanged from earlier versions...
    }
}
```

The pattern for this applet is established in the first component. No longer is there a separate, user-defined *OKButton* class. The OK button is now simply an object of class *Button*. The *OKButtonHandler* listener class is still present, but now it's defined on the very next line in order to highlight the association it has with the *button* object. The *OKButtonHandler* class implements *Action-Listener* by providing the single function *actionPerformed*. Since *OKButton-Handler* has access to the internals of the parent applet, it has no need to retain a reference to its parent. Gone is the constructor; absent is the *IParentApplet* interface. The result is a simpler applet that is easier to read and therefore easier to maintain.

The *init* function here is virtually identical to its preceding version. The calls to *addActionListener* and *addItemListener* are still necessary to associate a listener object with the component. Of course, because the *FontCheckbox* objects add their own listener automatically, the set of calls that adds listeners to each font type is no longer necessary.

OTHER INNER CLASS CONSIDERATIONS

Inner classes introduce a few linguistic problems to the Java language. Consider the following outer class, *TestApp*:

```
import java.applet.*;
import java.awt.*;

public class TestApp extends Applet
{
    class Inner
    {
        public void aMethod()
        {
            showStatus("Inside aMethod()");

            // The following statement is incorrect.
            // MyPanel mypanel = new MyPanel(this); // WRONG!

            // The following statement is correct.
            MyPanel mypanel = new MyPanel(TestApp.this);
        }
    }
}

class MyPanel extends Panel
{
    MyPanel(Applet parent)
    {
    }
}
```

Notice the *aMethod* function within the inner class *Inner*. The first statement within *aMethod* is a call to the *showStatus* method. To resolve this call, Java first looks to see whether *Inner* contains such a method directly. Seeing that it does not, Java then checks whether *Inner* inherits such a method from some base class. This can't be the case because *Inner* does not extend any other class. (This will be the case whenever we use inner classes for event delegation.) Having no luck there either, Java then checks whether the outer class includes such a method, either directly or by inheritance. There it finds the method *Applet.showStatus*, and the call is allowed.

Now let's consider the next statement, the call to *new MyPanel(this)*. As you can see, for whatever reason, the constructor for *MyPanel* takes a reference to the parent class *Applet*. In the past, I have always used just the keyword *this* to refer

>>

>>

to the current object. Here, however, a problem arises. In *new MyPanel(this)*, to which object does *this* refer? Do I mean the outer object of class *TestApp* or the inner object of class *Inner* (actually, *TestApp.Inner*)?

An unqualified reference to *this* always refers to the innermost class. Thus, *this* would be of class *TestApp.Inner*. Because there is no *MyPanel* constructor that takes an object of class *TestApp.Inner*, this call generates a compiler error.

To specify a particular *this*, Java allows the programmer to prepend the name of the class. Thus, *TestApp.this* is the name of the current object of class *TestApp*.

Finally, inner classes are not limited to other classes. An inner class can be defined within any block type, including methods. For further information, see the Visual J++ online help.

AN ANONYMOUS SOLUTION

The introduction of inner classes made a noticeable increase in the readability by decreasing the size of applets that use event delegation. In an attempt to further increase the terseness of such applets, version 1.1 of the Java standard also introduced anonymous classes.

Anonymous classes are inner classes that are defined without a name directly at the point where an object of that class is created. To understand anonymous classes, consider again the following inner class example:

```
class MyClass
{
    class InnerClass implements ISomeMethod
    {
        void someMethod()
        {
            // Whatever this method does...
        }
    }

    void init()
    {
        addMethod(new InnerClass());
    }
}
```

The *InnerClass* class has been defined for the sole purpose of creating a class to pass to *addMethod*. Wouldn't it be clearer if we could implement the *ISomeMethod* interface directly? And, while we're at it, wouldn't it be better to move the implementation of *ISomeMethod* closer to the *addMethod* call?

Anonymous classes give the programmer that ability. The anonymous version of this code snippet is shown here:

```
class MyClass
{
    void init()
    {
        addMethod
        (
            new ISomeMethod()
            {
                void someMethod()
                {
                    // Whatever this method does...
                }
            }

        );
    }
}
```

Here the statement *new ISomeMethod()* creates an object that implements the *ISomeMethod* interface. The definition of this class appears immediately following the *new* statement.

The following code demonstrates anonymous classes in use. The App3_3 applet is an anonymous class implementation of App3_2.

```
// App3_3 - The App3_2 applet implemented using anonymous classes
//          instead of simple inner classes
import java.applet.*;
import java.awt.*;
import java.awt.event.*;
import FileDescr;

public class App3_3 extends Applet
{
    // Define the Button and Choice components.
    // (The handlers have been moved down into
    // the code as anonymous classes.)
    Button      button = new Button("OK");
    Choice      choice = new Choice();
```

```
// Finally, define the check boxes.
Panel       checks = new Panel();
CheckboxGroup grp = new CheckboxGroup();
FontCheckbox  bold   = new FontCheckbox("Bold",   Font.BOLD);
FontCheckbox  italic = new FontCheckbox("Italic", Font.ITALIC);
FontCheckbox  normal = new FontCheckbox("Normal", Font.PLAIN);

// (The FontCheckbox class includes its
// handler class internally.)
class FontCheckbox extends Checkbox
{
    Font    font;

    FontCheckbox(String label, int nFontType)
    {
        super(label);
        font = new Font("Arial", nFontType, 12);

        // Here is where the ItemListener implementation
        // is defined.
        addItemListener
        (
            new ItemListener()
            {
                public void itemStateChanged(ItemEvent e)
                {
                    if (e.getStateChange() == ItemEvent.SELECTED)
                    {
                        txtfld.setFont(getFont());
                        repaint();
                    }
                }

            }
        );
    }

    public Font getFont()
    {
        return font;
    }
}
```

>>

>>

```java
// The text field has no handler class.
TextField txtfld = new TextField();

// init - Set up the components in the applet window.
public void init()
{
    // Use BorderLayout.
    setLayout(new BorderLayout());

    // Create an item list consisting of the names
    // of the files in the C:\ directory.
    updateChoiceList();

    // Update the Choice component with the item list
    // and position it on the left.
    Panel choiceWin = new Panel();
    choiceWin.setLayout(new BorderLayout());
    Label label = new Label("Selections:");
    choiceWin.add("North", label);
    choiceWin.add("Center", choice);
    add("West", choiceWin);

    // Add an event handler.
    choice.addItemListener
    (
        new ItemListener()
        {
            public void itemStateChanged(ItemEvent e)
            {
                if (e.getStateChange() == ItemEvent.SELECTED)
                {
                    String s = choice.getSelectedItem();
                    txtfld.setText(s);
                }
            }
        }
    );

    // Position the OK button at the bottom.
    add("South", button);
```

```
        button.addActionListener
        (
            new ActionListener()
            {
                public void actionPerformed(ActionEvent e)
                {
                    setVisible(false);
                }
            }
        );

        // Create a window in the middle with the three
        // check boxes in it.
        checks.setLayout(new BorderLayout());
        checks.add("North",  normal);
        checks.add("Center", bold);
        checks.add("South",  italic);
        add("Center", checks);

        // Adding the check boxes to the group will ensure
        // that only one of them is selected at a time.
        // (Start with normal set to true.)
        bold.setCheckboxGroup(grp);
        italic.setCheckboxGroup(grp);
        normal.setCheckboxGroup(grp);
        normal.setState(true);

        // Now add a text field at the top to display
        // the selected entry.
        txtfld.setEditable(false);
        txtfld.setFont(normal.getFont());
        add("North", txtfld);

        // Now that we've finished, make the whole thing visible.
        setVisible(true);
    }

    // updateChoiceList - Update items with a listing
    //                    of a specific directory.
    public void updateChoiceList()
    {
        // Unchanged from earlier versions...
    }
}
```

By comparing this applet to its predecessor, you can see how the interface definitions have been moved down into the body of the *init* function. Extracting the following code snippet makes this distinction clearer:

```
add("South", button);
button.addActionListener
(
    new ActionListener()
    {
        public void actionPerformed(ActionEvent e)
        {
            setVisible(false);
        }
    }
);
```

WHAT'S NEXT

Event delegation makes clever use of the listener interface to provide a direct, extensible solution to the processing of user events. The event delegation model is a worthwhile addition to the Java specification, one that AFC fully supports.

The introduction of inner classes to the Java syntax will go a long way toward easing the acceptance of event delegation by reducing the complexity of the extra classes the programmer must invent in order to use this feature. Personally, however, I don't think anonymous classes add any clarity at all. In fact, I think they are more difficult to read than their inner class brethren. They are presented here only in the interest of completeness.

In the next chapter, we'll use our knowledge of event delegation and the AWT to begin investigating AFC. We'll look at how AFC is organized and some of the general characteristics of AFC applets.

Laying the AFC Foundation

So far, we've looked at background material for Application Foundation Classes (AFC)—most notably, the workings of the Abstract Windowing Toolkit (AWT), including some of the major additions in version 1.1. While this information is certainly important in developing an understanding of AFC, by now you're probably getting anxious to see AFC itself.

In this chapter, you'll get an overview of AFC. First I'll explain the organization of AFC, and then we'll run through a few AFC applications just to get a feel for how AFC applets are put together. In the process, you'll get the preparation you'll need in order to use the code examples in Part Two, which will help you build your own powerful applets.

THE STRUCTURE OF AFC

AFC is divided into the following four packages:

- **com.ms.ui**—Contains the majority of AFC, including such classes as *UIApplet*.

- **com.ms.ui.event**—Defines AFC's event classes, including AFC's implementation of the Java 1.1 event delegation model.

- **com.ms.ui.resource**—Includes a couple of classes that are used to load resource files such as those created inside the Visual J++ Interactive Development Environment (IDE) by the Resource Wizard. Visual J++ converted these resource files to Java source files; AFC extends this capability by allowing these resource files to be read directly.

- **com.ms.fx**—Includes classes that are used to modify the AFC components of com.ms.ui. The com.ms.fx package includes classes that significantly extend and enhance the AWT Color and Font classes to make drawing and text operations more flexible.

NOTE

For the most part, the classes included within com.ms.ui, com.ms.ui.event, and com.ms.ui.resource begin with the extension *UI*. Interfaces contained within these classes begin with the letters *IUI*. Classes contained within com.ms.fx begin with *Fx*, and the interfaces contained within these classes begin with *IFx*. In rough terms, you might think of the classes within com.ms.ui as the nouns (the components), the classes within com.ms.ui.event as the verbs (the events) that act on those nouns, and the classes within com.ms.fx as the adjectives (the properties) used to modify those nouns.

AFC Components

AFC components exist for all of the user interface doodads to which users have become accustomed. Figure 4-1 shows a single display with an assortment of such fixtures.

As you can see, the window in this figure is displaying the Assorted tab. By clicking on the tabs arranged along the top, the user can quickly switch from one view to another.

The first (top) row contains three menus: one normal, one raised, and one raised that includes a graphic along with the text label. The second row also includes menus, but these are attached to what is known as a *band*. Dragging the band thumb (the set of vertical lines) that is on the right to the left carries the menu options with it—making them visible but at the cost of obscuring the menu options on the left. The next row down shows an assortment of buttons, including a push button outfitted with a graphic as well as text (Favorites). A drop-down list box and a list box much like those present in the AWT appear in the

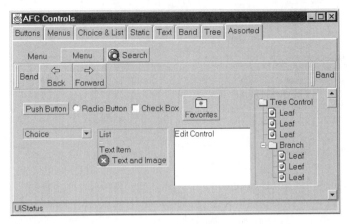

FIGURE 4-1   *A single window containing an assortment of AFC components.*

lower left. Notice, however, that AFC lists allow the same graphic/text combinations allowed on menu options and buttons. To the right of the list box is a text box. Last, in the lower right is the tree control. This component is particularly useful for examining hierarchical data such as a directory listing.

In Part Two, I will demonstrate how to create each of these components. Before we get into that, however, let's examine a little more of the inner workings of AFC.

AFC's Interface-Based Model

Whereas the AWT has a class-based model, AFC uses an interface-based model. The difference can be significant.

Remember that all AWT components are based on the class *Component*. This class includes the basic building blocks that all AWT components use. For example, all window management methods needed for the user interface are defined in this class. The basic class relationship within the AWT is shown in Figure 4-2 on the following page. Simple classes, such as *Button* and *Label*, extend the class *Canvas*. Containers of components, such as *Applet* and *Panel*, are based on the class *Container*. However, even *Container* is a subclass of *Component*.

There is elegance in this approach. Basing all classes on the single class *Component* means that AWT components are largely interchangeable. Extending *Container* from *Component* means that even a panel containing multiple buttons can be positioned where a single button might have appeared.

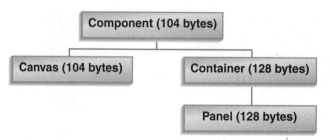

FIGURE 4-2
Relationship between the AWT base classes.

One of the limitations of this approach, however, is that each AWT component can be no smaller than the base class *Component*. This can lead to a considerable amount of overhead, as the sizes listed in Figure 4-2 demonstrate.

By comparison, AFC bases its components on a single interface, *IUIComponent*. All of the *UI* classes that make up AFC implement the *IUIComponent* interface either directly or indirectly through the base class *UIComponent*. The class relationship in AFC is shown in Figure 4-3.

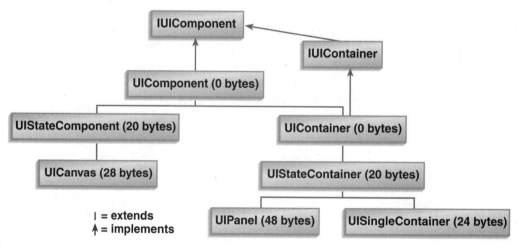

FIGURE 4-3 *Relationship between AFC base classes and interfaces.*

Basing the class structure on an interface has several benefits. It retains the elegance of the AWT model—AFC containers can accept any *IUIComponent*. However, because an interface has no data members, this technique does not inflict any size penalty on the different classes that implement the *IUIComponent* interface. The AFC model frees each component to retain only the amount of data it needs in order to implement the *IUIComponent* interface and no more. This lack of overhead is reflected in the sizes shown in Figure 4-3.

USING AFC

Part Two demonstrates how to use the majority of AFC classes, complete with examples. It is arranged like a reference, with information organized around the different types of objects, including the objects we just looked at. Before you jump into this uncharted territory, let's test the waters by examining a few AFC applets from the ground up.

Your First AFC Applet

As is the custom of most programming books, the first AFC applet I'll demonstrate is the venerable "Hello, World" applet, disguised here as App4_1:

```
// App4_1 - Hello, World as an AFC applet

// Start with AWT classes.
import java.applet.*;
import java.awt.*;

// We'll need the AFC classes as well.
import com.ms.ui.*;
import com.ms.fx.*;

// App4_1 - AFC applets extend AwtUIApplet
//          instead of Applet.
public class App4_1 extends AwtUIApplet
{
    public App4_1()
    {
        // Pass our applet to the
        // AwtUIApplet(UIApplet) constructor.
        super(new MyUIApplet());
    }
}
```

>>

>>

```
// MyUIApplet - The actual "applet/application" extends
//              UIApplet; UIApplet contains the same
//              methods as Applet.
class MyUIApplet extends UIApplet
{
    // paint - Invoked when it's necessary to repaint
    //         the applet window
    public void paint(FxGraphics fxg)
    {
        fxg.drawString("Hello, World - AFC style", 10, 20);
    }
}
```

By importing the java.applet and java.awt packages, this applet starts out like conventional AWT applets. In addition to these packages, all AFC applets must import the com.ms.ui AFC package. Most applets will also want to import the com.ms.ui.event and com.ms.fx packages. In this case, we won't need the event package since this applet does not process any events of its own. (Be patient—the next example applet will.)

Notice that *App4_1* is based on the class *AwtUIApplet*—this is true of all AFC applets. Because AFC is designed to work with all Java-compliant browsers, you might be wondering how this class structure is supposed to work because "applets are supposed to extend the class *Applet.*"

In fact, *AwtUIApplet* extends the class *Applet*. Therefore, *App4_1* is a subclass of *Applet* as is required of all applets even if the relationship is achieved through an intermediate class. As we will see shortly, classes that begin with *AwtUI* play a particular role.

NOTE

A class that follows the naming convention *AwtUIXxxx* is an AFC class that extends the AWT class *Xxxx*.

The *AwtUI* classes form a bridge between AFC and the AWT in the same way that an adapter plug converts a North American electrical appliance to fit a European wall socket. This conversion is necessary because the AWT is based on the *Component* class model, whereas AFC is based on an interface model.

The *AwtUIApplet* class has only one method of interest to us—the constructor *AwtUIApplet(UIApplet)*. The *UIApplet* class being passed to the *AwtUIApplet* constructor is the current AFC applet—in this case, an instance of *MyUIApplet*. The *UIApplet* class includes most of the methods that *Applet* does. In particular, the *start, stop, init,* and *destroy* methods of *UIApplet* serve the same role as they do in *Applet. AwtUIApplet* overrides the *Applet* methods of the same name to invoke the *UIApplet* methods. For example, when the browser invokes *init* to allow the applet to set itself up, the *AwtUIApplet.init* method passes the request to *UIApplet.init* for processing.

In this particular example, *MyUIApplet* overrides *paint* to output the requisite "Hello, World" message. The *FxGraphics* object passed to *UIApplet.paint* is an AFC extension to the standard *Graphics* class. *FxGraphics.drawString* draws the string in the current window in the same way that *Graphics.drawString* did in a previous example.

That's all there is to it! When the browser asks the applet to display its window, it calls *Applet.paint. Applet.paint* is overridden by *AwtUIApplet.paint* to invoke *UIApplet.paint*, which draws the string. The resulting window is shown in Figure 4-4.

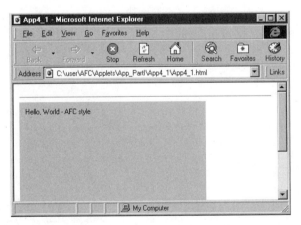

FIGURE 4-4   *The "Hello, World" output from the applet App4_1.*

HOW DO THE *AwtUI* CLASSES WORK?

You might be interested in how the *AwtUI* interface classes actually work internally. (If you're not interested or if you find these details too confusing, feel free to skip this sidebar without fear of shame or embarrassment.)

The bridge between the AWT and AFC is actually managed by a pair of classes named *AwtUIHost* and *UIRoot*. The *AwtUIHost* class extends *Panel*, the base AWT window class; and *UIRoot* extends *UIPanel*, the AFC equivalent. The *AwtUIHost* class forms the AWT side of the AWT-AFC interface, and *UIRoot* forms the AFC side.

There is a one-to-one relationship between the *AwtUIHost* class and the *UIRoot* class. *UIRoot* does all the AFC work for the *AwtUI* class. The *AwtUIHost* class acts as a gateway between *AwtUI* and *UIRoot*.

Consider, for example, the class *AwtUIApplet*. If the programmer attempts to add a *UI* component such as *UIApplet* to *AwtUIApplet*, as we did in App4_1, the *AwtUIApplet* class forwards the add request to the *AwtUIHost* class, which attaches the *UI* component to the *UIRoot* class.

Now consider what happens when an event such as mouse click is sent to the AWT for processing. The AWT sends the event to the *AwtUIApplet* class for processing. The *AwtUIApplet* class then forwards the request to *AwtUIHost*. The *AwtUIHost* class converts the AWT event to an AFC event and forwards it to the *UIRoot* class for processing.

This communication works in the other direction as well. When an AFC component invokes a method such as *repaint*, the request makes its way up to the *UIRoot* class, where it is forwarded through the *AwtUIHost* back to the AWT *Panel* class for processing.

Notice that you should not add conventional AWT components to an *AwtUIApplet* class. The call to the *add* method is supported because *AwtUIApplet* is a *Container* object; however, these components will be ignored because all messages from the AWT are diverted by the *AwtUIApplet* class to the associated *UIRoot* class for processing.

Another AFC Conversion

Let's take the next step—converting the relatively simple AWT applet App2_3 to a minimalist AFC applet. As you might remember, this applet displayed a label, a user-editable text field, and an OK button in a pop-up window. When the user clicked the OK button, the window read any text the user entered in the text field and transmitted it back to the main applet. The main applet displayed this text in the applet window.

The AFC version of App2_3 appears here as App4_2:

```
// App4_2 - App2_3 implemented as an AFC applet
import java.applet.*;
import java.awt.*;

// AFC classes
import com.ms.ui.*;

// ReportName - Provides the setName method for
//              reporting the user-entered name
interface ReportName
{
    void reportName(String sName);
}

public class App4_2 extends AwtUIApplet
{
    App4_2()
    {
        super(new MyApplet());
    }
}

class MyApplet extends UIApplet implements ReportName
{
    // Name entered in dialog box
    UIDrawText name = new UIDrawText("Nothing entered yet.");

    // Component container
    MyUIFrame frame = new MyUIFrame(this, "Important Input");
```

>>

```
    // init - Set the dialog box frame's size, and display it.
    public void init()
    {
        // Add the text entered by the user.
        name.setLocation(20, 20);
        add(name);

        // Make the frame resizable, and
        // set its initial size.
        frame.setResizable(true);
        frame.setSize(100, 100);

        // Now make the whole thing visible.
        frame.setVisible(true);
    }


    // reportName - Update the name field and repaint the
    //              applet in order to redisplay the name.
    public void reportName(String sName)
    {
        if (sName != null)
        {
            name.setValueText(sName);
            repaint();
        }
    }
}


// MyFrame - Creates a frame with three components
class MyUIFrame extends UIFrame
{
    // The parent applet
    ReportName applet = null;

    // Components within the dialog box
    UIEdit      txtfld = new UIEdit();
    UIText      label  = new UIText("Enter name:");
    UIButton    button = new UIPushButton("OK");

    MyUIFrame(ReportName applet, String sTitle)
    {
        // Pass the frame title to the
        // Frame(String) constructor.
        super(sTitle);
```

```
        // Now save the applet - we'll need this information
        // to call setName when the user clicks OK.
        this.applet = applet;

        // Add the label, the text field, and the OK button.
        add(label, "North");
        add(button, "South");

        txtfld.setBackground(Color.white);
        add(txtfld, "Center");
    }


// handleEvent - This method is called whenever
//                anything happens within the dialog box.
public boolean handleEvent(Event evt)
{
    // Retrieve the target object from the
    // event.
    Object oTarget = evt.target;

    // If this is the OK button...
    if (oTarget == button)
    {
        // ...save the contents of
        // the text field...
        if (evt.id == Event.MOUSE_DOWN)
        {
            String sName = txtfld.getValueText();

        // ...and pass the contents to the applet.
            applet.reportName(sName);
            return true;
        }
    }
    return false;
    }
}
```

You can see considerable similarity between this AFC applet and its conventional AWT predecessor. The applet, now a *UIApplet*, first adds a *UIDrawText* field to the applet window to display the name entered by the user. (The *UIDrawText* component simply displays the text it is given, much like an AWT *Label*.) The applet sets the location of the text field at 20 pixels from the top of the applet window and 20 pixels from the left. The initial contents of the text string are "*Nothing entered yet.*".

The *init* method continues by creating a resizable frame of class *MyUIFrame*. Such frames are created invisible; the call to *setVisible* is required so that the user can see the frame.

MyUIFrame defines the same three objects as App2_3—*txtfld*, *label*, and *button*—only this time the class of each has changed to match the AFC equivalents. The *UIEdit* object is a user-editable text field. The *UIText* object, on the other hand, is a string of text that cannot be edited. Finally, the *UIPushButton* object is a general-purpose button.

The three *UI* components are added to the frame in the *"North"*, *"Center"*, and *"South"* positions. The user can edit the *txtfld* object by entering whatever text is desired. Once the text has been entered, clicking the push button creates an *Event* object that is handled by the *handleEvent* method in the same way it was in App2_3.

AFC Using Event Delegation

App4_2 used the older and clumsier Java 1.0 event processing mechanism. AFC supports the more elegant Java 1.1–style event delegation model through its own classes contained in the package com.ms.ui.event. The applet App4_3, shown here, updates the previous applet to make use of this AFC flavor of event delegation:

```
// App4_3 - Same as App4_2 except this time, implements
//          event handling using event delegation
import java.applet.*;
import java.awt.*;

// AFC classes (notice the addition of event class)
import com.ms.ui.*;
import com.ms.ui.event.*;

// ReportName - Provides the setName method for
//              reporting the user-entered name
interface ReportName
{
    void reportName(String sName);
}
```

```java
public class App4_3 extends AwtUIApplet
{
    App4_3()
    {
        super(new MyApplet());
    }
}


class MyApplet extends UIApplet implements ReportName
{
    // Name entered in dialog box
    UIDrawText name = new UIDrawText("Nothing entered yet.");

    // Component container
    MyUIFrame frame = new MyUIFrame(this, "Important Input");

    // init - Set the dialog box frame's size, and display it.
    public void init()
    {
        // Add the text entered by the user.
        name.setLocation(20, 20);
        add(name);

        // Make the frame resizable, and
        // set its initial size.
        frame.setResizable(true);
        frame.setSize(100, 100);

        // Now make the whole thing visible.
        frame.setVisible(true);
    }


    // reportName - Update the name field and repaint the applet
    //              in order to redisplay the name.
    public void reportName(String sName)
    {
        if (sName != null)
        {
            name.setValueText(sName);
            repaint();
        }
    }
}
```

>>

```
// MyFrame - Creates a frame with three components
class MyUIFrame extends UIFrame
{
    // The parent applet
    ReportName applet = null;

    // Components within the dialog box
    UIEdit    txtfld = new UIEdit();
    UIText    label  = new UIText("Enter name:");

    UIPushButton button = new UIPushButton("OK");
    class OKButtonListener implements IUIActionListener
    {
        public void actionPerformed(UIActionEvent e)
        {
            // Get the contents of
            // the text field...
            String sName = txtfld.getValueText();

            // ...and pass it to the applet.
            applet.reportName(sName);
        }
    }

    MyUIFrame(ReportName applet, String sTitle)
    {
        // Pass the frame title to the
        // Frame(String) constructor.
        super(sTitle);

        // Now save the applet - we'll need this information
        // to call setName when the user clicks OK.
        this.applet = applet;

        // Add the label, the text field, and the OK button.
        add(label, "North");

        button.addActionListener(new OKButtonListener());
        add(button, "South");

        txtfld.setBackground(Color.white);
        add(txtfld, "Center");
    }
}
```

App4_3 is very similar to its App4_2 predecessor, as you would expect. Of course, this applet must import the AFC event package com.ms.ui.event in order to gain access to the AFC event delegation classes, but all other changes are limited to the *MyUIFrame* class.

MyUIFrame shows the same types of changes one would expect with any event delegation model conversion. The inner class *OKButtonListener* has been added to handle the action of clicking the OK button. This class implements *IUIAction-Listener*, rather than the conventional *ActionListener* interface, to read the action event invoked when the user clicks the push button. The internal workings of the *actionPerformed* method are predictable: the method reads the contents of the text field and conveys that information back to the applet by calling *reportName*.

An "AFC-Improved" Applet

This high degree of similarity between the AFC versions of applets and their conventional AWT-only predecessors illustrates how easy it is to become familiar with the AFC components. A few of the names have changed, but the concepts that exist in the AWT carry over into AFC, thereby reducing the learning curve. The long hours you've already spent learning where things are in the AWT class hierarchy can still be applied in AFC.

However, if AFC were merely the AWT with the names changed, there wouldn't be any reason to bother. But AFC contains extensive features that allow the programmer to enhance the appearance of her applet relatively easily. For example, consider the "AFC-improved" appearance of the Important Input dialog frame shown in Figure 4-5 on the following page. (This frame is taking the place of a dialog box.)

This version now sports an image in the background of the user input area and a small graphic on the OK button. (There are other, more subtle, differences, such as the fact that the OK button is optionally raised and is hot-tracked. See Chapter 6, "Buttons," for a detailed discussion of both topics.)

FIGURE 4-5   *An AFC-enhanced input dialog frame.*

Because it includes the utility class *Images*, you must include the AppCommon directory in the list of directories searched by Visual J++ before you can compile and execute App4_4.

The listing for this AFC-improved applet is shown here as App4_4:

```
// App4_4 - An AFC-improved version of App4_3
import java.applet.*;
import java.awt.*;

// AFC classes (notice the addition of event class)
import com.ms.ui.*;
import com.ms.ui.event.*;
import com.ms.fx.*;

// Images is one of the utility classes defined in AppCommon.
import Images;

// ReportName - Provides the setName method for
//              reporting the user-entered name
interface ReportName
{
    void reportName(String sName);
}
```

```
public class App4_4 extends AwtUIApplet
{
    App4_4()
    {
        super(new MyApplet());
    }
}

class MyApplet extends UIApplet implements ReportName
{
    // Name entered in dialog box
    UIDrawText name = new UIDrawText("Nothing entered yet.");

    // Component container
    MyFrame frame = null;

    // init - Set the dialog box frame's size, and display it.
    public void init()
    {
        // Note: The frame cannot be created as part of the
        // constructor because the base applet does not
        // yet exist!
        frame = new MyFrame(this, this, "Important Input");

        // Add the text entered by the user.
        name.setLocation(20, 20);
        add(name);

        // Now make the whole thing visible.
        frame.setVisible(true);
    }

    // reportName - Update the name field and repaint the applet
    //              in order to redisplay the name.
    public void reportName(String sName)
    {
        if (sName != null)
        {
            name.setValueText(sName);
            repaint();
        }
    }
}
```

>>

```
// MyFrame - Creates a frame with three components
class MyFrame extends UIFrame
{
    // The parent applet
    ReportName report = null;
    UIApplet   applet = null;

    // Components within the dialog box
    UIText      label  = new UIText("Enter name:");
    UIEdit      txtfld = new UIEdit();

    UIPushButton button = null;
    class OKButtonListener implements IUIActionListener
    {
        public void actionPerformed(UIActionEvent e)
        {
            String sName = txtfld.getValueText();
            report.reportName(sName);
        }
    }

    // The following images are used as the background
    // for the text field and as an image for the OK button.
    Images   images;
    String[] imageNames = {"TextBG.gif", "OK.jpg"};
    final int IMAGE_TEXTBG = 0;
    final int IMAGE_OK      = 1;

    MyFrame(ReportName report,
            UIApplet   applet,
            String     sTitle)
    {
        // Pass the frame title to the
        // UIFrame(String) constructor.
        super(sTitle);

        // Now save the applet - we'll need this information
        // to call setName when the user clicks OK.
        this.applet = applet;
        this.report = report;

        // Make the frame resizable, and
        // set its initial size.
        setResizable(true);
        setSize(200, 200);
```

```
setLayout(new UIBorderLayout());
setFont(new Font("Helvetica", Font.BOLD, 24));

// Load the images we will need for the button
// and text fields.
images = new Images(applet, imageNames);
images.load();

// Add the label, the text field, and the OK button.
add(label, "North");
UIItem okButtonLabel = new UIItem(images.getImage(IMAGE_OK),
                                  "OK",
                                  UIItem.CENTERED|UIItem.HOTTRACK);
button = new UIPushButton(okButtonLabel);
button.addActionListener(new OKButtonListener());
add(button, "South");

FxColor color = new FxTexture(images.getImage(IMAGE_TEXTBG),
                             FxTexture.STRETCH_ALL,
                             0, 0, -1, -1,
                             false,
                             Color.white);
txtfld.setBackground(color);
add(txtfld, "Center");
    }
}
```

The key to the differences in this applet's output from its predecessor's output lies in the way the *button* and *txtfld* objects are created. The *button* object example is the more direct:

```
UIItem okButtonLabel = new UIItem(images.getImage(IMAGE_OK),
                                  "OK",
                                  UIItem.CENTERED|UIItem.HOTTRACK);
button = new UIPushButton(okButtonLabel);
```

In the App4_3 example, the button label was nothing more than the ASCII string *"OK"*. Here you see that a label can be more complicated. In this example, the label consists of a *UIItem* object that contains a text-graphic pair. (The class *Images* is described in Appendix B, "Utility Classes Used in This Book." The function call *images.getImage(IMAGE_OK)* returns a previously loaded image.)

Even more impressive is the ease with which a graphic can be placed in the background of a text field, as demonstrated in the code snippet on the top of the following page, which creates the *txtfld* object.

```
FxColor color = new FxTexture(images.getImage(IMAGE_TEXTBG),
                              FxTexture.STRETCH_ALL,
                              0, 0, -1, -1,
                              false,
                              Color.white);
txtfld.setBackground(color);
```

The *FxTexture* class looks and acts like a color. In fact, *FxTexture* extends the class *FxColor*. Once this class is created, the programmer can apply the *FxTexture* class just as he might apply an *FxColor* class. Rather than containing a single color, however, *FxTexture* represents an image of some type. Here *FxColor* contains the grayed image of a bicyclist; this image is subsequently applied as the background color for the *txtfld* object. The remaining arguments to the constructor indicate that the image should fill the entire available space (that's the *0, 0, –1, –1* part), that the image should be stretched to fit the available space (rather than centered or tiled), and that the color white should be used if the image is not available because of a loading error.

AFC Applications

Just because I have been concentrating on applets, don't get the idea that AFC does not support applications just as well. Executing a *UIApplet* class from an application involves tricking the applet into thinking that it's being invoked from a browser. To simplify this task for the purposes of this book, I have created the general utility class *Application*. This class is quite simple to use, as the applet App4_5 (a combined applet/application version of the applet-only App4_1) demonstrates:

```
// App4_5 - Demonstrates the class Application,
//          which can be used to execute applets without
//          a browser
import java.applet.*;
import java.awt.*;

import com.ms.ui.*;
import com.ms.fx.*;

// The utility class Application is included in AppCommon;
// this simplifies the task of executing a UIApplet as an
// application.
import Application;
```

```
public class App4_5 extends AwtUIApplet
{
    // constructor - Where the applet starts
    public App4_5()
    {
        super(new MyApplet());
    }

    // main - Where the application begins
    public static void main(String[] arg)
    {
        // The class Application starts an
        // application around your applet code;
        // you must provide the applet, of course.
        // You can also provide the name of the window
        // frame, the width, and the height...
        /*
        new Application(new MyApplet(),
                        "Hello Application",
                        200, 200);
        */

        // ...or you can use the defaults.
        new Application(new MyApplet());
    }
}

// MyApplet - Just a standard applet
class MyApplet extends UIApplet
{
    public void paint(FxGraphics fxg)
    {
        fxg.drawString("Hello, World", 10, 20);
    }
}
```

When executed as an applet, this program is exactly the same as App4_1, on which it is based. When it is executed as an application, however, the sequence of events is considerably different.

Execution of the program as an application begins with the *static void main* method. This method creates a *UIApplet* object from our applet and passes it to the *Application* class in the same way that the *Applet* object was passed to *AwtUIApplet* in the applet implementation. That's all there is to it! The work of executing the *UIApplet* as an application is performed by the *Application* class.

The *Application* class isn't all that complicated, as this listing shows:

```
// Application - Allows a UIApplet class to be
//               executed by a program; simply creates
//               an application by passing it a UIApplet object
import java.awt.*;
import com.ms.ui.*;

public class Application extends UIFrame
{
    // The applet within the frame
    UIApplet uiapplet = null;

    // Small constructor - defaults the name,
    //                     width, and height
    Application(UIApplet uiapplet)
    {
        this(uiapplet,
            "AFC Application",
            300, 200);
    }

    // Full constructor - specifies the name and size
    //                    of the applet frame
    Application(UIApplet uiapplet,
            String sName,
            int nWidth,
            int nHeight)
    {
        // Open a frame with the specified name,
        // width, and height.
        super(sName);
        setSize(nWidth, nHeight);

        // Save the applet.
        this.uiapplet = uiapplet;
```

```
        // Now add the applet to the frame.
        setLayout(new UIBorderLayout());
        add(uiapplet, "Center");

        // Invoke the applet's init and
        // start methods. (If this were an
        // applet, the browser would have done
        // this when the applet was loaded and
        // entered.)
        uiapplet.init();
        uiapplet.start();

        // Display the results.
        setVisible(true);
        repaint();
    }


    // handleEvent - When the user clicks the
    //               upper right button,
    //               exit the application.
    public boolean handleEvent(Event e)
    {
        if (e.id == Event.WINDOW_DESTROY)
        {
            // Invoke the stop and destroy methods
            // as the browser would.
            uiapplet.stop();
            uiapplet.destroy();

            // Now exit.
            System.exit(0);
        }
        return super.handleEvent(e);
    }
}
```

The class *Application* extends *UIFrame*. This way, *Application* can provide a frame in which to execute the *UIApplet* program. The small constructor, which takes only a reference to the *UIApplet* object, does nothing more than invoke the full constructor, providing a default title and size. The full constructor first initializes the *UIFrame* class with the frame title and then sets the size as specified.

The constructor adds the *UIApplet* to the center of the frame, which gives the *UIApplet* class a place to display its applet window. *Application* then performs those steps the applet would expect a browser to perform: it calls *uiapplet.init* and then calls *uiapplet.start*. Finally, *Application* makes the frame containing the applet visible.

The *handleEvent* method is provided here to catch the WINDOW_DESTROY event, which is created when the user destroys the window (usually by clicking the Close button in the upper right corner of the window). When that occurs, *handleEvent* first calls *uiapplet.stop* and *uiapplet.destroy*, the same way a browser would, and then terminates the application. All other events are ignored by this *handleEvent* method and are passed on to the parent class.

NOTE

Remember that because *Application* is one of the utility classes contained in the AppCommon directory, AppCommon must be one of the directories listed in the file search list.

WHAT'S NEXT

In Part One, we've laid the groundwork for a study of classes that make up AFC. First we saw how to combine AWT components into different types of applets. Then we saw the newly introduced event delegation model for event handling. Finally, we saw how to use the same component-based approach to build AFC applets.

Part Two is conceived as an AFC reference book. It's intended to be kept next to your terminal. Included within its pages are example applets for each of the major classes in AFC. These classes are organized by functionality. For example, all of the button types are contained in a single chapter. Thus, if you have a question about the proper use of buttons, you should be able to find the answer quickly and easily. At the very least, you will be able to find example code for each of the button types.

Good luck and good hunting.

Part Two builds on the basic AFC concepts presented in Part One and describes the classes that make up AFC. The format for Part Two is a little bit different in that it is styled as a reference book. Each chapter covers a different set of classes. A class diagram at the beginning of each chapter shows the classes described in that chapter.

Each section begins by describing a class and then provides numerous examples showing how that class is used. So if you have a question about AFC buttons, you can refer to Chapter 6, which has more than 10 application examples that use various subclasses of the *UIButton* class in different ways. You will find examples of push buttons, radio buttons, check buttons (also called check boxes), and repeat buttons. Among the many examples, you should be able to find a solution for your particular problem.

Of course, this approach involves some repetition. For example, labels are discussed in Chapter 5 (labels are one subclass of *UICanvas*), Chapter 6 (button labels) and Chapter 9 (menu options are also labels). I've tried to avoid needless repetition by using cross-references. Thus, I demonstrate the most common form of menu labels in Chapter 9, but I direct you to the discussion of canvases in Chapter 5 for the more esoteric forms of labels, even though those esoteric forms can be applied to menus.

Many example applets in Part Two perform similar types of functions. For example, many classes read a local image file. Because the code for performing such mundane jobs as loading images can obscure the point the example is trying to show, and repeating this image-loading code would lead to book bloat, I've created several helper classes and collectively placed them in the folder AppCommon. You've already seen one of these helper classes—App 4_5 used the *Application* class.

Regarding what these helper classes do, *Application* contains the majority of code necessary for the example to execute as an application as well as an applet. All examples in Part Two can be executed as applets. Roughly 80 percent of these programs can also be executed as applications with the help of *Application*. (See App4_5.) *Images* simplifies the job of dealing with images. *FileDescr* performs directory operations. *FileDescr* can be used only by applications and trusted applets. (Appendix B, "Utility Classes Used in This Book," explains how these helper classes work.) You are encouraged to use and improve these classes in your own programs.

Here's a word of caution: it is critical that AppCommon be in the directory search path in order for these examples to execute properly. Select Tools/Options, and click on the Directories tab. Select Class Files from the Show Directories For list, and be sure that the path to AppCommon appears in the Directories list. When uploading an applet to your Web page, be sure that any necessary *AppCommon* classes are also uploaded.

PART TWO

MODERN COMPONENTRY

Canvases

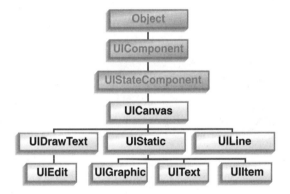

The *Canvas* classes, which are a set of classes that extend the abstract base class *UICanvas*, provide a canvas on which the user can write or draw. The *UICanvas* classes are not containers. (*UICanvas* is extended from *UIStateComponent*, which extends *UIComponent*.) Most of these classes can be edited programmatically only; however, the class *UIEdit* can also be updated by the applet user. The classes *UIGraphic* and *UIItem* can contain a graphical object. The remaining classes are designed to contain only text.

All of the *Canvas* objects support *FxColor*, which means that both the foreground and the background can be drawn in different colors and patterns, including background images. See Chapter 10, "Dialog Boxes," for details on *FxColor*.

THE *DRAWTEXT* OBJECT

The *DrawText* objects are *UIComponent* class objects that represent blocks of text. A *DrawText* object does not have its own border. Two classes make up the *DrawText* group: *UIDrawText* and *UIEdit*.

The *UIDrawText* Class

The *UIDrawText* class represents your basic read-only text component. Although it cannot be changed directly by the user, *UIDrawText* can be changed programmatically. Its use is demonstrated in the following simple applet:

```
// Text01 - Simple applet demonstrating the UIDrawText class

// AWT classes
import java.applet.*;
import java.awt.*;

// AFC classes
import com.ms.ui.*;
import com.ms.ui.event.*;

import Application;

public class Text01 extends AwtUIApplet
{
    Text01()
    {
        super(new MyApplet());
    }

    public static void main(String[] arg)
    {
        new Application(new MyApplet());
    }
}

class MyApplet extends UIApplet
{
    public void init()
    {
        setLayout(new UIBorderLayout());

        // Create a UIDrawText object, and add it to the
        // applet's window. That's all there is to it!
        UIDrawText text = new UIDrawText("some text");
        add(text, "Center");
```

```
        // The following button will demonstrate that
        // the text field can be edited (but not by
        // the user).
        add(new MyUIButton(text), "South");
    }
}


// MyUIButton - Updates the text field
//              by adding the string " plus more" to
//              whatever is there already
class MyUIButton extends UIPushButton
{
    UIDrawText text;
    class PBAction implements IUIActionListener
    {
        public void actionPerformed(UIActionEvent e)
        {
            text.setValueText(text.getValueText() + " plus more");
        }
    }

    MyUIButton(UIDrawText text)
    {
        super("Add text", UIPushButton.RAISED);
        this.text = text;
        addActionListener(new PBAction());
    }
}
```

The results of executing this applet and clicking the Add Text button twice are shown in Figure 5-1.

FIGURE 5-1   *Using the* UIDrawText *class can display a text string like this.*

When the *init* method is called, this applet creates a *UIDrawText* object containing the text *some text*, which it adds to the center of the applet window as follows:

```
// Create a UIDrawText object, and add it to the
// applet's window. That's all there is to it!
UIDrawText text = new UIDrawText("some text");
add(text, "Center");
```

The *UIBorderLayout* layout manager expands the *UIDrawText* component to fill the applet window.

The *MyUIButton* push button object that is created at the bottom of the applet window is used to edit the *UIDrawText* object. Clicking this push button invokes the *PBAction.actionPerformed* method, which first reads the value in the *UIDrawText* object by calling *getValueText*, appends the string " *plus more*", and then updates the *UIDrawText* object with the resulting string by calling *setValueText*:

```
text.setValueText(text.getValueText() + " plus more");
```

Remember that the *Application* class is provided to allow the applet to be executed as an application.

The *UIEdit* Class

The *UIEdit* class represents a *UIDrawText* object that is editable by the user. The *UIEdit* class even understands control characters such as backspace and newline and processes them appropriately.

Programmatically, the *UIEdit* class hardly differs from the *UIDrawText* class. In fact, you can replace the *UIDrawText* object in Text01 with a *UIEdit* object to create a user-editable text window:

```
// Create a UIEdit object, and add it to the
// applet's window.
UIEdit text = new UIEdit("some text");
add(text, "Center");
```

The output from this applet is identical to that of Text01 except that it can be edited as well, as shown in Figure 5-2. (The entire code for this applet is in Text02 on the companion CD.)

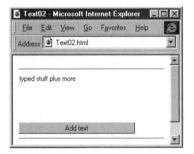

FIGURE 5-2   *The Text02 applet's user-editable window.*

Using *UIDrawText* and *UIEdit* with Viewers

Normally, a *UIDrawText* or *UIEdit* object would be placed within a viewer such as *UIScrollViewer*, *UISplitViewer*, or *UIColumnViewer*. Not only do such viewers provide the text area with a border to define the editable area, but they also extend the text area's features in useful ways. For example, *UIScrollViewer* attaches scrollbars when the amount of text cannot be viewed within the text area provided.

A simple viewer

The following applet, Text03a, demonstrates how a *UIEdit* object can be placed within a *UIScrollViewer* viewer to create a multiline, scrollable area. The applet also demonstrates how to read the text from this area for subsequent processing. (It does nothing more than display the read text.)

```
// Text03a - Places a UIEdit object within a scrollable text
//           area; uses an OK button to read the contents
//           of the window

// AWT classes
import java.applet.*;
import java.awt.*;

// AFC classes
import com.ms.ui.*;
import com.ms.ui.event.*;

import Application;
```

>>

```
public class Text03a extends AwtUIApplet
{
    Text03a()
    {
        super(new MyApplet());
    }

    public static void main(String[] arg)
    {
        new Application(new MyApplet());
    }
}

class MyApplet extends UIApplet
{
    // showStatus - If MyApplet is being invoked as an
    //              applet, output message in status
    //              bar; otherwise, just output.
    public void showStatus(String s)
    {
        if (getApplet() != null)
        {
            super.showStatus(s);
        }
        else
        {
            System.out.println(s);
        }
    }

    public void init()
    {
        setLayout(new UIBorderLayout());

        // Place the UIEdit object in a UIScrollViewer;
        // this will let the text area scroll when it
        // grows too large to fit in the assigned
        // space.
        UIEdit text = new MyTextArea();
        UIScrollViewer viewer = new UIScrollViewer(text);
        add(viewer, "Center");

        add(new MyUIButton(this, text), "South");
    }
}
```

```
// MyTextArea - Several properties can be set in a
//              UIDrawText object; a word wrap property
//              is just one of these.
class MyTextArea extends UIEdit
{
    MyTextArea()
    {
        setWordWrap(wwKeepWordIntact);
    }
}


// MyUIButton - Read the contents of the text
//              window, and process them in some way.
class MyUIButton extends UIPushButton
{
    UIApplet   parent;
    UIDrawText text;

    class PBAction implements IUIActionListener
    {
        public void actionPerformed(UIActionEvent e)
        {
            // Read the text field.
            String sText = text.getValueText();

            // Now you can do anything you want with it.
            parent.showStatus(sText);
        }
    }

    MyUIButton(UIApplet parent, UIDrawText text)
    {
        super("Read Text", UIPushButton.RAISED);
        this.parent = parent;
        this.text = text;
        addActionListener(new PBAction());
    }
}
```

When executed as an application, this applet generates output like that shown in Figure 5-3 on the following page.

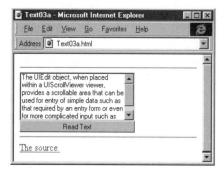

FIGURE 5-3   *Sample output from Text03a showing updated editable text area.*

This applet creates a *UIScrollViewer* class containing the user-defined text area of class *MyTextArea*. It then adds this viewer to the center of the applet window:

```
UIEdit text = new MyTextArea();
UIScrollViewer viewer = new UIScrollViewer(text);
add(viewer, "Center");
```

The *MyTextArea* subclass extends the *UIEdit* class by simply setting certain properties in the constructor. In this case, I have set the word wrap property to *wwKeepWordIntact*, meaning that entire words are wrapped (hyphenation is not allowed).

A *MyUIButton* object is attached to the bottom of the applet window. When clicked, this push button reads the contents of the editable window and passes them to *showStatus*. When invoked as an applet, *showStatus* calls *UIApplet-.showStatus* to display the text string in the status bar. When invoked as an application, *showStatus* calls *println* to display the string to your standard output.

You might want to do several things with the text read from the *UIEdit* window shown in Figure 5-3. For example, if the user were providing her name and address, you might want to record such information in a database. For this type of application, the approach demonstrated by Text03a is ideal. The *UIEdit* object also forms the beginnings of a simple word processor, but the approach used here won't work for a word processor without some modifications.

A word processor–like applet and the document/view model

Before Text03a can be used as a word processor–like applet, several changes must be made. Modern applications use what is known as the document/view model. In this model, the view handles interaction with the user while the document handles the storage of data, as shown in Figure 5-4.

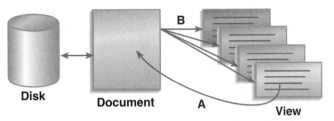

Disk   Document   A   View

A - Input is sent from the view to the document.
B - The changes to the document are sent to each of the views.

FIGURE 5-4   *The flow of data in the document/view model.*

As the user types, the input is captured by the view. The view passes this input to the document for processing. Once the input has been processed, the document passes the information back to the view for display.

While this may seem somewhat circuitous, the document/view model has numerous advantages. For one, the view tends to be the same, independent of what type of processing is actually going on behind the scenes. The document, which is processing the information, doesn't really care how the data is being displayed or how it is being collected. Thus, a spreadsheet document doesn't care whether its data is being displayed in matrix format, as a pie chart, or as a scattergram; while a view doesn't care how the data is processed as long as it continues to be displayed in its original format, be it a matrix format, a pie chart, or a scattergram.

Another advantage is that separating the document from the view allows multiple views to be attached to the same document. Using our spreadsheet example again, a matrix view and a pie chart view can both examine data from one document at the same time. The user can also view the same document in a word processor in two or more windows simultaneously.

If the data the user entered were kept in the view, the possibility would always exist that the two views could get out of sync, with one view showing updated data and the other showing out-of-date data. Keeping the actual data in the document means that all views stay in sync at all times. Users insist on this type of functionality in modern applications such as Microsoft Word and Microsoft Excel.

The example Text03b, beginning on the next page, demonstrates how *UIEdit* can be used as a view in a word processor–like applet.

```
// Text03b - A "real" word processor application
//           using the document/view model. Here
//           MyTextArea is used as a viewer into
//           the class Document. Note that this is
//           a bare-minimum application - it
//           doesn't attempt to handle keypresses
//           such as Backspace and Delete.

// AWT classes
import java.applet.*;
import java.awt.*;

// AFC classes
import com.ms.ui.*;
import com.ms.ui.event.*;
import com.ms.fx.*;

import Application;

public class Text03b extends AwtUIApplet
{
    Text03b()
    {
        super(new MyApplet());
    }

    public static void main(String[] arg)
    {
        new Application(new MyApplet());
    }
}


class MyApplet extends UIApplet
{
    // showStatus - If MyApplet is being invoked as an
    //              applet, output message in status
    //              bar; otherwise, just output.
    public void showStatus(String s)
    {
        if (getApplet() != null)
        {
            super.showStatus(s);
        }
        else
        {
            System.out.println(s);
        }
    }
```

```
    public void init()
    {
        // Create two text areas. Attach them
        // to the same document, and they will stay
        // in sync.
        Document doc = new Document();

        // Arrange the text areas vertically.
        Dimension d = new Dimension(200, 200);
        setSize(d);
        int nWidth  = d.width - 10;
        int nHeight = d.height/2 - 10;

        setLayout(new UIBorderLayout());
        UIEdit text1 = new MyTextArea(this, doc,
                                    nWidth, nHeight);

        add(text1, "North");

        UIEdit text2 = new MyTextArea(this, doc,
                                    nWidth, nHeight);

        add(text2, "South");
    }
}

// MyTextArea - Simple text area with an attached
//              document
class MyTextArea extends UIEdit
{
    UIApplet parent;
    Document doc;
    Dimension d;

    MyTextArea(UIApplet parent, Document doc,
             int nWidth, int nHeight)
    {
        this.parent = parent;
        d = new Dimension(nWidth, nHeight);

        // Set the current size.
        setSize(nWidth, nHeight);

        // Remember our document, and attach this text area to that
        // document. (Updates will come through that document.)
        this.doc = doc;
        doc.addTextArea(this);
```

>>

```
            setBordered(true);
    }

    public Dimension getPreferredSize() { return d; }

    // keyDown - Captures keypresses.
    public boolean keyDown(Event e, int nKey)
    {
        // Get the key, and display it in the status bar.
        char c = (char)nKey;
        parent.showStatus("Key = " + c);

        // Remember the current output position.
        int nOffset = getCurrIndex();

        // Add the character to the document.
        doc.addChar(c, nOffset);

        // Update the output position.
        setCurrIndex(nOffset + 1);
        return true;
    }

    // update - Updates the current text area;
    //          called by the document whenever the
    //          document is modified
    public void update(char c, int nOffset)
    {
        String s = getValueText();
        StringBuffer sb = new StringBuffer(s);
        sb.insert(nOffset, c);
        setValueText(sb.toString());
    }
}

// Document - The repository of information; the Document
//            class would correspond to the DOC file in
//            Microsoft Word.
class Document
{
    // Here contents refers to the contents of the document;
    // normally, the contents would be saved on disk.
    FxText contents = new FxText();
```

```
// The Document class keeps a container of all of the text
// fields attached to this document; each of these
// text fields represents a view into the document.
MyTextAreaPtr first = null;
class MyTextAreaPtr
{
    MyTextAreaPtr next;
    MyTextArea    data;
    MyTextAreaPtr(MyTextArea data)
    {
        this.data = data;
        next = first;
        first = this;
    }
}

// addChar - Add a character to the document at the
//           indicated offset.
public void addChar(char c, int nOffset)
{
    contents.insert(c, nOffset);

    // Now update all text areas.
    MyTextAreaPtr textAreaPtr = first;
    while(textAreaPtr != null)
    {
        textAreaPtr.data.update(c, nOffset);
        textAreaPtr = textAreaPtr.next;
    }
}

// addTextArea - Add another view to the document.
public void addTextArea(MyTextArea textArea)
{
    new MyTextAreaPtr(textArea);
}
}
```

This applet creates two text areas, arranged one above the other. These two views are attached to a single document. The result of executing this applet is shown in Figure 5-5 on the following page.

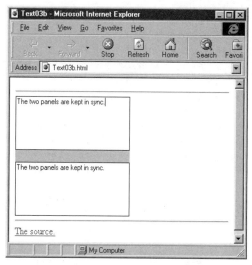

FIGURE 5-5   *Output from Text03b showing how the two text windows stay in sync regardless of which window is used for input.*

Execution begins with the *init* method, which creates two *MyTextArea* objects, one attached to the top and the other to the bottom of the applet window. The width of each text area is set to the width of the applet window (minus 10 pixels for insets), and the height is set to half the height of the applet window (again, minus 10 pixels). Each *MyTextArea* object is passed the same *Document* object.

The *MyTextArea* class looks much like the constructor shown in Text03a except that it also saves its *Document* object and then attaches itself to the document. This version of *MyTextArea* provides two extra methods of critical importance.

The first method, *keyDown*, is invoked automatically whenever the user presses a key while the cursor is within the text area. This method outputs the key entered to the applet's status bar. (Obviously, this step is optional.) Next *keyDown* passes the keypress to the *Document* object by calling *addChar* before updating the insertion point. The insertion point must be passed to the *Document* object so that *Document* knows where to insert the character. (Remember that the user can insert characters in the middle of existing text and not just at the end.) The *keyDown* method rereads the current insertion point on each keystroke in case the user has clicked the mouse somewhere within the text area and thereby moved the insertion point.

The second critical method is the *update* method. This method is called by the *Document* object when the text changes. The *update* method inserts the new character in the text string and displays the results.

The *Document* class for this applet is overly simplistic. It maintains a linked list of attached *MyTextArea* objects. When the text area calls the *addTextArea* method, this method adds the text area onto the beginning of the linked list.

The *Document.addChar* method is called by *MyTextArea* each time the user presses a key. The *addChar* method first adds the character passed to it to the document's contents at the offset specified. It then loops through the list of *MyTextArea* objects attached to the *Document* object and passes the character to the *update* function of each. In this way, each view is given a chance to update itself with the new document data.

Even though this applet adequately demonstrates the principles of the document/view model, it is lacking in several notable ways. For one, it does not handle control characters such as backspace and delete. This capability could be added to the view without too much trouble. Further, in a real-world application, you would want to provide a document that actually does something. A spreadsheet document would provide some type of calculator engine. A word processor would provide word processing capabilities. In addition, most documents maintain their data on disk either in a database of some sort or in some type of proprietary file structure. Maintaining all of the data in memory limits the amount of data that the applet can deal with.

STATICS

The classes that make up the *Static* group derive from *UIStatic*. These classes can contain small amounts of text, an image, or both. These classes are used primarily as labels for buttons, as menu items, and as labels on tabs or anywhere else a fixed text or text and graphic label is required. *UIStatic* objects come in three flavors: *UIText*, *UIGraphic*, and *UIItem*.

The *UIText* Class

Before we look at the *UIText* class, you should be absolutely clear that a simple *String* object can also be used as a label in almost every case. Using a string object as a label is demonstrated in the following example applet, Static01a.

```
// Static01a - Strings can serve as labels, much as they
//            do in the AWT.
import java.applet.*;
import java.awt.*;

import com.ms.ui.*;
import com.ms.ui.event.*;

import Application;

public class Static01a extends AwtUIApplet
{
    Static01a()
    {
        super(new MyApplet());
    }

    public static void main(String[] arg)
    {
        new Application(new MyApplet());
    }
}

class MyApplet extends UIApplet
{
    public void init()
    {
        // Create an example menu.
        UIMenuList fileList = new UIMenuList();
        fileList.add("Open");
        fileList.add("Save");
        fileList.add("Save as...");
        fileList.add("Close");
        fileList.add("Exit");

        UIMenuButton fileButton =
                    new UIMenuButton("File", fileList);

        UIBand editMenu = new UIBand();
        editMenu.add(fileButton);
```

```
        UIBandBox menu = new UIBandBox();
        menu.add(editMenu);

        setLayout(new UIBorderLayout());
        add(menu, "North");
    }
}
```

The output of this applet is shown in Figure 5-6.

Static01a - Microsoft Internet Explorer

File Edit View Go Favorites Help

Back   Forward   Stop   Refresh   Home

Address Static01a.html

File
Open
Save
Save as...
Close
Exit

The source.

My Computer

FIGURE 5-6   *A menu built using* String *objects as labels.*

The experienced AFC programmer is more likely to generate the same applet using the *UIText* class, as shown in the equivalent applet Static01b:

```
// Static01b - Using UIText fields instead of Strings for
//             labels gives the programmer control over such
//             features as whether the item is hot-tracked.
import java.applet.*;
import java.awt.*;

import com.ms.ui.*;
import com.ms.ui.event.*;

import Application;
```

```
public class Static01b extends AwtUIApplet
{
    Static01b()
    {
        super(new MyApplet());
    }

    public static void main(String[] arg)
    {
        new Application(new MyApplet());
    }
}

class MyApplet extends UIApplet
{
    public void init()
    {
        UIMenuList fileList = new UIMenuList();

        // Create the style to be used for the text
        // fields in the menu.
        int nStyle = UIText.LEFT|UIText.HOTTRACK;

        // Now create UIText objects for menu labels.
        fileList.add(new UIText("Open",     nStyle));
        fileList.add(new UIText("Save",     nStyle));
        fileList.add(new UIText("Save as...", nStyle));
        fileList.add(new UIText("Close",    nStyle));
        fileList.add(new UIText("Exit",     nStyle));

        UIMenuButton fileButton = new UIMenuButton("File", fileList);

        UIBand editMenu = new UIBand();
        editMenu.add(fileButton);

        UIBandBox menu = new UIBandBox();
        menu.add(editMenu);

        setLayout(new UIBorderLayout());
        add(menu, "North");
    }
}
```

A hot-tracked label changes color whenever the user points at it with the mouse. In addition, with the *UIItem* class the programmer can specify left, right, or center alignment.

NOTE

The *add(String)* method does nothing more than create a *UIItem* object for you and then pass that object to the *add(UIItem)* method. The *add(String)* method is provided for compatibility with the AWT.

Subclassing *UIText*

The *UIText* class can be subclassed to add functionality to a label. This technique is demonstrated in the following applet, Static01c:

```java
// Static01c - Using UIText enables the programmer to create
//             subclasses to perform the actual operation.
import java.applet.*;
import java.awt.*;

import com.ms.ui.*;
import com.ms.ui.event.*;

import Application;

public class Static01c extends AwtUIApplet
{
    Static01c()
    {
        super(new MyApplet());
    }

    public static void main(String[] arg)
    {
        new Application(new MyApplet());
    }
}

class MyApplet extends UIApplet
{
    // showStatus - If MyApplet is being invoked as an
    //              applet, output message in status
    //              bar; otherwise, just output.
    public void showStatus(String s)
    {
        if (getApplet() != null)
        {
            super.showStatus(s);
        }
```

>>

```
        else
        {
            System.out.println(s);
        }
    }


// UIOpenText - Represents the Open menu item, including
//              the code to perform the actual operation
class UIOpenText extends UIText
{
    UIOpenText(int nStyle)
    {
        super("Open", nStyle);
    }

    // mouseUp - Perform the open operation. (Whatever
    //           that might be. Operations are normally
    //           performed on the mouse up and not on the
    //           mouse down - go figure.)
    public boolean mouseUp(Event e, int x, int y)
    {
        showStatus("Selected Open");
        return super.mouseUp(e, x, y);
    }
}


// UIExtText - The exit operation in a nutshell
class UIExitText extends UIText
{
    UIExitText(int nStyle)
    {
        super("Exit", nStyle);
    }
    public boolean mouseUp(Event e, int x, int y)
    {
        showStatus("Selected Exit");
        return super.mouseUp(e, x, y);
    }
}


public void init()
{
    UIMenuList fileList = new UIMenuList();

    // Now create UIText objects for menu labels.
    int nStyle = UIText.LEFT|UIText.HOTTRACK;
    fileList.add(new UIOpenText(nStyle));
```

```
        // The other menu items...
        fileList.add(new UIExitText(nStyle));

        // The remainder is the same.
        UIMenuButton fileButton = new UIMenuButton("File", fileList);

        UIBand editMenu = new UIBand();
        editMenu.add(fileButton);

        UIBandBox menu = new UIBandBox();
        menu.add(editMenu);

        setLayout(new UIBorderLayout());
        add(menu, "North");
    }
}
```

Here I have created the class *UIOpenText*, which extends the *UIText* class by overriding the *mouseUp* method. Using an object of class *UIOpenText* as the label for the File/Open menu item causes this locally defined *mouseUp* method to be invoked when the user chooses this menu item. Similarly, an object of class *UIExitText* is used as the label for the File/Exit menu option. Of course, this is not the only way to provide menu functionality, but it is a modular, extensible approach.

TIP

Don't provide button or menu functionality on the *mouseDown* event that is invoked when the user clicks on the label. Triggering the *mouseUp* method gives the user the opportunity to change her mind by moving the mouse pointer off the label before releasing the mouse button. This is the standard approach used by most applications and the one to which users have become accustomed.

The *UIGraphic* Class

The *UIText* class is useful for labeling objects using text strings. The *UIGraphic* class is used to label objects using images instead of text. In the following example applet, Static02, *UIGraphic* objects are used to label menu options in the same way that *UIText* objects were used earlier.

```
// Static02 - The UIGraphic class allows the use of
//           an image as a label in place of text.
import java.applet.*;
import java.awt.*;

import com.ms.ui.*;
import com.ms.ui.event.*;

import Images;
import Application;

public class Static02 extends AwtUIApplet
{
    Static02()
    {
        super(new MyApplet());
    }

    public static void main(String[] arg)
    {
        System.out.println("Cannot execute as an application");
    }
}

class MyApplet extends UIApplet
{
    // Names of the images to associate with the
    // menu options
    String[] sImageNames = new String[4]
        {"open.gif", "save.gif", "close.gif", "exit.gif"};
    final int OPEN  = 0;
    final int SAVE  = 1;
    final int CLOSE = 2;
    final int EXIT  = 3;

    public void init()
    {
        // Create the images we will need later.
        Images images = new Images(this, sImageNames);
        images.load();

        // Now continue with the menu.
        UIMenuList fileList = new UIMenuList();
```

```
        // Create the style to be used for the text
        // fields in the menu.
        int nStyle = UIGraphic.CENTERED|UIGraphic.HOTTRACK;

        // Now create UIText objects for menu labels.
        fileList.add(new UIGraphic(images.getImage(OPEN), nStyle));
        fileList.add(new UIGraphic(images.getImage(SAVE), nStyle));
        fileList.add(new UIGraphic(images.getImage(CLOSE), nStyle));
        fileList.add(new UIGraphic(images.getImage(EXIT), nStyle));

        UIMenuButton fileButton = new UIMenuButton("File", fileList);

        UIBand editMenu = new UIBand();
        editMenu.add(fileButton);

        UIBandBox menu = new UIBandBox();
        menu.add(editMenu);

        setLayout(new UIBorderLayout());
        add(menu, "North");
    }
}
```

In outline, this applet is identical to the earlier *UIText* applet (Static01b). One additional complication, however, is the loading of the image files into *Image* objects. This process is made much easier by the *Images* class, one of the App-Common classes described in Appendix B, "Utility Classes Used in This Book."

NOTE

The *Application* class does not support the loading of images.

The graphical menu items are created using statements such as the following:

```
        fileList.add(new UIGraphic(images.getImage(OPEN), nStyle));
```

The call to *images.getImage(OPEN)* returns an *Image* object. This technique is used to construct a *UIGraphic* object that is used as the menu option label.

Figure 5-7 on the following page shows the Static02 applet menu with graphical labels.

FIGURE 5-7   *The same menu as in Figure 5-6 (without the Save As option) using graphics images for menu labels.*

You wouldn't normally use *UIGraphic* objects alone as labels for a menu; this was just an example to demonstrate their use.

The *UIItem* Class

The *UIItem* class serves as a combination of the *UIText* and *UIGraphic* classes: it contains a text string like *UIText* and a graphics object like *UIGraphic*. The following applet, Static03, demonstrates the same menu using *UIItem* objects for labels:

```
// Static03 - The UIItem class allows an image and a label to be
//            combined and treated like a single entity.
import java.applet.*;
import java.awt.*;

import com.ms.ui.*;
import com.ms.ui.event.*;

import Images;
import Application;
```

```
public class Static03 extends AwtUIApplet
{
    Static03()
    {
        super(new MyApplet());
    }

    public static void main(String[] arg)
    {
        System.out.println("Cannot execute as an application.");
    }
}


class MyApplet extends UIApplet
{
    // Names of the images to associate with
    // the labels
    String[] sImageNames = new String[4]
        {"open.gif", "save.gif", "close.gif", "exit.gif"};
    String[] sLabel = new String[4]
        {"Open", "Save", "Close", "Exit"};
    final int OPEN  = 0;
    final int SAVE  = 1;
    final int CLOSE = 2;
    final int EXIT  = 3;

    public void init()
    {
        // Load the images we will need later.
        Images images = new Images(this, sImageNames);
        images.load();

        // Now continue with the menu.
        UIMenuList fileList = new UIMenuList();

        // Create UIText objects for menu labels -
        // each UIItem needs an image, a label, a style,
        // and an indication of where the image should be
        // positioned relative to the text.
        int nStyle = UIItem.LEFT;
        int nImagePos = UIItem.ONLEFT;
```

>>

>>

```
            fileList.add(new UIItem(images.getImage(OPEN),
                        sLabel[OPEN], nStyle, nImagePos));
            fileList.add(new UIItem(images.getImage(SAVE),
                        sLabel[SAVE], nStyle, nImagePos));
            fileList.add(new UIItem(images.getImage(CLOSE),
                        sLabel[CLOSE],nStyle, nImagePos));
            fileList.add(new UIItem(images.getImage(EXIT),
                        sLabel[EXIT], nStyle, nImagePos));

            // Again, no changes from here on.
            UIMenuButton fileButton = new UIMenuButton("File", fileList);

            UIBand editMenu = new UIBand();
            editMenu.add(fileButton);

            UIBandBox menu = new UIBandBox();
            menu.add(editMenu);

            setLayout(new UIBorderLayout());
            add(menu, "North");
        }
}
```

Here the constructor for the *UIItem* takes both a text string and an image:

```
int nStyle = UIItem.LEFT;
int nImagePos = UIItem.ONLEFT;
fileList.add(new UIItem(images.getImage(OPEN),
            sLabel[OPEN], nStyle, nImagePos));
```

The *nImagePos* argument positions the image with respect to the text—in this case, the image is to be displayed to the left of the text. The result of executing this applet appears in Figure 5-8.

When the *Image* Object Isn't Available

As noted, the *Application* class does not support the loading of images. (This is because the *MediaTracker* class requires the current *Applet* object as one of its arguments. If you don't know what that means, don't worry.) Does this limitation mean that an application that uses a *UIItem* object to label its menu or buttons cannot be executed as an application? Maybe not.

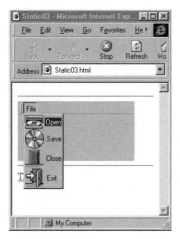

FIGURE 5-8   *Images and text strings combined in menu labels.*

It turns out that if the image reference passed to *UIItem* is *null*, *UIItem* acts like a *UIText*. In effect, *UIItem* simply ignores the graphics part. You can use this characteristic to your advantage in code like the following snippet:

```
Image image = null;
if (parent.getApplet() != null)
{
    Images images = new Images(parent, "Folder.gif");
    images.load();
    image = images.getImage();
}
UIItem label = new UIItem(image, "Label");
```

Here the *Image* reference is initialized to *null*. If the current program is an applet, an object of class *Images* is created to load the label image and that image is assigned to the variable *image*. If the program is an application, however, *image* retains its *null* value, which allows the application to continue to execute with text labels—only the graphics portions are missing. (This example was taken from the Tree02 applet in Chapter 7, "Panels and Windows," in case you would like to examine the code further.)

THE *UILINE* CLASS

The final class in this category is the *UILine* class. This simple class does nothing more than draw a line separator in a menu or a band box. The following simple example applet demonstrates:

```
// Line01 - The UILine class is useful for creating a line in
//          menu lists to separate groups of menu items.
import java.applet.*;
import java.awt.*;

import com.ms.ui.*;
import com.ms.ui.event.*;

import Application;

public class Line01 extends AwtUIApplet
{
    Line01()
    {
        super(new MyApplet());
    }

    public static void main(String[] arg)
    {
        new Application(new MyApplet());
    }
}

class MyApplet extends UIApplet
{
    public void init()
    {
        UIMenuList fileList = new UIMenuList();
        fileList.add("Open");
        fileList.add("Save");
        fileList.add("Save as...");
        fileList.add("Close");

        // Insert a line separator in the menu.
        fileList.add(new UILine());
        fileList.add("Print");

        // Add another one.
        fileList.add(new UILine());
        fileList.add("Exit");
```

```
        UIMenuButton fileButton = new UIMenuButton("File", fileList);

        UIBand editMenu = new UIBand();
        editMenu.add(fileButton);

        UIBandBox menu = new UIBandBox();
        menu.add(editMenu);

        setLayout(new UIBorderLayout());
        add(menu, "North");
    }
}
```

The resulting menu is shown in Figure 5-9.

FIGURE 5-9   *A similar menu with line separators.*

WHAT'S NEXT

The *Canvas* classes are some of the simplest classes in AFC. The *UIDrawText* class represents the simple text output class, and the *UIEdit* class allows for both output and input. In addition to these two classes, *UIItem* and its siblings, *UIText* and *UIGraphic*, are used primarily as labels for other AFC components.

Buttons

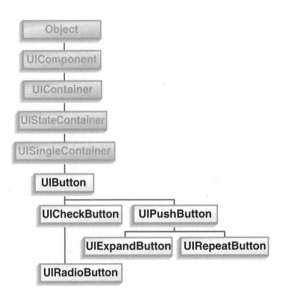

Under the AW I, the programmer must make do with a single *Button* class that's intended to serve in all the different places where buttons are used. Under AFC, the *UIButton* class is an abstract base class for several classes, each designed to provide a different type of button: *UIPushButton, UICheckButton, UIRadioButton, UIRepeatButton,* and *UIExpandButton.*

THE *UIPUSHBUTTON* CLASS

The most basic of all buttons is the push button, so we will examine it first. Because the push button is the most basic, most of the push button features described in this section also apply to the other button types.

Creating Buttons

The following applet demonstrates the creation of two buttons in an applet window:

```
// Button01 - Basic button applet
import java.applet.*;
import java.awt.*;
import com.ms.ui.*;
import Application;

public class Button01 extends AwtUIApplet
{
    Button01()
    {
        super(new MyApplet());
    }

    public static void main(String[] arg)
    {
        new Application(new MyApplet());
    }
}

class MyApplet extends UIApplet
{

    public void init()
    {
        // Use an extremely simple layout.
        setLayout(new UIFlowLayout());

        // Create two labeled push buttons;
        // use strings for labels.
        add(new UIPushButton("Go"));
        add(new UIPushButton("Stop"));
    }
}
```

This applet begins by establishing *UIFlowLayout* as the layout manager. (Remember that *UIFlowLayout* is the simplest of the layout managers.) The *UIFlowLayout* layout manager allocates components from left to right in a single row for as long as there is room in the row; it then drops down to the next row and continues the process.

The *UIPushButton(String)* constructor creates a push button with the given label. The call to the *add* method adds the button to the parent applet window in the next available slot. In the absence of other considerations, the size of the button is determined by the size of the label or by a call to the *setSize* method. The size of a button can also be influenced by overriding the *getPreferredSize* method. As we will see shortly, these considerations are often overridden by the layout manager, which might resize the component to fit its own display needs.

The output from the Button01 applet is shown in Figure 6-1.

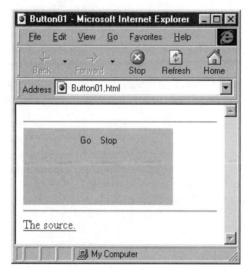

FIGURE 6-1   *The output from the most basic of all button applets.*

 NOTE

> In Figure 6-1, all you can see are labels—you can't tell the labels represent buttons until you move your mouse pointer over them. The properties that affect button appearance and the mouseover actions that effect changes in button appearance are discussed later in this chapter.

Laying Out Buttons

UIFlowLayout is not the most convenient layout manager for buttons. For one thing, users generally prefer that all their buttons be the same size. In addition, they like similar buttons to be aligned either vertically or horizontally (or both if there are a lot of buttons).

You can align buttons by carefully setting the size of the applet window to contain the buttons appropriately when displayed on a PC running Microsoft Windows. However, this technique doesn't guarantee that the applet will appear properly on all platforms that support Java. The *UIFlowLayout* layout manager just doesn't give the programmer much help in laying out buttons.

For laying out buttons horizontally, as in the Button01 applet, two other layouts are a better choice. The first of these options, the *UIRowLayout* layout manager, divides the available horizontal space equally into the requested number of rows. Adding our buttons to these columns ensures that the buttons are all the same size, as demonstrated in the following applet, Button02:

```
// Button02 - The arrangement of buttons can be controlled
//            using different layouts by placing buttons
//            in subpanels; here the buttons are placed
//            along the bottom of the applet window. Using
//            the UIRowLayout layout manager ensures that both
//            buttons are the same size.
import java.applet.*;
import java.awt.*;
import com.ms.ui.*;
import Application;

public class Button02 extends AwtUIApplet
{
    Button02()
    {
        super(new MyApplet());
    }

    public static void main(String[] arg)
    {
        new Application(new MyApplet());
    }
}
```

```
class MyApplet extends UIApplet
{
    public void init()
    {
        // Use an extremely simple layout
        // for the parent applet window.
        setLayout(new UIBorderLayout());

        // Create a new panel for the buttons.
        UIPanel buttonPanel = new UIPanel();

        // Divide the available space into
        // equally spaced rows.
        buttonPanel.setLayout(new UIRowLayout(2));

        // Now add the two labeled push buttons...
        buttonPanel.add(new UIPushButton("Go"));
        buttonPanel.add(new UIPushButton("Stop"));

        // ...and position this panel along the bottom
        // of the applet window.
        add(buttonPanel, "South");
    }
}
```

This applet begins by creating a separate panel intended solely for the buttons. A *UIRowLayout* object with two columns is assigned to this new *buttonPanel* object. The Go button is added to the *buttonPanel* object to become the first column, and the Stop button is added as the second column. Last the *buttonPanel* object is added at the bottom of the applet window.

The net result is shown in Figure 6-2 on the following page.

A similar effect can be achieved using the *UIButtonFlowLayout* layout manager. This layout manager also makes all buttons the same width, but rather than basing this width on the available window area, this layout manager sizes all buttons to be the same width as the largest button. The size of this largest button is whatever is required to display the largest button label.

FIGURE 6-2   *A more pleasing button layout.*

Assigning Activities to Buttons

Buttons are not of much use if nothing happens when the user clicks them. To avoid this bit of embarrassment, we need to be able to assign activities to our buttons. There are a lot of different ways of doing this. My personal preference is to create a button subclass that defines an inner class to implement the appropriate listener. The following applet, Button03a, demonstrates this technique:

```
// Button03a - Adding an EventListener is the most
//             straightforward way to assign an activity
//             to a button. Here this is done using
//             subclassing.
import java.applet.*;
import java.awt.*;
import com.ms.ui.*;
import com.ms.ui.event.*;

import Application;

public class Button03a extends AwtUIApplet
{
    Button03a()
    {
        super(new MyApplet());
    }
```

```
    public static void main(String[] arg)
    {
        new Application(new MyApplet());
    }
}

class MyApplet extends UIApplet
{
    // showStatus - If MyApplet is being invoked as an
    //              applet, output the message in the status
    //              bar; otherwise, just output.
    public void showStatus(String s)
    {
        if (getApplet() != null)
        {
            super.showStatus(s);
        }
        else
        {
            System.out.println(s);
        }
    }

    // init - Set up panel with buttons.
    public void init()
    {
        // Use an extremely simple layout.
        setLayout(new UIBorderLayout());

        // Create a new panel for the buttons.
        UIPanel buttonPanel = new UIPanel();
        buttonPanel.setLayout(new UIRowLayout(2));

        // Now add the two labeled push buttons.
        buttonPanel.add(new MyUIPushButton(this, "Go"));
        buttonPanel.add(new MyUIPushButton(this, "Stop"));

        add(buttonPanel, "South");
    }
}

// MyUIPushButton - Subclass of UIPushButton that adds
//                  the event listener.
class MyUIPushButton extends UIPushButton
{
    UIApplet parent;
```

>>

```
// PBAction - This event listener simply displays
//               the button label in the status bar.
class PBAction implements IUIActionListener
{
    public void actionPerformed(UIActionEvent e)
    {
        parent.showStatus("User clicked on " + getName());
    }
}

// MyUIPushButton - Constructor
MyUIPushButton(UIApplet parent, String label)
{
    // Pass the argument to the base class constructor.
    super(label);

    // Save the other argument.
    this.parent = parent;

    // Attach the listener.
    addActionListener(new PBAction());
}
}
```

The *MyApplet* class for this applet goes through the same steps as in the Button02 applet with one exception: here the *MyUIPushButton* class takes the place of the *UIPushButton* class.

Of course, *MyUIPushButton* is nothing more than a *UIPushButton* with the appropriate action added to it. This bit of trickery is performed by passing a *PBAction* object to *addActionListener*. Selecting a *UIPushButton* object results in a *UIActionEvent* class being passed to the *actionPerformed* method of the registered *IUIActionListener* interface. This particular *actionPerformed* method does nothing more than display the button label in the applet's status bar.

The fact that the *MyApplet* class in Button03a is virtually identical to that in Button02 is the strength of this approach—the main application doesn't have to deal with the implementation of the button. The button class handles all the details, and that's an advantage.

In this example applet, however, both buttons do the same thing. In a real-world application, it wouldn't make sense for two buttons to do the same thing. Using the current approach, fixing this problem would mean creating a different subclass for each button. In a real-world application, that would mean lots of different subclasses. Some might consider that a disadvantage.

The following applet, Button03b, demonstrates how to assign an activity to a button without creating new button subclasses:

```
// Button03b - Defines a button activity in a
//             separate class, which avoids the
//             creation of different button subclasses
import java.applet.*;
import java.awt.*;
import com.ms.ui.*;
import com.ms.ui.event.*;

import Application;

public class Button03b extends AwtUIApplet
{
    Button03b()
    {
        super(new MyApplet());
    }

    public static void main(String[] arg)
    {
        new Application(new MyApplet());
    }
}

class MyApplet extends UIApplet
{
    // showStatus - If MyApplet is being invoked as an
    //              applet, output the message in the status
    //              bar; otherwise, just output.
    public void showStatus(String s)
    {
        if (getApplet() != null)
        {
            super.showStatus(s);
        }
        else
        {
            System.out.println(s);
        }
    }
```

>>

```
        // init - Perform the actual work.
        public void init()
        {
            // Use an extremely simple layout.
            setLayout(new UIBorderLayout());

            // Create a new panel for the buttons.
            UIPanel buttonPanel = new UIPanel();
            buttonPanel.setLayout(new UIRowLayout(2));

            // Now add the two labeled push buttons.
            // This time, add the action listener here rather than
            // in the button constructor.
            UIPushButton goButton = new UIPushButton("Go");
            goButton.addActionListener(
                            new MyPBAction(this, goButton));
            buttonPanel.add(goButton);

            UIPushButton stopButton = new UIPushButton("Stop");
            stopButton.addActionListener(
                            new MyPBAction(this, stopButton));
            buttonPanel.add(stopButton);

            add(buttonPanel, "South");
        }
    }

// MyPBAction - Event listener for my buttons
class MyPBAction implements IUIActionListener
{
    UIApplet parent;
    UIButton button;

    // actionPerformed - This event listener simply displays
    //                   the button label in the status bar.
    public void actionPerformed(UIActionEvent e)
    {
        parent.showStatus("User clicked on " + button.getName());
    }
```

```
// MyUIPushButton - Constructor
MyPBAction(UIApplet parent, UIButton button)
{
    // Save the other argument.
    this.parent = parent;

    // We'll need the button as well.
    this.button = button;
}
}
```

This approach does not require numerous button subclasses; however, it still requires multiple implementations of *IUIActionListener*, which I don't find to be a better solution. (I get by with only one implementation here because both buttons perform the same action.) A further disadvantage of this approach is that it complicates the main applet class by requiring the *init* function to assign listeners.

 NOTE

> A variation on this theme is to create an "active" subclass of *UIPushButton* that accepts the *IUIActionListener* interface as an argument to the constructor—this is the approach taken in applet Button07, which we examine later in this chapter. The approach is basically the same, but the code may be a little easier to read.

Button Labels

In the applets demonstrated so far, I have used *String* objects to label the buttons. *UICanvas* objects (discussed in Chapter 5, "Canvases") can also be used as button labels. In this section, I will demonstrate both how and why to do so.

UIText labels

An object of class *UIText* can be used as a button label. (See Chapter 5, "Canvases," for a discussion of *UIText*.) Using a *UIText* object gives the programmer more control over the button label, as applet Button04, which begins on the next page, demonstrates.

```
// Button04 - UIButtons have various properties -
//            for example, hot-tracking.
//            This applet demonstrates how these
//            properties are controlled using a UIText
//            object as a button label.
import java.applet.*;
import java.awt.*;
import com.ms.ui.*;
import com.ms.ui.event.*;

import Application;

public class Button04 extends AwtUIApplet
{
    Button04()
    {
        super(new MyApplet());
    }

    public static void main(String[] arg)
    {
        new Application(new MyApplet());
    }
}

class MyApplet extends UIApplet
{
    // showStatus - If MyApplet is being invoked as an
    //              applet, output the message in the
    //              status bar; otherwise, just output.
    public void showStatus(String s)
    {
        if (getApplet() != null)
        {
            super.showStatus(s);
        }
        else
        {
            System.out.println(s);
        }
    }
```

```
// newRow - This function creates a new row of buttons
//          with the specified styles.
public UIPanel newRow(String label, int nHot, int nStyle)
{
    // Create a row with two columns:
    // one for the text and the other for the two buttons.
    UIPanel rowPanel = new UIPanel();
    rowPanel.setLayout(new UIRowLayout(2));

    // The left-hand column is the text.
    rowPanel.add(new MyText(label));

    // The right-hand column is itself a panel
    // with two buttons.
    UIPanel buttonPanel = new UIPanel();
    buttonPanel.setLayout(new UIRowLayout(2));
    rowPanel.add(buttonPanel);

    // The left button is the Go button.
    // (Note: The "hotness" is carried by the UIText
    // object label; the remaining styles are passed
    // directly to the UIButton object.)
    UIText goLabel = new UIText("Go", nHot);
    UIPushButton goButton = new MyUIPushButton(this,
                                               goLabel,
                                               nStyle);

    buttonPanel.add(goButton);

    // And the right button is the Stop button.
    UIText stopLabel = new UIText("Stop", nHot);
    UIPushButton stopButton = new MyUIPushButton(this,
                                                 stopLabel,
                                                 nStyle);

    buttonPanel.add(stopButton);

    return rowPanel;
}

public void init()
{
    // Use a vertical layout.
    // (This will stack the rows of buttons vertically.)
    setLayout(new UIVerticalFlowLayout());
```

>>

>>

```
                        // Now create different types of rows.
                        add(newRow("Hot-Tracked/Raised",   // Label
                                    UIText.HOTTRACK,         // "Hot-tracking"
                                    UIPushButton.RAISED));   // Button properties

                        add(newRow("Hot-Tracked/Raised Toggle",
                                    UIText.HOTTRACK,
                                    UIPushButton.RAISED | UIPushButton.TOGGLE));

                        add(newRow("Nothing",
                                    0,
                                    0));
            }
}


// MyText - Fixed-length text area
class MyText extends UIDrawText
{
        MyText(String text)
        {
            super(text);
        }

        static Dimension size = new Dimension(250, 12);
        public Dimension getPreferredSize()
        {
            return size;
        }
}


// MyUIPushButton - Push button with its own action listener
//                  already built in
class MyUIPushButton extends UIPushButton
{
        UIApplet parent;

        class PBAction implements IUIActionListener
        {
            public void actionPerformed(UIActionEvent e)
            {
                IUIComponent comp = e.getActionItem();
                parent.showStatus("User clicked on " +
                                                    comp.getName());
            }
        }
```

```
MyUIPushButton(UIApplet parent, UIText label, int nStyle)
{
    super(label, nStyle);
    this.parent = parent;

    addActionListener(new PBAction());
}
}
```

The output from this applet appears in Figure 6-3. Notice that the Stop toggle button is in the depressed state and the Go toggle button is not. When you click the Go toggle button, the Stop toggle button remains depressed.

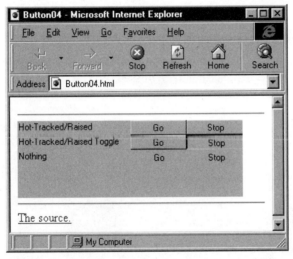

FIGURE 6-3   *Three rows of buttons, each created using a different set of properties.*

Here the *init* function adds three *UIPanel* objects, each created by calling *new-Row* with different parameters. The three rows are created as follows:

```
add(newRow("Hot-Tracked/Raised",       // Label
        UIText.HOTTRACK,               // UIText property
        UIPushButton.RAISED));         // UIButton property

add(newRow("Hot-Tracked/Raised Toggle",
        UIText.HOTTRACK,
        UIPushButton.RAISED | UIPushButton.TOGGLE));

add(newRow("Nothing",
        0,
        0));
```

The first button is created by assigning the *UIText* label a property named *HOTTRACK*.

NOTE

> When a button is hot-tracked, it changes color in a subtle way when the mouse pointer is positioned on it. All buttons that are created using *String* objects for labels (and thus all buttons we have seen so far) are hot-tracked. In AFC, the hot-tracked color and non-hot-tracked color are the same so that there is no obvious difference when the cursor moves across a hot-tracked object.

The first button pair is raised; the second row contains buttons that are both raised and toggled.

NOTE

> The *raised* property gives the buttons their chiseled appearance. A toggle button has two states: raised and depressed.

Finally, the third row of buttons has none of these properties set.

CONTROLLING THE SIZE OF AN OBJECT

In AFC, the size of an object is determined by the size of its contents, so a *UIText* object, for example, would be sized according to the text it has to display. You can change this default behavior by overriding the *getPreferredSize* method.

In order to make all of the labels the same size in the example applet, I created a subclass of *UIText* that overrides the *getPreferredSize* method. This new *getPreferredSize* method returns a fixed size irrespective of the amount of text contained:

```
static Dimension size = new Dimension(250, 12);
public Dimension getPreferredSize()
{
    return size;
}
```

This technique ensures that all of the labels are the same 250 units wide.

The *UIVerticalFlowLayout* layout manager for the applet window aligns the rows vertically. Each row object created by *newRow* contains a label on the left that identifies the type of row and two buttons on the right. The *newRow* method does this by creating one *UIPanel* object with a column of text on the left and a separate *UIPanel* object on the right containing the two buttons. Using two separate panels in this way lets you make the two buttons the same size and the label a different size from the buttons.

Graphics labels

The following applet, Button05a, creates button labels that include both a text string and a small graphic:

```
// Button05a - Using the UIItem class, you can label a button using
//              both an image and text.
import java.applet.*;
import java.awt.*;

import com.ms.ui.*;
import com.ms.ui.event.*;

import Images;
import Application;

public class Button05a extends AwtUIApplet
{
    Button05a()
    {
        super(new MyApplet());
    }

    public static void main(String[] app)
    {
        System.out.println("Cannot execute as application.");
    }
}

class MyApplet extends UIApplet
{
    Images images;
    String[] sNames = new String[2] {"go.gif",
                                      "stop.gif"};
    final int GO   = 0;  // Index into sNames
    final int STOP = 1;
```

>>

>>

```
public void init()
{
    // Start by loading the images.
    images = new Images(this, sNames);
    images.load();

    // Now we will need a panel to hold the buttons.
    UIPanel buttonPanel = new UIPanel();
    buttonPanel.setLayout(new UIRowLayout(2));

    // Create the first button:
    // create a UIItem with the Go image on the left
    // and the text on the right.
    UIItem goLabel = new UIItem(images.getImage(GO),
                               "Go",
                               UIItem.HOTTRACK,
                               UIItem.ONLEFT);

    // Now create a button with those labels.
    UIPushButton goButton =
                new MyUIPushButton(this,
                                      goLabel,
                                      UIPushButton.TOGGLE);
    buttonPanel.add(goButton);

    // Do the same thing for the Stop button.
    UIItem stopLabel = new UIItem(images.getImage(STOP),
                               "Stop",
                               UIItem.HOTTRACK,
                               UIItem.ONLEFT);
    UIPushButton stopButton =
                new MyUIPushButton(this,
                                      stopLabel,
                                      UIPushButton.TOGGLE);
    buttonPanel.add(stopButton);

    // Then position the resulting button panel at the
    // bottom of the applet window.
    setLayout(new UIBorderLayout());
    add(buttonPanel, "South");
}
}
```

```
// MyUIPushButton - Push button with its own action listener
//                  already built in
class MyUIPushButton extends UIPushButton
{
    UIApplet parent;

    class PBAction implements IUIActionListener
    {
        public void actionPerformed(UIActionEvent e)
        {
            IUIComponent comp = e.getActionItem();
            parent.showStatus("User clicked on " +
                                        comp.getName());

        }
    }

    MyUIPushButton(UIApplet parent,
                   UIItem label,
                   int nStyle)
    {
        super(label, nStyle);
        this.parent = parent;

        addActionListener(new PBAction());
    }
}
```

Two images, go.gif and stop.gif, are used to provide the images for the Go and Stop button labels. (These images are included on the companion CD.) The *init* method begins by loading these two images using the help class *Images* contained in AppCommon. (See Appendix B, "Utility Classes Used in This Book," for an explanation of this class.)

An object of class *UIItem* is created as a label for the Go button as follows:

```
UIItem goLabel = new UIItem(images.getImage(GO),
                            "Go",
                            UIItem.HOTTRACK,
                            UIItem.ONLEFT);
```

The first argument to *UIItem* is the image to be used (of class *Image*). The second argument is the actual text. The third argument defines such properties as hot-tracking. The final argument specifies the orientation of the image relative to the text. This *UIItem* object is then passed to the button to be used as its label.

The result of the Button05a applet is shown in Figure 6-4.

FIGURE 6-4   *The* UIItem *class lets you combine images and text to create a button label.*

Dynamic graphics labels

Normal hot-tracking affects only the text part of a button label. However, if you want to give your applet real sex appeal, you'll want to hot-track the image as well. You can do this by manually changing the image portion of the *UIItem* label as the mouse pointer moves into and out of the button area.

This technique is demonstrated in the following applet, Button05b:

```
// Button05b - Using the mouseEnter and mouseExit methods,
//              you can change the button image as
//              part of hot-tracking.
import java.applet.*;
import java.awt.*;

import com.ms.ui.*;
import com.ms.ui.event.*;

import Images;
import Application;
```

```java
public class Button05b extends AwtUIApplet
{
    Button05b()
    {
        super(new MyApplet());
    }

    public static void main(String[] app)
    {
        System.out.println("Cannot execute as application.");
    }
}

class MyApplet extends UIApplet
{
    Images images;
    String[] sNames = new String[4]{"Back.gif",
                                    "Forward.gif",
                                    "HotBack.gif",
                                    "HotForward.gif"};
    final int GO   = 0;  // "Cool" images
    final int STOP = 1;
    final int GH   = 2;  // "Hot" images
    final int STPH = 3;

    public void init()
    {
        // Start by loading the images.
        images = new Images(this, sNames);
        images.load();

        // Now we need a panel to hold the buttons.
        UIPanel buttonPanel = new UIPanel();
        buttonPanel.setLayout(new UIRowLayout(2));

        // Create a HotColdPushButton, and pass it the
        // images and text it will need for both the
        // hot and cool images.
        UIPushButton goButton = new MyGoButton(this,
                                    images.getImage(GO),
                                    "Go",
                                    images.getImage(GH),
                                    "Go!");
        buttonPanel.add(goButton);
```

```
        // Do the same thing for the Stop button.
        UIPushButton stopButton = new MyStopButton(this,
                                        images.getImage(STOP),
                                        "Stop",
                                        images.getImage(STPH),
                                        "Stop!");
        buttonPanel.add(stopButton);

        // And then position the resulting button panel
        // at the bottom of the applet window.
        setLayout(new UIBorderLayout());
        add(buttonPanel, "South");
    }
}

// HotColdPushButton - Push button that changes labels as it
//                     goes from hot to cold
class HotColdPushButton extends UIPushButton
{
    UIApplet parent;

    // Current button label
    UIItem coolLabel;
    UIItem hotLabel;

    HotColdPushButton(UIApplet parent,
                    Image coolImg, String coolText,
                    Image hotImg,  String hotText)
    {
        coolLabel = new UIItem(coolImg,
                            coolText,
                            0,
                            UIItem.ONLEFT);
        hotLabel  = new UIItem(hotImg,
                            hotText,
                            0,
                            UIItem.ONLEFT);

        setHeader(coolLabel);
        setStyle(UIPushButton.TOGGLE);

        this.parent = parent;
    }
```

```
    // mouseEnter - Change images when mouse moves over the button.
    public boolean mouseEnter(Event e, int x, int y)
    {
        // Replace the cool label with the hot label.
        replace(hotLabel, coolLabel);

        // Be sure to perform any other processing.
        return super.mouseEnter(e, x, y);
    }

    // mouseExit - Set the image back to normal on exit.
    public boolean mouseExit(Event e, int x, int y)
    {
        // Put the cool label back.
        replace(coolLabel, hotLabel);

        return super.mouseExit(e, x, y);
    }
}

// Create subclasses of HotColdPushButton.
class MyGoButton extends HotColdPushButton
{
    class PBAction implements IUIActionListener
    {
        public void actionPerformed(UIActionEvent e)
        {
            parent.showStatus("User clicked Go.");
        }
    }

    MyGoButton(UIApplet parent,
               Image coolImg, String coolText,
               Image hotImg,  String hotText)
    {
        super(parent, coolImg, coolText, hotImg, hotText);

        // Assign the action listener (as usual).
        addActionListener(new PBAction());
    }

}
```

>>

```
class MyStopButton extends HotColdPushButton
{
    class PBAction implements IUIActionListener
    {
        public void actionPerformed(UIActionEvent e)
        {
            parent.showStatus("User clicked Stop.");
        }
    }

    MyStopButton(UIApplet parent,
                 Image coolImg, String coolText,
                 Image hotImg,  String hotText)
    {
        super(parent, coolImg, coolText, hotImg, hotText);

        // Assign the action listener (as usual).
        addActionListener(new PBAction());
    }

}
```

This applet begins like its simpler predecessor by loading the images that will be used to label the buttons. In this case, however, rather than load two images, the applet loads four: two to be used as "cool" images and two to be used as "hot" images.

The *HotColdPushButton* class uses these images to create two *UIItem* labels, one contained in *coolLabel* and the other in *hotLabel*. The call to *setHeader* sets the initial label of the button to *coolLabel*. (Here I'm assuming that the mouse does not initially point to the button. If it does, the label will not update until the mouse pointer moves out of the button area and then back into it.)

TIP

> Normally, a button's label is specified when the button is constructed. If this is impossible, however, you can create the button without a label and then use the *setHeader* function to set the button label at a later time.

HotColdPushButton overrides the *UIPushButton mouseEnter* and *mouseExit* functions to change the button label as the mouse enters and exits the button area. The *replace* method can be used to replace any component attached to a container. In this example, I use *replace* to replace the button label with *hotLabel* in the case of *mouseEnter* and with *coolLabel* in the case of *mouseExit*.

NOTE

UIButton (extended by *UIPushButton*) extends the *UISingleContainer* class, which is a type of container that contains a single child component—the header.

The *init* function creates two buttons: a button of class *MyGoButton* and a button of class *MyStopButton*. Both classes extend *HotColdPushButton* by adding button-specific action listener functions.

TIP

I could have put the label creation code directly in the *MyGoButton* and *MyStop-Button* classes, but it's better to combine common features in a common base class because coding is more efficient (there is only one place to code and debug the label conversion code) and the code is easier to follow mentally. When I deal with *HotColdPushButton*, I need worry myself only with those features necessary to change the label as the button changes temperature.

The results of this applet are shown in Figure 6-5.

FIGURE 6-5   *The output of Button05b, showing the Go button as hot and the Stop button as cool.*

THE *UICheckButton* AND *UIRadioButton* CLASSES

The *UICheckButton* and *UIRadioButton* classes share most of the properties of the *UIPush-Button* class described earlier in this chapter. Check buttons and radio buttons differ from each other only in appearance. A check button (sometimes also referred to as a check box) consists of a square box that contains a check mark when the button has been selected, and a radio button consists of a circle that is "colored in" when the button is selected.

NOTE

> Both check buttons and radio buttons are typically used to represent options that a user can select. To enable users to select more than one option at a time, standard coding practice is to use check buttons with properties that are independent of one another. To enable users to select only one option (that is, the choices are mutually exclusive), radio buttons should be used. See the section "Grouping Radio Buttons" later in this chapter for more details about radio buttons.

The following applet, Button06, demonstrates the appearance of the *UICheckButton* and *UIRadioButton* components:

```
// Button06 - This applet creates two simple check buttons and
//            one radio button.
import java.applet.*;
import java.awt.*;
import com.ms.ui.*;
import com.ms.ui.event.*;

import Application;

public class Button06 extends AwtUIApplet
{
    Button06()
    {
        super(new MyApplet());
    }

    public static void main(String[] arg)
    {
        new Application(new MyApplet());
    }
}
```

```
class MyApplet extends UIApplet
{
    public void init()
    {
        // Use a vertical layout for the buttons.
        setLayout(new UIVerticalFlowLayout());

        // Create two check buttons and one radio button, and add
        // them to the applet window.
        add(new UICheckButton("Action 1"));
        add(new UICheckButton("Action 2"));
        add(new UIRadioButton("Action 3"));
    }
}
```

The results of this applet are shown in Figure 6-6. Notice the difference in appearance between the two check buttons and the single radio button.

FIGURE 6-6   *The output from Button06, showing simple check buttons and a radio button.*

Adding Activities to Check Buttons

To be of any use, check buttons and radio buttons need to do something when the user selects or deselects them. The following applet, Button07, demonstrates how to assign an action to three check boxes.

```
// Button07 - The check buttons used here have been
//              assigned activities.
import java.applet.*;
import java.awt.*;
import com.ms.ui.*;
import com.ms.ui.event.*;

import Application;

public class Button07 extends AwtUIApplet
{
    Button07()
    {
        super(new MyApplet());
    }

    public static void main(String[] arg)
    {
        new Application(new MyApplet());
    }
}

class MyApplet extends UIApplet
{
    // showStatus - If MyApplet is being invoked as an
    //              applet, output the message in the status
    //              bar; otherwise, just output.
    public void showStatus(String s)
    {
        if (getApplet() != null)
        {
            super.showStatus(s);
        }
        else
        {
            System.out.println(s);
        }
    }

    public void init()
    {
        // Assign a layout to the applet window.
        setLayout(new UIBorderLayout());
```

```
        // Create a group for the check buttons.
        // This grouping makes the relationship between
        // the buttons more evident to the user.
        UICheckGroup group = new UICheckGroup("Check buttons");
        group.setLayout(new UIVerticalFlowLayout());

        // Now create the check b  .uttons, each with its own
        // listener. Notice that not all listeners need
        // to have the same constructor with the same arguments.
        ActionCB button2 = new ActionCB("Action 2",
                            new Action2(this));
        ActionCB button1 = new ActionCB("Action 1",
                            new Action1(this, button2));
        ActionCB button3 = new ActionCB("Action 3",
                            new Action3(this));

        // Add the buttons to the group.
        group.add(button1);
        group.add(button2);
        group.add(button3);

        // And add the group to the applet window.
        add(group, "Center");
    }
}


// ActionCB - This subclass simply allows the item
//            listener to be passed in the constructor.
class ActionCB extends UICheckButton
{
    ActionCB(String label, IUIItemListener listener)
    {
        super(label);

        addItemListener(listener);
    }
}
```

>>

```
// Action1 - The item listener for button 1. In addition
//           to outputting in the status bar, this
//           listener also enables and disables
//           button 2.
class Action1 implements IUIItemListener
{
    MyApplet container;
    UIButton button;

    Action1(MyApplet container, UIButton button)
    {
        this.container = container;
        this.button    = button;

        // Start the other button off disabled.
        button.setEnabled(false);
    }

    // itemStateChanged - Invoked when button is selected
    public void itemStateChanged(UIItemEvent e)
    {
        // The following sets bSelected to true if the
        // button is selected and false otherwise.
        boolean bSelected =
                    e.getStateChange() == UIItemEvent.SELECTED;

        // The action taken is simply to output a message.
        container.showStatus("Button 1 clicked " +
                                (bSelected ? "on" : "off"));
        button.setEnabled(bSelected);
        if (!bSelected)
        {
            button.setChecked(false);
        }
    }
}

// Action2 - Simply output to the status bar.
class Action2 implements IUIItemListener
{
    MyApplet container;

    Action2(MyApplet container)
    {
        this.container = container;
    }
```

```
    // itemStateChanged - Invoked when button is selected
    public void itemStateChanged(UIItemEvent e)
    {
        boolean bSelected =
                e.getStateChange() == UIItemEvent.SELECTED;

        container.showStatus("Button 2 clicked " +
                        (bSelected ? "on" : "off"));
    }
}

// Action3 - Same as Action2
class Action3 implements IUIItemListener
{
    MyApplet container;

    Action3(MyApplet container)
    {
        this.container = container;
    }

    // itemStateChanged - Invoked when button is selected
    public void itemStateChanged(UIItemEvent e)
    {
        boolean bSelected =
                e.getStateChange() == UIItemEvent.SELECTED;

        container.showStatus("Button 3 clicked " +
                        (bSelected ? "on" : "off"));
    }
}
```

The results of this more sophisticated check button applet are shown in Figure 6-7 on the following page.

Rather than add the buttons directly to the applet window, where they can easily get lost among the other components, this applet creates a *UICheckGroup* object to contain the check buttons. *UICheckGroup* is a type of panel outfitted with a small label in the upper left corner and surrounded by a narrow edge. As you can see in Figure 6-7, such groups set off the buttons nicely from their surroundings. Using the vertical flow layout ensures that the check boxes are aligned vertically within this group.

FIGURE 6-7 *The output from Button07. On the left, check button 2 has been deactivated; checking check button 1 on the right activates check button 2.*

The approach used to assign activities to the check buttons in this applet is slightly different from the approach we looked at earlier in this chapter. Here I have created a subclass of *UICheckButton* that differs only in accepting its event listener object as one of the constructor arguments. This is similar to the approach taken in Button03b—the introduction of the *ActionCB* class simply allows several steps to be combined into one. Once the buttons have been created, they are added to the check button group and the group is added to the applet window.

The event listeners used here also differ from those used in the preceding examples. The *UIPushButton* class uses the *IUIActionListener* interface. Unlike push buttons, check buttons and radio buttons invoke an event both when they are selected and when they are deselected. The *UIItemEvent* object passed to *IUIItemListener* includes this type of state information. You can see how this information is read in the *itemStateChanged* methods.

Finally, *button1* enables *button2* when it is selected and disables *button2* when it is deselected. This enabling and disabling is handled by the *setEnabled* method, a common function demonstrated in the *Action1* class.

Grouping Radio Buttons

As mentioned, other than subtle differences in appearance, radio buttons are nearly identical to check buttons. Thus, *UICheckButton* could have been replaced by *UIRadioButton* in the previous examples. Radio buttons have one additional property, however: mutual exclusiveness.

The mutual exclusiveness property of radio buttons is implemented not in the *UIButton* class but in the *UIRadioGroup* class that is used to contain the buttons. This technique is demonstrated in the following simple example applet:

```
// Button08a - Implements a mutually exclusive set of radio
//             buttons. The UIRadioGroup class ensures that
//             only one button is selected at a time.

import java.applet.*;
import java.awt.*;
import com.ms.ui.*;
import com.ms.ui.event.*;

import Application;

public class Button08a extends AwtUIApplet
{
    Button08a()
    {
        super(new MyApplet());
    }

    public static void main(String[] arg)
    {
        new Application(new MyApplet());
    }
}

class MyApplet extends UIApplet
{
    // showStatus - If MyApplet is being invoked as an
    //              applet, output the message in the status
    //              bar; otherwise, just output.
    public void showStatus(String s)
    {
        if (getApplet() != null)
        {
            super.showStatus(s);
        }
```

>>

```
                                else
                                {
                                    System.out.println(s);
                                }
                        }

                        public void init()
                        {
                            add(new MyUIGroup(this));
                        }
                }

                // MyUIGroup - The radio group is designed to contain radio
                //              buttons.
                class MyUIGroup extends UIRadioGroup
                {
                    UIApplet parent = null;

                    MyUIGroup(UIApplet parent)
                    {
                        super("Radio control");

                        this.parent = parent;

                        // Arrange the radio buttons vertically.
                        setLayout(new UIVerticalFlowLayout());

                        // Add the three buttons.
                        MyUIRadioButton r1 = new MyUIRadioButton(parent,
                                                            "Option 1");
                        add(r1);

                        MyUIRadioButton r2 = new MyUIRadioButton(parent,
                                                            "Option 2");
                        add(r2);

                        MyUIRadioButton r3 = new MyUIRadioButton(parent,
                                                            "Option 3");
                        add(r3);

                        // At least one of the buttons must be set.
                        r1.setChecked(true);
                    }
                }
```

```
// MyUIRadioButton - Subclass of UIRadioButton that adds
//                    the event listener
class MyUIRadioButton extends UIRadioButton
{
    UIApplet parent;

    // PBAction - This event listener simply displays
    //            the button label in the status bar.
    class PBAction implements IUIItemListener
    {
        public void itemStateChanged(UIItemEvent e)
        {
            // Perform whatever action is necessary.
            parent.showStatus("User clicked on " + getName());
        }
    }

    // MyUIRadioButton - Constructor
    MyUIRadioButton(UIApplet parent, String label)
    {
        // Pass the argument to the base class constructor.
        super(label, 0);

        // Save the other argument.
        this.parent = parent;

        // Attach the listener.
        addItemListener(new PBAction());
    }

    Dimension d = new Dimension(100, 20);
    public Dimension getPreferredSize() { return d; }
}
```

Using a *UIRadioGroup* object to enclose the three *UIRadioButton* objects ensures that no two radio buttons can be selected at the same time. The circular
check area cues the user that these are mutually exclusive radio buttons. The
result is shown in Figure 6-8 on the following page.

FIGURE 6-8   *The output of the Button08a applet, showing a group of three mutually exclusive radio buttons.*

Occasionally, the programmer wants to take extra action when a radio button is deselected. Unfortunately, the *UIRadioGroup* class does not pass a *UIItem-Event* object to the button being deselected to indicate that it is passing out of favor. We can make up for this shortcoming by implementing the mutual exclusiveness property of the *UIRadioGroup* manually, as shown in the following example applet, Button08b:

```
// Button08b - Demonstrates how to implement
//             mutually exclusive buttons manually

// This applet is the same as Button08a except that MyUIGroup
// extends UICheckGroup instead of UIRadioGroup.

// MyUIRadioButton - Subclass of UIRadioButton that adds
//                   the event listener
class MyUIRadioButton extends UIRadioButton
{
    UIApplet parent;

    // PBAction - This item listener simply displays
    //            the button label in the status bar.
    class PBAction implements IUIItemListener
    {
        public void itemStateChanged(UIItemEvent e)
        {
            parent.showStatus("User clicked on " + getName());
```

```
        // Invoke radioToggle to select the current
        // button while deselecting all other buttons.
        radioToggle();
    }
}


// MyUIRadioButton - Constructor
MyUIRadioButton(UIApplet parent, String label)
{
    // Pass the argument to the base class constructor.
    super(label, 0);

    // Save the other argument.
    this.parent = parent;

    // Attach the listener.
    addItemListener(new PBAction());
}

Dimension d = new Dimension(100, 20);
public Dimension getPreferredSize() { return d; }

// radioToggle - Ensure that the buttons
//               are mutually exclusive.
void radioToggle()
{
    // First turn off all other buttons; then
    // find the group that owns the buttons.
    IUIContainer group = getParent();

    // Loop through all of the children of this group.
    int nNumChildren = group.getChildCount();
    for(int i = 0; i < nNumChildren; i++)
    {
        // For each radio button...
        IUIComponent child = group.getChild(i);
        if (child instanceof UIRadioButton)
        {
            // ...deselect it.
            UIRadioButton button = (UIRadioButton)child;
            button.setChecked(false);
        }
    }

    // Now turn on the selected button.
    setChecked(true);
}
```

Here the work of ensuring that only one button is selected at a time is performed by the *radioToggle* method. This method is written to be as general as possible. It starts by calling *getParent* to get the parent of the button (the *UICheckGroup* class to which the buttons were added). It then loops through each of the children of this container. If a child is a *UIRadioButton* object (which they all should be because we didn't add anything else, but it's always good to check), the function deselects it. Once this loop has finished, we can be certain that all buttons have been deselected. Last *radioToggle* selects the "current" radio button (the one that the user selected).

NOTE

Obviously, in a different application you could select the existing buttons before deselecting them to be sure that the selection represented a change, and if it did, you could take whatever action you deemed necessary.

THE *UIREPEATBUTTON* CLASS

The *UIRepeatButton* class is a variation of *UIPushButton*. *UIRepeatButton* implements the *TimerListener* interface in order to provide repeated events while the user holds down the mouse button.

In use, the repeat button might appear identical to the push button. The action listener for the repeat button is identical to that of the push button. The differences begin to arise if the applet needs to keep track of when the user releases the mouse button and then presses and holds down the mouse button again. This situation is demonstrated in the following applet, Button09:

```
// Button09 - Generates action events over and over
//            as long as the mouse button is held down
//            over the repeat button
import java.applet.*;
import java.awt.*;
import com.ms.ui.*;
import com.ms.ui.event.*;

import Application;
```

```
public class Button09 extends AwtUIApplet
{
    Button09()
    {
        super(new MyApplet());
    }

    public static void main(String[] arg)
    {
        new Application(new MyApplet());
    }
}

class MyApplet extends UIApplet
{
    // showStatus - If MyApplet is being invoked as an
    //              applet, output the message in the status
    //              bar; otherwise, just output.
    public void showStatus(String s)
    {
        if (getApplet() != null)
        {
            super.showStatus(s);
        }
        else
        {
            System.out.println(s);
        }
    }


    public void init()
    {
        // Use an extremely simple layout.
        setLayout(new UIBorderLayout());

        // Create a new panel for the buttons.
        UIPanel buttonPanel = new UIPanel();
        buttonPanel.setLayout(new UIRowLayout(2));

        // Now add the two labeled push buttons.
        buttonPanel.add(new MyUIRepeatButton(this, "Go"));
        buttonPanel.add(new MyUIRepeatButton(this, "Stop"));

        add(buttonPanel, "South");
    }
}
```

```
// MyUIRepeatButton - Subclass of UIRepeatButton
class MyUIRepeatButton extends UIRepeatButton
{
    UIApplet parent;
    int      nSelectCount = 0;
    boolean  bReleased = true;

    // PBAction - This event listener simply displays
    //           the button label in the status bar.
    class PBAction implements IUIActionListener
    {
        public void actionPerformed(UIActionEvent e)
        {
            // bPressed will be true as long as the
            // mouse button is held down. (This filters
            // out events queued up and processed after
            // the mouse button has actually been
            // released.)
            boolean bPressed = isPressed();
            if (!bPressed)
            {
                return;
            }

            // If bReleased is true, the user has
            // just pressed the mouse button.
            if (bReleased)
            {
                nSelectCount = 0;
                bReleased = false;
            }

            // Increment the count.
            nSelectCount++;

            String status = getName() + " clicked " +
                            Integer.toString(nSelectCount) +
                            " times";
            parent.showStatus(status);
        }
    }
```

```
// mouseUp - Flagging when the mouse is released allows
//           the repeat button to start over from one
//           extended mouse click to another.
public boolean mouseUp(Event e, int x, int y)
{
    bReleased = true;
    return super.mouseUp(e, x, y);
}


// MyUIRepeatButton - Constructor
MyUIRepeatButton(UIApplet parent, String label)
{
    // Pass the argument to the base class constructor.
    super(label);

    // Save the other argument.
    this.parent = parent;

    // Attach the listener.
    addActionListener(new PBAction());
}
}
```

Here the *mouseUp* method records the fact that the user has released the mouse button. When the next action event is generated, *actionPerformed* can detect the event and use it to reset the event counter. The result is shown in Figure 6-9.

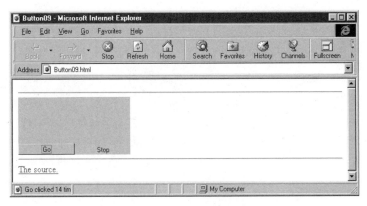

FIGURE 6-9   *The output of the Button09 applet, showing the click count in the status bar after the Go button has been clicked and held down.*

THE *UIEXPANDBUTTON* CLASS

The final class among the subclasses of *UIButton* is the *UIExpandButton* class. This class creates a button that is used exclusively as the small plus or minus sign in front of the nodes in a *UITree* object. For an example of the care and feeding of trees, see the section titled "Trees" on page 231 in Chapter 8, "Choices."

WHAT'S NEXT

The *UIButton* class provides a rich set of buttons, including push buttons, check buttons, and radio buttons. In the next chapter, we will look at some of the different types of windows provided by AFC. Not only do these windows include some of the group components that we've seen so far but also some really nifty viewers for combining text and graphics in a single applet or for easily scrolling large windows.

Panels and Windows

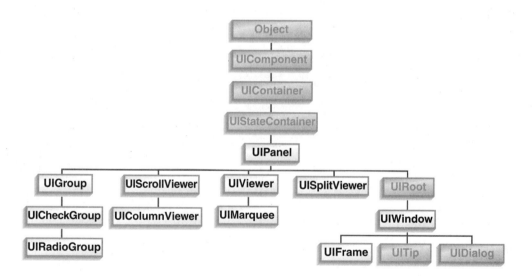

This chapter deals with the classes that make up panels and windows. You can write an applet without ever dealing with windows—the applet itself provides a perfectly usable window. It is unlikely, however, that you can write much of an applet without dealing with panels. If you glance through the chapters in Part Two, you'll notice a variety of panels. Panels allow the programmer to group components for layout purposes. In this chapter, you'll see a number of other uses for panels. (AFC handles panels, windows, and frames in much the same way as the AWT. However, AFC provides more subclasses than the AWT, and with additional capabilities.)

What's the Difference Between Panels and Windows?

Before we get started, I should stress the distinction between panels and windows. A panel is a rectangular portion of a window. It may be clearly delineated, as is the case with the *UIGroup* class, or its boundaries may be invisible, as is the case with the plain *UIPanel* class.

A window, on the other hand, has a life of its own, independent of any other window. Here too a window may be clearly separated from its surroundings, as is the case with the *UIFrame* class, or not, as with the *UIWindow* class. This distinction is most clear when you compare the *UIFrame* and *UIPanel* classes. Because *UIFrame* is independent, the user can resize, minimize, maximize, and close a *UIFrame* object without affecting other windows. The user cannot resize a *UIPanel* object except by resizing the *UIFrame* object in which the panel resides.

FRAMING WINDOWS

The most basic of all windows is represented by the *UIWindow* class. The following applet creates a small window and populates it with a single text message:

```
// Window01 - The UIWindow class represents a freestanding window
//            that can be independent of the applet window.
//            Notice that the UIWindow object created here is not
//            "added" to the applet window. The window
//            has no title bar or border.
import java.applet.*;
import java.awt.*;

import com.ms.ui.*;
import com.ms.fx.*;

import Application;

public class Window01 extends AwtUIApplet
{
        Window01()
    {
        super(new MyApplet());
    }

    public static void main(String[] arg)
    {
        new Application(new MyApplet());
    }
}
```

```
class MyApplet extends UIApplet
{
    // Create a window. Again, notice that this window
    // is not added to the applet window. Ensure that
    // the reference to the window does not go out of
    // scope.
    UIWindow window = null;
    public void init()
    {
        window = new MyUIWindow();
    }
}


// MyUIWindow - Creates a 200x200-pixel window located
//              down and to the right of the upper left
//              corner of the screen
class MyUIWindow extends UIWindow
{
    MyUIWindow()
    {
        // Invoke the UIWindow constructor.
        super(new Frame());

        // Set the size and location.
        setSize(200, 200);
        setLocation(100, 100);

        // You can set a new font.
        // (This step is strictly optional.)
        setFont(new FxFont("Arial", FxFont.PLAIN, 18));

        // Components can be added to a UIWindow window in the
        // same way that they are added to an applet's
        // window - the default layout manager for a
        // UIWindow is UIBorderLayout.
        add(new UIText("This is a UIText control."), "Center");

        // Windows are created hidden.
        setVisible(true);
    }
}
```

If you examine the *MyApplet.init* function, you'll see that *init* creates a *UIWindow* object in much the same way that the *init* functions of other applets create buttons or menus. However, if you look carefully, you'll notice that the *UIWindow* object is not attached to the applet's window. Unlike a panel or other component, a window is not the child of a container—a window enjoys an existence of its own.

You will probably find the output from this applet, shown in Figure 7-1, to be somewhat lacking. I certainly do. The window simply sits there on top of the browser display. It has no border to highlight where it begins and ends. It has no title bar or window dressings across the top. Clicking anywhere within the browser brings the browser display to the foreground, thereby obscuring the *UIWindow* object. Without a frame, the user cannot manipulate the window. There isn't even a way to retrieve the window once it is obscured. To add these advanced features, you must look to the *UIFrame* class.

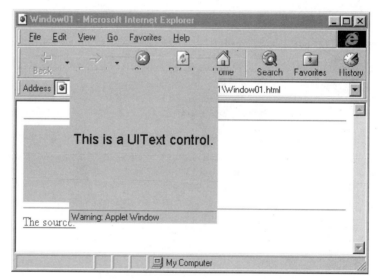

FIGURE 7-1   *The appearance of the* UIWindow *object is rather plain.*

UIFrame extends the lowly *UIWindow* class into a truly useful class by adding features such as a title bar, window dressing, and a window frame, without adding much, if any, complexity to the code. The *UIFrame* class is demonstrated in the following applet, Window02:

```
// Window02 - The UIFrame class is more useful than UIWindow.
//            The frame has a title bar, including window
//            dressings such as the Minimize, Maximize, and
//            Close buttons.
import java.applet.*;
import java.awt.*;

import com.ms.ui.*;
import com.ms.ui.event.*;
import com.ms.fx.*;

import Application;

public class Window02 extends AwtUIApplet
{
    Window02()
    {
        super(new MyApplet());
    }

    public static void main(String[] arg)
    {
        new Application(new MyApplet());
    }
}

class MyApplet extends UIApplet
{
    UIFrame frame = null;
    public void init()
    {
        // Create a frame the same way we created
        // a window earlier.
        frame = new MyUIFrame();

        // This time, add a push button to
        // display the frame.
        setLayout(new UIBorderLayout());
        add(new ShowButton(frame), "South");
    }
}
```

```
// MyUIFrame - This frame displays the same information
//            as the earlier window; however, it includes
//            minimal logic to hide itself when the user
//            clicks the Close button.
class MyUIFrame extends UIFrame
{
    MyUIFrame()
    {
        // These steps are the same as in the Window01 applet,
        // except here the UIFrame constructor takes an
        // optional title that appears in the title bar.
        super("Window02 Frame");
        setSize(200, 200);
        setLocation(100, 100);

        setFont(new FxFont("Arial", FxFont.PLAIN, 18));

        add(new UIText("This is a UIText control."), "Center");

        setVisible(true);
    }

    // handleEvent - When the user clicks the
    //               Close button, hide the frame.
    //               The user can make the frame
    //               visible again by clicking the
    //               Display Frame button.
    public boolean handleEvent(Event e)
    {
        if (e.id == Event.WINDOW_DESTROY)
        {
            setVisible(false);
        }
        return super.handleEvent(e);
    }
}

// ShowButton - When the user clicks this button,
//              show the frame again.
class ShowButton extends UIPushButton
{
    UIFrame frame = null;
```

```
class PBAction implements IUIActionListener
{
    public void actionPerformed(UIActionEvent e)
    {
        frame.setVisible(true);
    }
}

ShowButton(UIFrame frame)
{
    super("Display Frame", UIPushButton.RAISED);
    this.frame = frame;

    // Attach the action listener.
    addActionListener(new PBAction());
}
}
```

The parts of this applet have been moved around a bit, but at its core, it is simply the Window01 applet with *UIWindow* replaced by *UIFrame*—except here the constructor for *UIFrame* wants a *String* argument to be displayed in the title bar. Nevertheless, the results of this applet, shown in Figure 7-2, are much more pleasing.

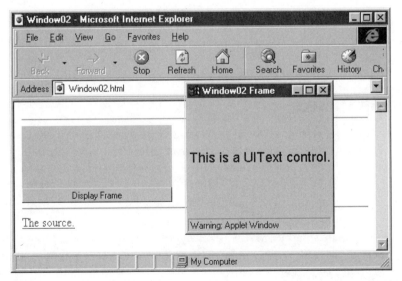

FIGURE 7-2   *The output of the Window02 applet, showing an independent window with a title bar and window dressing.*

The frame can be moved about, resized, and manipulated independent of the browser that created it.

UIFrame provides the same types of window dressing the modern GUI user is accustomed to. By manipulating the frame, the user can minimize, maximize, and resize the *UIFrame* object. The base *UIFrame* class handles these operations automatically.

UIFrame needs help to handle the Close button, however. When the user clicks the Close button, AFC passes a WINDOW_DESTROY event to the frame. The *handleEvent* method in *UIFrame* ignores this event. Window02 overrides the default *handleEvent* method in order to catch this WINDOW_DESTROY event. When such an event is detected, the *handleEvent* method in Window02 calls *setVisible(false)* to hide the frame. That done, *handleEvent* passes the *Event* object to the default *handleEvent* in *UIFrame* for further processing.

CAUTION

> When you override the *handleEvent* method, if you forget to pass unhandled events to *UIFrame.handleEvent*, operations that *UIFrame* normally handles on its own, such as minimizing, will no longer be processed properly because *UIFrame.handleEvent* will never see them.

A push button is added to the applet window to redisplay the frame after the user has closed it. See Chapter 6, "Buttons," for details on the use of push buttons.

GROUPING PANELS

Because the panel is invisible to the user, you might wonder what purpose it serves. However, if you've read Chapter 5, "Canvases," and Chapter 6, "Buttons," you have already seen how panels are used to group components so that the components can be handled as a single unit by the layout manager. Panels themselves also have layout managers to handle the layout of components within the panel. The layout manager of the child panel can be different from the layout manager of the panel's parent, giving the programmer considerable flexibility in the appearance of the final applet. This flexibility is demonstrated in the following example applet, Panel01:

```
// Panel01 - The most common use for panels is to group
//            components, especially when you are using layout
//            managers such as UIBorderLayout.
import java.applet.*;
import java.awt.*;

import com.ms.ui.*;

import Application;

public class Panel01 extends AwtUIApplet
{
    Panel01()
    {
        super(new MyApplet());
    }

    public static void main(String[] arg)
    {
        new Application(new MyApplet());
    }
}

class MyApplet extends UIApplet
{
    // showStatus - If MyApplet is being invoked as an
    //              applet, output the message in the status
    //              bar; otherwise, just output.
    public void showStatus(String s)
    {
        if (getApplet() != null)
        {
            super.showStatus(s);
        }
        else
        {
            System.out.println(s);
        }
    }
```

>>

```
public void init()
{
    // Create a right-hand-panel that is vertically
    // aligned, like a row of data.
    UIPanel panelRight = new UIPanel();
    panelRight.setLayout(new UIVerticalFlowLayout());
    panelRight.add(new UIText("line 1"));
    panelRight.add(new UIText("line 2"));
    panelRight.add(new UIText("line 3"));
    panelRight.add(new UIText("line 4"));

    // Do the same along the left side of the window.
    UIPanel panelLeft = new UIPanel();
    panelLeft.setLayout(new UIVerticalFlowLayout());
    panelLeft.add(new UIText("line 1"));
    panelLeft.add(new UIText("line 2"));
    panelLeft.add(new UIText("line 3"));

    // Create a pair of evenly spaced buttons at
    // the bottom of the window.
    UIPanel panelBottom = new UIPanel();
    panelBottom.setLayout(new UIRowLayout(2));
    panelBottom.add(new UIPushButton("OK"));
    panelBottom.add(new UIPushButton("Exit"));

    // Create a center panel with explanations.
    UIPanel panelCenter = new UIPanel();
    panelCenter.setLayout(new UIBorderLayout());
    panelCenter.add(new UIText("Label on top"),
                    "North");
    panelCenter.add(new UIText("Row along left"),
                    "West");
    panelCenter.add(new UIText("Row along right"),
                    "East");
    panelCenter.add(new UIText("Buttons at bottom"),
                    "South");

    // Now position the panels along the borders.
    setLayout(new UIBorderLayout());
    add(new UIText("Example Layout Using Panels"),
                    "North");
    add(panelLeft,   "West");
    add(panelRight,  "East");
    add(panelBottom, "South");
    add(panelCenter, "Center");
}
}
```

The results, shown in Figure 7-3, demonstrate what this applet is about. Complicated format control is made possible by using the interaction between panels and layout managers.

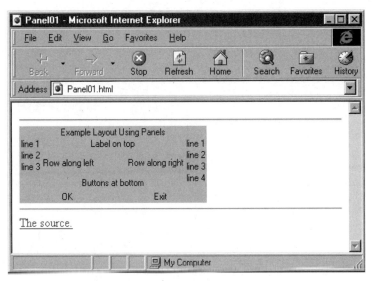

FIGURE 7-3   *The output from the Panel01 applet.*

The row of items along the left side of the applet window (*line1*, *line 2*, and *line 3*) is created by the panel named *panelLeft*. This panel uses a *UIVerticalFlow-Layout* layout manager, which aligns its components vertically. The same trick is used to create *panelRight*.

The *panelBottom* panel houses two buttons, OK and Exit. The *UIRowLayout* layout manager ensures that the available space is evenly allocated to the two buttons. Last a *panelCenter* panel is created, with explanatory text to describe the surrounding panels.

The panels are added to the applet window using the *UIBorderLayout* layout manager, to create the output shown in Figure 7-3.

You can create a slightly more sophisticated panel by using the *UIGroup*, *UI-CheckGroup*, and *UIRadioGroup* classes. These classes act like a simple panel except they are surrounded by a border and they include a label in the upper left corner. Groups differ from frames in that they cannot be resized and they do not include window dressings such as the Maximize, Minimize, and Close buttons. Groups are used to contain components in such a way that they are visually set apart from the other components within the window. In particular, *UICheckGroup* is used primarily to group check buttons, and *UIRadioGroup* is used primarily to group radio buttons.

> See the discussion of *UICheckButton* and *UIRadioButton* in Chapter 6, "Buttons," for examples of the *UICheckGroup* and *UIRadioGroup* classes in action.

VIEWERS

The group of classes collectively known as viewers extends the *UIPanel* class by providing features such as scrolling, panning, and splitting. Viewers let the user view an image larger than the available window by panning the actual window over a virtual window containing the image. Viewers come in a number of flavors. The first two types we'll cover are *UIViewer* and *UIMarquee*. Because the latter is easier to use, I will cover it first, and then also cover three additional types of viewers: *UIScrollViewer*, *UIColumnViewer*, and *UISplitViewer*.

The *UIMarquee* Class

The *UIMarquee* class is a specialized version of a viewer. The marquee viewer pans a component in a constant direction and at a constant rate specified by the programmer, using a timer as input. Once the contents have completely scrolled off the viewer, *UIMarquee* rolls them around to begin again on the other side.

The component being scrolled can be anything the programmer wants; however, it is generally a *UIText* object containing a text string. The following applet, Viewer01, demonstrates the use of *UIMarquee* to scroll text read from an HTML page:

```
// Viewer01 - Implements the UIMarquee class
import java.applet.*;
import java.awt.*;

import com.ms.ui.*;
import com.ms.ui.event.*;
```

```
import Application;

public class Viewer01 extends AwtUIApplet
{
    Viewer01()
    {
        super(new MyApplet());
    }

    public static void main(String[] arg)
    {
        System.out.println("Cannot be executed as an application.");
    }
}

class MyApplet extends UIApplet
{
    // Set the marquee string and the period between movements.
    // (Both are read from the HTML file but are defaulted
    // here.)
    private String sMarquee = "Default string";
    private int nPeriod = 100;
    private int nXIncrement = 1;  // Default is to left
    private int nYIncrement = 0;

    private final String PARAM_string = "string";
    private final String PARAM_period = "period";
    private final String PARAM_xdir   = "xdir";
    private final String PARAM_ydir   = "ydir";

    public void init()
    {
        // Read parameters from the HTML page.
        // First the marquee string.
        String param;
        param = getParameter(PARAM_string);
        if (param != null)
        {
            sMarquee = param;
        }
```

```
// Now the pan rate...
param = getParameter(PARAM_period);
if (param != null)
{
    nPeriod = Integer.parseInt(param);
}

// ...and the direction
param = getParameter(PARAM_xdir);
if (param != null)
{
    nXIncrement = Integer.parseInt(param);
}
param = getParameter(PARAM_ydir);
if (param != null)
{
    nYIncrement = Integer.parseInt(param);
}

// Create a simple IUIComponent out of the string.
UIText text = new UIText(sMarquee);

// Put this component in a marquee viewer...
UIMarquee marquee = new UIMarquee(text,
                                  nPeriod,
                                  nXIncrement,
                                  nYIncrement);

// ...and add it to the applet.
setLayout(new UIBorderLayout());
add(marquee, "Center");
    }
}
```

As is typical for marquee applets, the example reads the text to be displayed, the speed, and the direction of travel from the HTML page. Once the marquee string has been read, it is converted to a *UIText* object and passed to the *UI-Marquee* constructor. Notice in particular the *nXIncrement* and *nYIncrement* arguments. A value of *1* for *nXIncrement* results in a string that pans from right to left. A value of *–1* pans from left to right. In similar fashion, a value of *1* for *nYIncrement* pans the component from bottom to top, and a value of *–1* pans from top to bottom.

Once constructed, the *UIMarquee* object is added to the applet window.

The following HTML excerpt results in a window that pans from the lower left corner up and to the right:

```
<applet
    code=Viewer01.class
    name=Viewer01
    width=400
    height=100 >
    <param name="string" value="AFC makes marquees easy.">
    <param name="xdir" value=-1>
    <param name="ydir" value=1>
</applet>
```

The results of this code are shown in Figure 7-4.

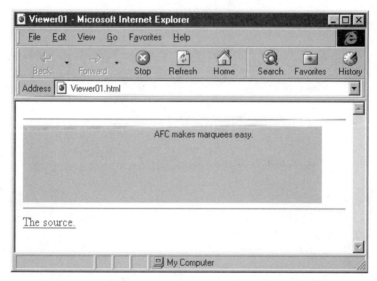

FIGURE 7-4 *The output of the Viewer01 applet, which demonstrates the* UIMarquee *class.*

The *UIViewer* Class

The generic *UIViewer* class is considerably more powerful than *UIMarquee* but is also more difficult to use. Whereas the *UIMarquee* class panned the contents of the viewer automatically (based on time), the contents of the *UIViewer* class can be panned according to whatever input the programmer chooses to use. However, it is left up to the applet to perform the panning.

The following applet, Viewer02, allows the user to drag the image within the applet window:

```
// Viewer02 - You can use the UIViewer class to provide
//            a small viewing area into a larger virtual
//            window. In this example, the applet window
//            is smaller than the image being displayed.
//            The user can move the image in the
//            applet window by using the mouse.
import java.applet.*;
import java.awt.*;

import com.ms.ui.*;
import com.ms.ui.event.*;

import Images;
import Application;

public class Viewer02 extends AwtUIApplet
{
    Viewer02()
    {
        super(new MyApplet());
    }

    public static void main(String[] arg)
    {
        System.out.println("Cannot execute as an application.");
    }
}

class MyApplet extends UIApplet
{
    public void init()
    {
        setLayout(new UIBorderLayout());

        // Load an image for this viewer to view.
        Images images = new Images(this, "Hubble.jpg");
        images.load();

        // Create a custom viewer with this image...
        UIViewer viewer = new MyViewer(images.getImage());
```

```
        // ...and add it to the applet window.
        add(viewer, "Center");
    }
}

// MyViewer - Provides a UIViewer object that moves its contents
//            when the user drags the mouse within the
//            viewer's display area
class MyViewer extends UIViewer
{
    // The previous location of the mouse pointer during
    // a drag operation
    Point dragPt = new Point(0, 0);

    // The difference between the current drag location
    // and the previous drag location
    Point deltaPt = new Point(0, 0);


    // Constructor
    MyViewer(Image image)
    {
        // Create a graphics object out of this image,
        // and add it to the viewer.
        super(new UIGraphic(image));
    }

    // mouseDown - The mouse drag begins with a
    //             mouse down event; record the
    //             location of the mouse.
    public boolean mouseDown(Event e, int x, int y)
    {
        dragPt.x = x;
        dragPt.y = y;
        return super.mouseDown(e, x, y);
    }

    // mouseDrag - Mouse drag events are created as
    //             the user drags the mouse;
    //             process these movements.
    public boolean mouseDrag(Event e, int x, int y)
    {
        // Calculate how far the mouse moved since
        // the last event.
        deltaPt.x = x - dragPt.x;
        deltaPt.y = y - dragPt.y;
```

>>

>>

```
        // Add this offset to the current viewer position.
        Point currentPt = getPosition();
        currentPt.x -= deltaPt.x;
        currentPt.y -= deltaPt.y;

        // Make this the new viewer position.
        setPosition(currentPt);

        // Remember the new location of the mouse pointer
        // so that it can be compared with the next mouse
        // pointer location.
        dragPt.x = x;
        dragPt.y = y;

        return super.mouseDrag(e, x, y);
    }
}
```

Viewer02 begins by using the *Images* class to load an image from the file Hubble.jpg, an impressive picture of Jupiter taken by the Hubble Space Telescope showing the moon Io and its shadow. (The *Images* class is contained on the companion CD in the directory AppCommon and is described in Appendix B, "Utility Classes Used in This Book.")

The class *MyViewer* extends the *UIViewer* class by overriding the *mouseDown* and *mouseDrag* methods. The *mouseDrag* method is called as the user moves the mouse with the mouse button held down. Each time a mouse drag event is reported, *mouseDrag* calculates how far the mouse has moved (*deltaPt*) since the last time a mouse drag was reported. It updates the image offset (*currentPt*) by that amount and sets the viewer position accordingly by calling *setPosition*. The *mouseDown* method records the location of the mouse at the time the user first presses the mouse button. This location is used to process the first mouse drag event report.

The static result shown in Figure 7-5 doesn't do this applet justice. The user can pan the image by dragging the mouse anywhere within the window.

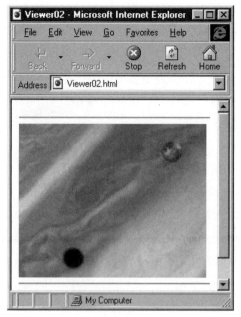

FIGURE 7-5   *The output of the Viewer02 applet, showing the moon Io and its shadow on the surface of Jupiter.*

Scroll Viewer

The class *UIScrollViewer* provides a viewer similar to the *UIViewer* class except that where *UIViewer* left it up to the applet to determine how the image was to be panned, the *UIScrollViewer* class adds scrollbars to handle the pan operations. Both horizontal and vertical scrollbars are added as they are needed. The scroll viewer provides a convenient means to view components that are larger than the applet window but not too large to fit completely into memory.

TIP

A scroll viewer would not be a good choice for implementing scrolling in an application such as a word processor because the amount of text might be quite large.

The following applet, ScrollViewer01, demonstrates a *UIScrollViewer*-based applet designed to display the same Hubble Space Telescope image of Jupiter seen in Figure 7-5 on page 203:

```
// ScrollViewer01 - The UIScrollViewer class provides scrollbars
//                  when the content exceeds the available size
//                  of the viewer; here we put a largish image
//                  into a much too small viewer.
import java.applet.*;
import java.awt.*;

import com.ms.ui.*;
import com.ms.fx.*;

import Application;
import Images;

public class ScrollViewer01 extends AwtUIApplet
{
    ScrollViewer01()
    {
        super(new MyApplet());
    }

    public static void main(String[] arg)
    {
        System.out.println("Cannot execute as an application.");
    }
}


class MyApplet extends UIApplet
{
    public void init()
    {
        // Create a labeled image to add to the scroll
        // viewer.
        Images images = new Images(this, "Hubble.jpg");
        images.load();
        UIItem item = new UIItem(images.getImage(),
                                 "Jupiter from HST",
                                 0,
                                 UIItem.ABOVE);
```

```
// Make the label 48 points (pretty big).
FxFont font = new FxFont("Arial", FxFont.PLAIN, 48);
item.setFont(font);

// Add the item to the scroll viewer.
// Note: The scroll viewer wraps your item with
// a UIViewer object and then adds the object
// to the scroll viewer.
UIScrollViewer viewer = new UIScrollViewer(item);

// Add the scroll viewer to the applet window.
setLayout(new UIBorderLayout());
add(viewer, "Center");
    }
}
```

This applet creates a *UIItem* object from the Hubble Space Telescope image, along with text intended as a label for the picture. A *UIScrollViewer* object is then created around this *UIItem* object and added to the applet window. That's all there is to creating a scrollable image! The result is shown in Figure 7-6.

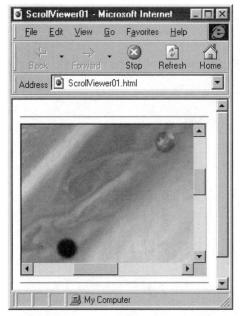

FIGURE 7-6   *The Hubble Space Telescope image displayed using a scrolling viewer.*

As written, the scroll viewer in this applet displays scrollbars only when they are necessary. Specifying *UIScroll.NOHIDE* to the *UIScrollViewer* constructor instructs the class to display the scroll bar at all times. Separate settings are available for the horizontal and vertical scroll bars.

Column Viewer

The column viewer is a variation on the scroll viewer theme. Like the scroll viewer, it allows the user to view more data than can fit at one time in the applet window. Unlike the simple scroll viewer, however, the column viewer is designed to handle columns of data, as demonstrated in the following applet, ColumnViewer01:

```
// ColumnViewer01 - The column viewer provides a scrollable
//                  multiple-column viewer. There are two ways
//                  to build up a column viewer - here we
//                  build the rows first and then use
//                  them to construct the column viewer.
import java.applet.*;
import java.awt.*;

import com.ms.ui.*;
import Application;

public class ColumnViewer01 extends AwtUIApplet
{
    ColumnViewer01()
    {
        super(new MyApplet());
    }

    public static void main(String[] arg)
    {
        new Application(new MyApplet());
    }
}

class MyApplet extends UIApplet
{
    // The column header consists of an array
    // of objects of class UIColumnHeader - here there
    // are three columns.
    UIColumnHeader[] hdrs = new UIColumnHeader[3]
```

```
{
    new UIColumnHeader("Decimal"),
    new UIColumnHeader("Octal"),
    new UIColumnHeader("Hexadecimal")
};

// The following data will be used to build the rows.
static final String[] sDecimal = new String[16]
{ "0",  "1",  "2",  "3",  "4",  "5",  "6",  "7",
  "8",  "9",  "10", "11", "12", "13", "14", "15"};
static final String[] sOctal   = new String[16]
{ "0",  "1",  "2",  "3",  "4",  "5",  "6",  "7",
 "10", "11", "12", "13", "14", "15", "16", "17"};
static final String[] sHex      = new String[16]
{ "0",  "1",  "2",  "3",  "4",  "5",  "6",  "7",
  "8",  "9",  "A",  "B",  "C",  "D",  "E",  "F"};

public void init()
{
    // A UIList class is used as a container of rows.
    UIList list = new UIList();

    // Here we will create 16 rows of three columns.
    for(int i = 0; i < 16; i++)
    {
        // Each row consists of an array of
        // strings - in this case, three.
        Object[] rowObjs = new Object[3];
        rowObjs[0] = sDecimal[i];
        rowObjs[1] = sOctal[i];
        rowObjs[2] = sHex[i];

        // Build a UIRow object from this array...
        UIRow row = new UIRow(rowObjs);

        // ...and add it to the list.
        list.add(row);
    }

    // Now create the column viewer from this
    // array of column headers and list of rows.
    UIColumnViewer viewer = new UIColumnViewer(hdrs, list);
    viewer.setWidths(98);
```

>>

```
        // Add it to the applet.
        setLayout(new UIBorderLayout());
        add(viewer, "Center");
    }
}
```

Looking ahead within the *init* method, one of the *UIColumnViewer* constructors accepts an array of *UIColumnHeader* objects—the column headers—to be used as the first row, and a list of *UIRow* objects, each row consisting of an array of objects to be displayed. The *UIColumnHeader* array is created in the following statement:

```
UIColumnHeader[] hdrs = new UIColumnHeader[3]
{
    new UIColumnHeader("Decimal"),
    new UIColumnHeader("Octal"),
    new UIColumnHeader("Hexadecimal")
};
```

Each row is created within the *for* loop and added to the *UIList* class *list* object. Once completed, both *hdrs* and *list* are used to create the column viewer.

The results of the column viewer applet are shown in Figure 7-7.

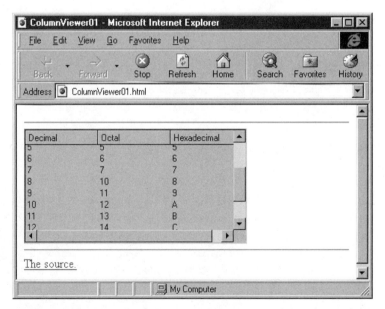

FIGURE 7-7   *The output from the ColumnViewer01 applet; the columns are kept "locked" together so that they all scroll together.*

This approach works fine when the data is known from the outset. There are cases, however, when the data is accumulated or when the contents of the column viewer need to change. The following applet uses the *UIColumnViewer* class to generate the same output, but it does so by adding rows to an already created column viewer:

```java
// ColumnViewer02 - The second way to build a column viewer
//                  is to first build it empty and then add
//                  rows to it one at a time.
import java.applet.*;
import java.awt.*;

import com.ms.ui.*;
import com.ms.ui.event.*;
import Application;

public class ColumnViewer02 extends AwtUIApplet
{
    ColumnViewer02()
    {
        super(new MyApplet());
    }

    public static void main(String[] arg)
    {
        new Application(new MyApplet());
    }
}

class MyApplet extends UIApplet
{
    // Column headers
    UIColumnHeader[] hdrs = new UIColumnHeader[3]
    {
        new UIColumnHeader("Decimal"),
        new UIColumnHeader("Octal"),
        new UIColumnHeader("Hexadecimal")
    };
```

>>

```
// The following data will be used to build the rows.
static final String[] sDecimal = new String[16]
{ "0", "1", "2", "3", "4", "5", "6", "7",
  "8", "9", "10", "11", "12", "13", "14", "15"};
static final String[] sOctal   = new String[16]
{ "0", "1", "2", "3", "4", "5", "6", "7",
 "10", "11", "12", "13", "14", "15", "16", "17"};
static final String[] sHex     = new String[16]
{ "0", "1", "2", "3", "4", "5", "6", "7",
  "8", "9", "A", "B", "C", "D", "E", "F"};

public void init()
{
    // Create the column viewer empty...
    UIList list = new UIList();
    UIColumnViewer viewer = new UIColumnViewer(hdrs, list);
    viewer.setWidths(98);

    // ...and add the viewer to the applet.
    setLayout(new UIBorderLayout());
    add(viewer, "Center");

    // Now add the columns one at a time.
    for(int i = 0; i < 16; i++)
    {
        // Each row consists of an array of
        // strings - in this case, three.
        Object[] rowObjs = new Object[3];
        rowObjs[0] = sDecimal[i];
        rowObjs[1] = sOctal[i];
        rowObjs[2] = sHex[i];

        // Add the row to the list. (The viewer
        // builds the UIRow object for us. The add method
        // returns the row; we can keep it if
        // we're interested.)
        UIRow row = (UIRow)viewer.add(rowObjs);
    }
}
```

Here the *UIColumnViewer* object is created with a header and an empty list. Once created, the applet adds each row by calling *viewer.add* and passing it an array of objects. In actual practice, these rows might be added in some other method, perhaps as a result of user input. Notice that the *add* method returns a reference to the *UIRow* object it creates, in case you need to do anything to it.

Finally, it is often the case that we want our applet to give the user the opportunity to select one of the columns for processing. This selection is handled by attaching an item listener to the column viewer, as demonstrated in the following applet:

```
// ColumnViewer03 - The column viewer generates an item
//                  event when the user selects one of the
//                  rows.
import java.applet.*;
import java.awt.*;

import com.ms.ui.*;
import com.ms.ui.event.*;
import Application;

public class ColumnViewer03 extends AwtUIApplet
{
    ColumnViewer03()
    {
        super(new MyApplet());
    }

    public static void main(String[] arg)
    {
        new Application(new MyApplet());
    }
}

class MyApplet extends UIApplet
{
    // Column headers
    UIColumnHeader[] hdrs = new UIColumnHeader[3]
    {
        new UIColumnHeader("Decimal"),
        new UIColumnHeader("Octal"),
        new UIColumnHeader("Hexadecimal")
    };
```

>>

```
// The following data will be used to build the rows.
static final String[] sDecimal = new String[16]
{ "0", "1", "2", "3", "4", "5", "6", "7",
  "8", "9", "10", "11", "12", "13", "14", "15"};
static final String[] sOctal   = new String[16]
{ "0", "1", "2", "3", "4", "5", "6", "7",
  "10", "11", "12", "13", "14", "15", "16", "17"};
static final String[] sHex     = new String[16]
{ "0", "1", "2", "3", "4", "5", "6", "7",
  "8", "9", "A", "B", "C", "D", "E", "F"};

// IL - Because we stuffed the column viewer with
//      rows of our own subclass, we can store
//      extra information in the subclass.
class IL implements IUIItemListener
{
    public void itemStateChanged(UIItemEvent e)
    {
        MyRow item = (MyRow)e.getItem();
        showStatus("Selected row " +
                    Integer.toString(item.nId));
    }
}

// showStatus - If MyApplet is being invoked as an
//              applet, output message in status
//              bar; otherwise, just output.
public void showStatus(String s)
{
    if (getApplet() != null)
    {
        super.showStatus(s);
    }
    else
    {
        System.out.println(s);
    }
}

public void init()
{
    // Create the column viewer empty.
    UIList list = new UIList();
    UIColumnViewer viewer = new UIColumnViewer(hdrs, list);
    viewer.setWidths(98);
```

```
        // Add an item listener...
        viewer.addItemListener(new IL());

        // ...and add the viewer to the applet.
        setLayout(new UIBorderLayout());
        add(viewer, "Center");

        // Now add the columns one at a time as before,
        // but this time make them a subclass of the UIRow
        // of our own making.
        for(int i = 0; i < 16; i++)
        {
            // Create a row of our own...
            Object[] rowObjs = new Object[3];
            rowObjs[0] = sDecimal[i];
            rowObjs[1] = sOctal[i];
            rowObjs[2] = sHex[i];

            UIRow row = new MyRow(rowObjs, i);

            // ...and add it to the list.
            viewer.add(row);
        }
    }
}


// MyRow - By creating a subclass of UIRow to add to
//         the column viewer instead of a simple UIRow,
//         we can add whatever information we want in
//         order to know what to do when the user
//         selects that row.
class MyRow extends UIRow
{
    // Row ID
    public int nId;

    MyRow(Object[] objs, int nId)
    {
        super(objs);
        this.nId = nId;
    }
}
```

An item listener object is attached to the column viewer in the *init* method. When the user selects one of the rows, the *itemStateChanged* method of the item listener is invoked with an item event containing the selected row. Often the row contains the data needed in order for the applet to know how to process the user's request. When it does not, however, the programmer can extend *UIRow* to include whatever data will be needed. Here I have created the class *MyRow* by adding some trivial information to demonstrate the principle. In a real-world application, *MyRow* can contain any data needed to process the selection.

Split Viewer

The split viewer is also similar to the scroll viewer except that the split viewer allows two different objects to be viewed simultaneously. You've seen this type of behavior already in programs like Microsoft Word. When you need to edit one part of a document while viewing another, you simply grab the tab in the upper right corner of the window (just above the scroll-up arrow) and pull it down to reveal an upper window and a lower window, each outfitted with its own scroll bars.

The following applet demonstrates how to use the *UISplitViewer* class to create both horizontally and vertically split displays:

```
// SplitViewer01 - The split viewer allows two images to be
//                 displayed simultaneously. This viewer is
//                 quite easy to set up.
import java.applet.*;
import java.awt.*;

import com.ms.ui.*;

import Application;
import Images;

public class SplitViewer01 extends AwtUIApplet
{
    SplitViewer01()
    {
        super(new MyApplet());
    }

    public static void main(String[] arg)
    {
        System.out.println("Cannot execute as application.");
    }
}
```

```
class MyApplet extends UIApplet
{
    public void init()
    {
        // Get an image that we will put in the top
        // window of the splitter.
        Images images = new Images(this, "Hubble.jpg");
        images.load();
        Image image = images.getImage();
        UIGraphic top = new UIGraphic(image);

        // Create a horizontally split viewer for the
        // bottom pane. Put an edit window on the left and
        // a button panel on the right. Put the split
        // in the middle, and disable the scroll bars.
        UIEdit edit = new UIEdit("Enter text here:");
        UIPanel panel = new MyPanel();
        UISplitViewer bot =
                new UISplitViewer(edit, panel,
                                  0, -50,
                                  false);

        // Now create an overall splitter by putting
        // the vertical splitter at the bottom and the
        // graphics object at the top. Give the graphics
        // object 80 percent of the view area initially
        // and enable scroll bars.
        UISplitViewer viewer =
                new UISplitViewer(top, bot,
                                  UISplitViewer.HORIZONTAL, -80,
                                  true);

        // Now add this to the applet window.
        setLayout(new UIBorderLayout());
        add(viewer, "Center");
    }
}
```

>>

```
// MyPanel - Creates a panel with text in the middle and
//              buttons at the bottom
class MyPanel extends UIPanel
{
    MyPanel()
    {
        setLayout(new UIBorderLayout());

        add(new UIText("Button Panel"), "Center");
        UIPanel subpanel = new UIPanel();

        UIPushButton button;
        button = new UIPushButton("Go", UIPushButton.RAISED);
        subpanel.add(button, "West");
        button = new UIPushButton("Stop", UIPushButton.RAISED);
        subpanel.add(button, "East");
        add(subpanel, "South");
    }
}
```

The results of this applet are shown in Figure 7-8.

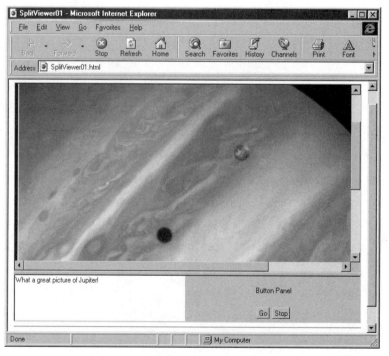

FIGURE 7-8   *The output of the SplitViewer01 applet; the split viewer can be used to create both horizontally and vertically split displays, even in the same applet.*

The upper image consists of a *UIGraphic* object named *top*. The lower image is itself a split viewer, split vertically. The left side of this lower split viewer is a simple *UIEdit* text field, and the right side is a custom-built panel. Notice that the constructor for *UISplitViewer* takes as arguments the two objects to appear on either side of the split along with a flag indicating whether to split horizontally or vertically and where to place the initial split. A positive number indicates the size, in pixels, of the splitter bar from the top. A negative number indicates a percentage, so *-50* means the splitter bar is positioned in the middle. The final argument to the constructor is a Boolean value indicating whether the splitter bar can be dragged by the user.

WHAT'S NEXT

The numerous classes that make up the *Panel* and *Window* groups form a powerful set. *UIPanel*, *UIGroup*, *UICheckGroup*, and *UIRadioGroup* are used primarily to group components within a window. The *UIFrame* class allows the applet to create independent windows replete with title bar, controls, and window frame. The *UIViewer* class and its subclass, *UIMarquee*, represent various forms of viewers for displaying images in windows that are too small to display an entire image at one time.

In the next chapter, we will start looking at the more advanced display components. For example, the first group of classes we'll examine, which is derived from *UIChoice*, allows the user to select one or more items from a list of some type—a significant enhancement to the output of your applet.

Choices

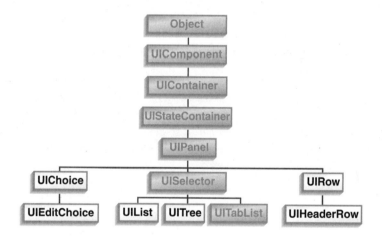

This chapter describes a set of classes that I have grouped together under the category *choices*. These classes enable the user to choose an item from a list of some type. The choices group breaks down into three basic object types: selection boxes, lists, and trees. All of these choices can be used with the *UIRow* class to allow the user to work with multiple objects simultaneously.

SELECTION BOXES

A selection box displays a drop-down list of options and allows the user to select one. Once the user has made her decision, the drop-down list disappears, leaving just the selected item. Selection boxes come in two flavors: uneditable *UIChoice* and user-editable *UIEditChoice*.

The *UIChoice* Class

The *UIChoice* class is probably the most generally useful class of the choices group because it provides the user with a drop-down selection box of options. Figure 8-1 shows a *UIChoice* object with the drop-down selection box visible and the same list after the user has made her selection.

FIGURE 8-1   *The* UIChoice *class drop-down selection box. On the left, the selection box is in the dropped-down state; on the right, it is in the normal state.*

The following applet, Choice01, was used to generate Figure 8-1:

```
// Choice01 - The UIChoice class presents the user with a
//            drop-down list of options and lets the user
//            select one.
import java.applet.*;
import java.awt.*;

import com.ms.ui.*;
import com.ms.ui.event.*;

import Application;

public class Choice01 extends AwtUIApplet
{
    Choice01()
    {
        super(new MyApplet());
    }
```

```
    public static void main(String[] arg)
    {
        new Application(new MyApplet());
    }
}

class MyApplet extends UIApplet
{
    public void init()
    {
        // Create the Choice object.
        UIChoice choice = new UIChoice();

        // Now add a few items to the list.
        choice.addString("Option 1");
        choice.addString("Option 2");
        choice.addString("Option 3");

        // Start with the first element in the list
        // as the selected element.
        choice.setSelectedIndex(0);

        // Display the selection to the applet.
        setLayout(new UIFlowLayout());
        add(choice);
    }
}
```

This applet begins by creating a *UIChoice* object. It then adds three items to the list of options. Here the additions are of type *String*, but you could just as easily make them a subclass of *UIStatic*—for example, *UIItem*. (See Chapter 5, "Canvases," for details.)

The call to *setSelectedIndex* displays the drop-down list with the first item in the list selected. Without this call, the selected item area of the selection box would initially appear empty. Last, the *choice* object is added to the applet panel.

A file list

While it does happen that the list of items to be added to a drop-down selection box is fixed and can therefore be hard coded, it is much more common that the list is calculated when the applet is executed. One of the most common uses for a drop-down selection box is to contain a list of files, such as the contents of a directory. The following applet, Choice02, demonstrates how to create this type of selection box:

```
// Choice02 - Fill the Choice object with a sorted list
//            of filenames, and then wait for the user to
//            select one. When she does, display the choice
//            by stuffing it into a Text object.
//            Use UIEditChoice if you want to allow the user
//            to edit the selection.
import java.applet.*;
import java.awt.*;

import com.ms.ui.*;
import com.ms.ui.event.*;

import FileDescr;
import Application;

public class Choice02 extends AwtUIApplet
{
    Choice02()
    {
        super(new MyApplet());
    }

    public static void main(String[] arg)
    {
        new Application(new MyApplet(), "File List", 100, 300);
    }
}

class MyApplet extends UIApplet
{
    // UIChoice does not allow editing of the selection.
    UIChoice choice = new UIChoice();
    // UIEditChoice does.
    // UIChoice choice = new UIEditChoice();

    UIDrawText text = new UIDrawText("No selection");
```

```
// PBActionListener - Invoked when the user clicks
//                    the OK button
class PBActionListener implements IUIActionListener
{
    public void actionPerformed(UIActionEvent e)
    {
        // Get the current selection from the Choice
        // object...
        String sSelection = choice.getValueText();

        // ...and stuff it into the Text object.
        text.setValueText(sSelection);
    }
}

public void init()
{
    // Create a sorted list of files.
    FileDescr fileList = new FileDescr("c:");
    fileList.sort(true);

    // Now add the items from the file list to
    // the choice list.
    int nLength = fileList.getChildCount();
    for (int i = 0; i < nLength; i++)
    {
        choice.addString(fileList.getChild(i));
    }

    // Start with the first item selected.
    choice.setSelectedIndex(0);

    // Now add the choices list to the window.
    setLayout(new UIBorderLayout());
    add(choice, "North");

    // Position a Select button at the bottom.
    UIPushButton button = new UIPushButton("OK");
    button.addActionListener(new PBActionListener());
    add(button, "South");

    // Display the selected text in the center.
    add(text, "Center");
}
}
```

This program begins by creating a *FileDescr* object for the directory C:\temp. Obviously, you can place any directory you want in this object.

FileDescr is another of those common classes contained in AppCommon and described in Appendix B, "Utility Classes Used in This Book." An object of class *FileDescr* can represent either a file or a folder on the disk. This class provides a number of convenient methods for accessing information about the file or folder. For example, if *fileList* is a folder, the *fileList* object contains an array of *String* objects, each containing the name of a file in that folder. The method *fileList.sort* sorts this list in ascending order. The *true* argument passed to the *sort* method indicates that the sort should be conducted without regard to capitalization—that is, treating uppercase and lowercase the same.

NOTE

The Java security model allows file operations only from the following:

- applications of all types
- trusted applets (see Appendix A, "Signing Applets," for instructions on how to flag an applet as trusted)
- applets being executed from the debugger

Once the *FileDescr* class has created the *fileList* object containing a sorted list of the contents of the specified folder, the program enters a loop, calling the *getChild* method. Each call to *getChild* returns the next name in the file list. Each name is added to the choice list by calling *addString*.

A further addition to *init* is a button that reads the contents of the *UIChoice* object, enabling the application to determine which file has been selected. The name of the selected file is displayed in a *UIDrawText* object positioned in the applet window. (This technique provides a way of reading the *UIChoice* object. If you prefer, you can attach a listener directly to the *UIChoice* object; the Choice03 example program, which follows, demonstrates how.)

Figure 8-2 shows the results of executing Choice02 on the C:\temp directory of my system.

FIGURE 8-2   *The* UIChoice *drop-down selection box populated with a file list.*

The *UIEditChoice* class

The standard *UIChoice* class allows the user only to select one of the options presented. It does not allow the user to edit that selection in any way. If you want the user to be able to edit her selection, use the *UIEditChoice* class instead. Both of the example programs, Choice01 and Choice02, have been commented to indicate where the *UIEditChoice* class could have been used in place of *UIChoice*.

LISTS

The *UIList* class represents AFC's implementation of the list. A list is like a drop-down selection box in that it presents a list of options to the user. It differs from the drop-down box in two critical ways, however. First, the *UIList* class does not provide the drop-down dynamics of *UIChoice*. All of the options appear all of the time. Second, the *UIList* class optionally allows the user to select more than one entry at a time.

The following program, Choice03, demonstrates the use of the *UIList* class:

```
// Choice03 - The list allows the user to select multiple
//            elements at one time. It does not have the
//            drop-down list dynamics of the UIChoice object.
import java.applet.*;
import java.awt.*;

import com.ms.ui.*;
import com.ms.ui.event.*;

import FileDescr;
import Application;

public class Choice03 extends AwtUIApplet
{
    Choice03()
    {
        super(new MyApplet());
    }

    public static void main(String[] arg)
    {
        new Application(new MyApplet());
    }
}


class MyApplet extends UIApplet
{
    // UIList - The list can be single-select, multiple-select,
    //          or extend-select, the last of these meaning that
    //          dragging the mouse selects a range.
    UIList list = new UIList(UIList.EXTENDSELECT,
                            UIVerticalFlowLayout.FILL);
```

```
// Container for selected items
UIGroup selGroup;

// ItemListener - Invoked when the state of the list changes
class ItemListener implements IUIItemListener
{
    public void itemStateChanged(UIItemEvent e)
    {
        // The UIItemEvent object has the particular item
        // selected; however, for a list, it's usually
        // easier to query the list for all selected
        // items.
        IUIComponent[] selComps = list.getSelectedItems();

        // Remove anything that's currently in the selected
        // group object.
        selGroup.removeAllChildren();

        // Now add the ASCII representation of the selected
        // items.
        for (int i = 0, i < selComps.length; i++)
        {
            selGroup.add(new UIText(selComps[i] getName()));
        }
    }
}

public void init()
{
    // Populating the list is the same as
    // populating a Choice object.
    FileDescr fileList = new FileDescr("c:/temp");
    fileList.sort(true);
    int nLength = fileList.getChildCount();
    for (int i = 0; i < nLength; i++)
    {
        // Use add(String) instead of addString(String).
        list.add(fileList.getChild(i));
    }
```

>>

```
// Set the item listener.
list.addItemListener(new ItemListener());

// Add the list to the window.
setLayout(new UIRowLayout(2));

// Put the list in a group on the left.
UIGroup listGroup = new UIGroup("List");
listGroup.add(list);
add(listGroup);

// Display the selected files on the right.
selGroup = new UIGroup("Selected items");
selGroup.setLayout(new UIVerticalFlowLayout());
add(selGroup);
    }
}
```

Choice03 exhibits several differences from Choice02—some of these stemming from differences between the *UIList* and the *UIChoice* classes. The first difference is the way in which the *UIList* object is created. Whereas the *UIChoice* class offered no options, the *UIList* constructor accepts two arguments. The first argument to the *UIList* constructor indicates how many items can be selected at one time. A value of *SINGLESELECT* indicates that only one item can be selected. A value of *MULTISELECT* specifies that multiple items can be selected simultaneously. *EXTENDSELECT* is like *MULTISELECT* except that it allows the user to select ranges of items by dragging over them with the mouse. Keep in mind that enabling the *EXTENDSELECT* feature changes the dynamics of the mouse somewhat.

The second argument to the *UIList* constructor specifies whether the list is to have one or multiple columns. The value *FILL* used here indicates that the list has one column and that all the fields are filled to the same width.

The second difference between Choice03 and its predecessors lies in the way that items are read from the list. Rather than defining a button to read the list, this program assigns an item listener directly to the list. (The item listener approach can be used with the *UIChoice* and *UIEditChoice* classes as well.)

The item listener in this program queries the list for all selected items and then adds these to a group that has been created specifically to display the selected filenames. Notice that *getSelectedItems* does not return an array of *String* objects, even though the program added *String* objects to the list. This occurs because *add(String)* changes the *String* object into an object of class *UIText* before adding it to the list. This technique is similar to using *UILabel.add(String)*.

The results of the Choice03 program are shown in Figure 8-3.

FIGURE 8-3   *My C:\temp directory showing multiple files selected.*

DEBUGGING TIP:
DETERMINING THE CLASS OF OBJECTS RECEIVED IN LISTENERS

Often when you are writing listener functions, it isn't obvious what type of object to expect either from the *UIEvent* or from the read methods such as *getSelected*. The documented return class of *IUIComponent* isn't much help in AFC since all components are subclasses of *IUIComponent*! You can often guess the class based on the class of object you're listening to or based on the type of class you added in the first place. The latter can be misleading, however, as we saw in the case of Choice03—even though we added *String* objects, that isn't what we got back.

I have found that the easiest approach is to write the program initially using a listener function that does nothing more than output the class name of the object that it retrieves in the applet's status bar. For example, my first item listener for Choice03 appeared as follows:

```
// ItemListener - Used to determine
//                the class of the objects
//                received from the list
class ItemListener implements IUIItemListener
{
    public void itemStateChanged(UIItemEvent e)
    {
        IUIComponent[] selComps = list.getSelectedItems();
        // getClass is a method of Object.
        Class c = selComps[0].getClass();
        // Now get the name of the class.
        String sType = c.getName();

        // Display the class name in the status bar of the
        // browser.
        showStatus("Class = " + sType);
    }
}
```

When I select an item from the list, the message "Class = com.ms.ui.UIText" is displayed in the status bar. I can now return armed with the knowledge that I need to write a real item listener.

TREES

The *UIChoice* and *UIList* classes are very good at presenting the user with a list of options and allowing him to pick one. However, both of these classes assume that all data is created equal, so they present the options in the form of a flat list.

Unlike the *UIChoice* and *UIList* classes, the *UITree* class allows the program to display hierarchical information. (*Hierarchical data* is data that has some type of precedence. For example, a cascading menu is hierarchical in that selecting one menu option opens a subsequent menu with a new set of options.)

Figure 8-4 demonstrates the appearance of a *UITree* object. You will instantly recognize this as the tree structure that Microsoft Windows applications such as File Manager and Windows Explorer made famous. The small plus sign next to Folder3 in the image on the left indicates that this folder has information "hidden" beneath it. Clicking on the plus sign expands the tree to display this information, as shown in the center image. Notice that the plus sign has changed to a minus sign to show that no subordinate information is hidden. Similarly, double-clicking on MyDisk hides the entire tree hierarchy, resulting in the image displayed on the right.

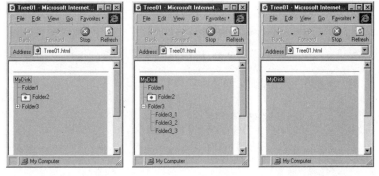

FIGURE 8-4   *A UITree tree list populated with a few simple options, showing the initial, fully open, and fully closed states.*

The program that was used to create Figure 8-4, Tree01, is shown here:

```
// Tree01 - The UITree class creates a tree control such as
//          that commonly used to display directories
//          of files.
import java.applet.*;
import java.awt.*;

import com.ms.ui.*;
import com.ms.ui.event.*;

import Images;
import Application;

public class Tree01 extends AwtUIApplet
{
    Tree01()
    {
        super(new MyApplet());
    }

    public static void main(String[] arg)
    {
        System.out.println("Cannot execute as an application.");
    }
}

class MyApplet extends UIApplet
{
    public void init()
    {
        setLayout(new UIBorderLayout());
        add(new TreePanel(this), "Center");
        setVisible(true);
    }
}

class TreePanel extends UIPanel
{
    TreePanel(UIApplet parent)
    {
        // Normally, you'll want to use a simple label...
        UITree files = new UITree("MyDisk");
        files.add("Folder1");
```

```
        // ...but you can also use a UIStatic object of some kind.
        Images images = new Images(parent, "Favorites.gif");
        images.load();
        Image image = images.getImage();
        UIItem item = new UIItem(image, "Folder2",
                                    UIItem.HOTTRACK);
        files.add(item);

        // Subtrees can hang off trees as well.
        UITree folder3 = new UITree("Folder3");
        files.add(folder3);
        folder3.add("Folder3_1");
        folder3.add("Folder3_2");
        folder3.add("Folder3_3");

        setLayout(new UIBorderLayout());
        add(files, "Center");
        files.setExpanded(true);
    }
}
```

The *init* function for Tree01 does nothing more than add a *TreePanel* object to the middle of the applet window. *TreePanel* is the class that I have created to craft a tree list using the *UITree* class. The constructor for *TreePanel* creates a *UITree* object named *MyDisk*. This name becomes the root of the tree. The three branches, *Folder1*, *Folder2*, and *Folder3*, all stem from this root.

The first limb, *Folder1*, is added simply by calling *UITree.add(String)*. This call generates a simple label. It is also possible to use a *UIStatic* object of some kind, most commonly a *UIItem* object, to hold both text and an image. I used this technique to display a small folder image next to the *Folder2* label.

Folder3 was created to simulate a directory containing several files. Notice that *Folder3* is itself a *UITree* object, which enables the program to continue adding limbs to this branch. Calling *files.setExpanded(true)* opens up the first layer of the tree hierarchy. Without this call, the initial state of the tree is the fully closed state shown on the right in Figure 8-4 on page 231.

A Practical Tree Example

Once again, it is often the case that the data you want to display cannot be hard coded as it was in the Tree01 example. The following program, Tree02, builds a tree with multiple branches from the contents of the hard disk:

```
// Tree02 - Demonstrates a serious use for the UITree class.
//          This applet displays the files contained
//          within a folder (directory) in the UITree class.
import java.applet.*;
import java.awt.*;

import com.ms.ui.*;
import com.ms.ui.event.*;

import Images;
import FileDescr;
import Application;

public class Tree02 extends AwtUIApplet
{
    Tree02()
    {
        super(new MyApplet());
    }

    public static void main(String[] arg)
    {
        // System.out.println("Cannot execute as an application.");
        new Application(new MyApplet());
    }
}

class MyApplet extends UIApplet
{
    // sBaseFolder - Folder from which the file tree is
    //               to start; initialize it to the default
    //               directory name. (The default can be
    //               overridden in an applet by the directory
    //               parameter in the HTML page.)
    String sBaseFolder = "C:/Program Files/DevStudio/Vj";

    // showStatus - If MyApplet is being invoked as an
    //              applet, output the message in the status
    //              bar; otherwise, just output.
    public void showStatus(String s)
```

```
    {
        if (getApplet() != null)
        {
            super.showStatus(s);
        }
        else
        {
            System.out.println(s);
        }
    }

    public void init()
    {
        // If this is an applet,...
        String param;
        if (getApplet() != null)
        {
            // ...get the base directory from the HTML file.
            param = getParameter("directory");
            if (param != null)
            {
                sBaseFolder = param;
            }
        }

        setLayout(new UIBorderLayout());
        add(new TreePanel(this, sBaseFolder), "Center");
        setVisible(true);
    }
}

// TreePanel - Base this object on the UIScrollViewer class so
//             that the user can scroll up and down to see
//             the entire file tree.
class TreePanel extends UIScrollViewer
{
    TreePanel(UIApplet parent, String sBaseFileName)
    {
        // The folder image is the little yellow symbol
        // to the left of the name of folders.
        // (If this applet is being executed from an application,
        // you can't load the image - sorry.)
        Image image = null;
```

>>

```
        if (parent.getApplet() != null)
        {
            Images images = new Images(parent, "Folder.gif");
            images.load();
            image = images.getImage();
        }

        // Create a label for the base folder.
        UIItem label = new UIItem(image, sBaseFileName);

        // Now open a file descriptor for the base folder.
        FileDescr baseFileDescr = new FileDescr(sBaseFileName);

        // Create an FTBranch node from this information.
        FTBranch baseNode = new FTBranch(parent,
                                         baseFileDescr,
                                         label);

        // Expand it. (UITree's nodes are created shrunk.)
        baseNode.setExpanded(true);

        // Last add the FTBranch node to the scroll viewer.
        setContent(baseNode);
    }
}

// FTBranch - Represents a branch in a file-based UITree object
class FTBranch extends UITree
{
    // fileDescr - File descriptor for this node
    FileDescr fileDescr;

    UIApplet parent;

    // IL - The item listener is invoked when any of
    //      the attached text labels (filenames) is
    //      selected by the user.
    class IL implements IUIItemListener
    {
        public void itemStateChanged(UIItemEvent e)
        {
            Object label = e.getItem();
```

```
        if (label instanceof UIText)
        {
            UIText fileLabel = (UIText)label;
            parent.showStatus("Selected " +
                                    fileLabel.getName());
        }
    }
}

// Constructor
FTBranch(UIApplet parent,
        FileDescr baseFileDescr,
        UIItem nodeLabel)
{
    // Create an FTBranch node with the specified name.
    super(nodeLabel);

    // Save the parent applet.
    this.parent = parent;

    // Add the item listener.
    addItemListener(new IL());

    // Sort the file list.
    baseFileDescr.sort(true);

    // Loop through the members of this folder (directory).
    // (The class FileDescr makes this process a lot easier.)
    // On the first pass, list only the subfolders.
    int nNoFiles = baseFileDescr.getChildCount();
    for (int i = 0; i < nNoFiles; i++)
    {
        String sFileName = baseFileDescr.getChild(i);

        // If this member is itself a folder,...
        FileDescr fileDescr = new FileDescr(baseFileDescr,
                                        sFileName);
        if (fileDescr.isDirectory())
        {
            // ...make a file tree branch out of it.
            // Start by creating the label.
            Image image = nodeLabel.getImage();
            UIItem label = new UIItem(image, sFileName);
```

>>

```
                // Now add the new branch.
                add(new FTBranch(parent, fileDescr, label));
            }
        }

        // Repeat the process for files (nonfolders).
        for (int i = 0; i < nNoFiles; i++)
        {
            String sFileName = baseFileDescr.getChild(i);

            // If this member is not a folder,...
            FileDescr fileDescr = new FileDescr(baseFileDescr,
                                                sFileName);
            if (!fileDescr.isDirectory());
            {
                // ...create a Text object from the name and add
                // it to the tree.
                add(new UIText(sFileName));
            }
        }
    }
}
```

The results of the Tree02 applet are shown in Figure 8-5.

FIGURE 8-5   *A UITree object that shows part of the contents of my hard disk.*

The structure of this program is different from those you've seen before. Although the program might seem confusing at first, it becomes clearer if we go through it one step at a time.

Tree02 starts out straightforwardly. First it defines the string *sBaseFolder* as the default directory to display. Obviously, I could have picked any directory I wanted, but I reasoned that the directory containing the Microsoft Visual J++ compiler is likely to be on your hard disk. In any case, when executing this program as an applet, the user can select any directory she wants by changing the *directory* parameter in the HTML page—which is the significance of the call to *getParameter* in *init*. The *init* method creates a *TreePanel* object in the base directory.

The class *TreePanel* extends *UIScrollViewer*. In this way, the *TreePanel* object will display scrollbars as soon as the number of files in the tree exceeds the capacity of the panel to display them all. The constructor for *TreePanel* starts by loading Folder.gif, the image of a small folder, which will be placed beside the name of directories in the file tree. *TreePanel* then goes on to create a *FileDescr* object in the base directory. From this object, *TreePanel* creates the base node of the tree by constructing an object of class *FTBranch*, a subclass of *UITree*. This base branch is then expanded and added to the *TreePanel*.

The class *FileDescr* is one of the common classes I created for this book to simplify some of the example applets. *FileDescr* creates a description of the "file" passed to the *FileDescr* constructor. If this "file" is a true file, *FileDescr* records information such as the length, date, and time of the last modification. If the "file" passed is actually a directory, *FileDescr* automatically queries the directory for its contents. The application can then call *getChild* to get the names of the files contained in the directory. See Appendix B, "Utility Classes Used in This Book," for more information about how this class works.

The key to the Tree02 program lies in the class *FTBranch* (short for "file tree branch"). Each branch of the file tree is represented by an object of class *FTBranch*. The root of the file tree, *TreePanel*, starts by creating an *FTBranch* object to represent the trunk of the tree. First the *FTBranch* has attached a listener to pick up the event generated when the user selects a particular branch. It then sorts the files contained within that branch. Passing *true* to *sort* tells the *sort* function to treat uppercase and lowercase the same in filenames.

Last, *FTBranch* adds the filenames to the *FTBranch* tree branch. Normally, a file tree lists subdirectories first. *FTBranch* does this by iterating through the file list twice. On the first pass, it processes only directories; on the second pass, it processes only nondirectories (simple files). This approach might not be very efficient, but it reduces code complexity significantly.

For each subdirectory that *FTBranch* finds, it opens another tree branch. It does this by creating a new *FTBranch* object. Of course, this new *FTBranch* object will in turn search its contents, adding new *FTBranch* nodes for each sub-directory that it finds and adding *UIText* objects for the simple files. In this way, the program makes its way recursively down each directory chain until all branches have been explored to their ends.

For simple files, *FTBranch* simply builds a *UIText* object from the filename and adds it to the list.

FALL–BACK APPLICATION MODE PROCESSING

Using the *Application* class, most of the sample programs in this book can be executed either as an application or an applet. Unfortunately, *Application* does not support certain applet-only operations such as loading an *Image* object from an application. Thus, most of the example programs that load graphics simply output an error message when they are executed as an application, without ever trying to run.

Tree02 is different from the other example programs in this book in that it can be executed as an application in what I call a "fall-back application" mode— the ability to execute a program as an application without full capabilities. When Tree02 is executed as an applet, it performs like a normal applet, load-ing graphics images or whatever else is required. When Tree02 is executed as an application, however, it knows to avoid operations that are not available.

To determine how it's being executed, Tree02 calls *getApplet*. When called from an applet, *getApplet* returns a reference to the current applet. When called from an application, however, *getApplet* returns a null value. For example, the following code created the folder labels:

>>

```
Image image = null;
if (parent.getApplet() != null)
{
Images images = new Images(parent, "Folder.gif");
images.load();
image = images.getImage();
}

// Create a label for the base folder.
UIItem label = new UIItem(image, sBaseFileName);
```

Here, when executed as an applet, the program creates an *images* object using the Folder.gif image. It then uses this object to load the *image* object, which is in turn used to create the *UIItem label* object. The *label* object is then passed to the *FTBranch* object to be used as the label for the subdirectories.

When Tree02 is executed as an application, however, because *getApplet* returns a null value, *image* retains its initial value of *null*. A *UIItem* object with a null value for *image* appears identical to a *UIText* object. No error is generated. The results are shown in the following image—compare it with the same program executed as an applet as shown in Figure 8-5. Except for the absence of cutesy folder icons, Tree02 appears practically the same whether executed as an application or an applet.

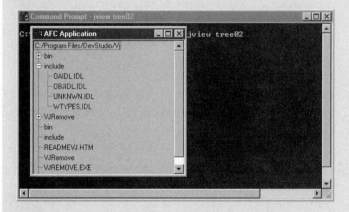

Although Tree02 doesn't do everything as an application that it does as an applet, it does support a large enough subset to be useful.

Improving Performance Using Multitasking

Although impressive in appearance, Tree02 is a little slow in starting up. This slowness occurs because the constructor for the base-level *FTBranch* class doesn't return to *TreePanel* until the entire tree has been constructed, even though only the topmost level of the tree is visible.

A relatively small change to the *FTBranch* class can increase the apparent performance of the applet without adding significantly to the complexity of the class. The following version of *FTBranch* populates the tree in a separate thread while the original thread returns to the browser to display the top level of the tree as soon as possible:

```
// FTBranch - Represents a branch in a file-based UITree object
class FTBranch extends UITree implements Runnable
{
    UIApplet parent;
    FileDescr baseFileDescr;
    UIItem   nodeLabel;

    // IL - The item listener is invoked when any of
    //      the attached text labels (filenames) is
    //      selected by the user.
    class IL implements IUIItemListener
    {
        public void itemStateChanged(UIItemEvent e)
        {
            Object label = e.getItem();
            if (label instanceof UIText)
            {
                UIText fileLabel = (UIText)label;
                parent.showStatus("Selected " +
                                fileLabel.getName());
            }
        }
    }

    // Constructor
    FTBranch(UIApplet parent,
            FileDescr baseFileDescr,
            UIItem nodeLabel,
            boolean bNewThread)
    {
        // Create an FTBranch node with the specified name.
        super(nodeLabel);
```

```
    // Save the parent applet.
    this.parent = parent;
    this.baseFileDescr = baseFileDescr;
    this.nodeLabel = nodeLabel;

    // Add the item listener.
    addItemListener(new IL());

    // Sort the file list.
    baseFileDescr.sort(true);

    // Perform the next step...
    if (bNewThread)
    {
        // ...either in a new Thread object...
        Thread thread = new Thread(this);
        thread.run();
    }
    else
    {
        // ...or in the same Thread object
        run();
    }
}

public void run()
{
    // Loop through the members of this folder (directory).
    // (The class FileDescr makes this process a lot easier.)
    // On the first pass, list only the subfolders.
    int nNoFiles = baseFileDescr.getChildCount();
    for (int i = 0; i < nNoFiles; i++)
    {
        String sFileName = baseFileDescr.getChild(i);

        // If this member is itself a folder,...
        FileDescr fileDescr = new FileDescr(baseFileDescr,
                                            sFileName);
        if (fileDescr.isDirectory())
        {
            // ...make a file tree branch out of it.
            // Start by creating the label.
            Image image = nodeLabel.getImage();
            UIItem label = new UIItem(image, sFileName);
```

>>

```
                        // Now add the new branch.
                        add(new FTBranch(parent,
                                         fileDescr,
                                         label,
                                         false));
            }
    }

    // Repeat the process for files (nonfolders).
    for (int i = 0; i < nNoFiles; i++)
    {
        String sFileName = baseFileDescr.getChild(i);

        // If this member is not a folder,...
        FileDescr fileDescr = new FileDescr(baseFileDescr,
                                            sFileName);
        if (!fileDescr.isDirectory());
        {

            // ...create a text object from the name and add
            // it to the tree.
            add(new UIText(sFileName));
        }
    }
}
}
```

The constructor for this version of *FTBranch* starts out the same as that in Tree02. However, rather than search the entire tree beneath it while the caller waits, this version starts a new thread to perform the search and returns to *TreePanel* immediately. *FTBranch* does this by first marking itself as *Runnable*, which means that *FTBranch* implements a *run* method. In addition, *Runnable* means that you can start a new *Thread* with this *FTBranch* object. The new *Thread* begins execution by calling the *run* method of the *Runnable* object passed to it.

In practice, this technique works as follows. I moved the two *for* loops that perform the actual search of the contents of the directory tree into the method *run*. I then added an argument to the *FTBranch* constructor to allow the caller to indicate whether a new thread should be created to handle the tree search. If *bNewThread* is *true*, the applet executes the statement *new Thread(this).run*. This statement creates a new thread using the current object and then runs it, thereby passing control to the *run* method. Once the *Thread* has been created, the constructor returns immediately, allowing the browser to display the applet window even as threads are created in the background.

I could have started a new thread for every *FTBranch* object created, but then I would have had numerous threads all trying to execute simultaneously. It's really necessary for only the first *FTBranch* to create a single background thread. Thus, when the root *FTBranch* finds subdirectories, it creates new *FTBranch* objects with the *bNewThread* flag set to *false*. In this case, the *FTBranch* constructor simply executes *run* out of the same thread rather than creating a new thread.

> This technique of creating a thread in the background to perform lengthy operations while returning to the user as soon as possible is an effective one that should be in the toolbox of every Java programmer.

ROWS OF DATA

The *UIRow* class represents several objects that can be treated as a single object. Logically, a *UIRow* object is like a single row in a table. *UIRow* can be effectively combined with the various types of choices to allow the user to handle multiple objects simultaneously. This technique is demonstrated in the following applet, Row01:

```
// Row01 - A row can be used to tie multiple objects in
//         one place. Here I use a filename and the
//         originating path in place of the filename
//         itself as we did in our list example.
import java.applet.*;
import java.awt.*;

import com.ms.ui.*;
import com.ms.ui.event.*;

import FileDescr;
import Application;
```

>>

>>

```
public class Row01 extends AwtUIApplet
{
    Row01()
    {
        super(new MyApplet());
    }

    public static void main(String[] arg)
    {
        new Application(new MyApplet(), "c:/temp", 500, 100);
    }
}

class MyApplet extends UIApplet
{
    // UIList - The list can be single-select, multiple-select
    //          or extend-select, the last of these meaning that
    //          dragging the mouse selects a range.
    UIList list = new UIList(UIList.EXTENDSELECT,
                            UIVerticalFlowLayout.FILL);

    // Container for selected items
    UIGroup selGroup;

    // PBActionListener - Invoked when the user clicks
    //                    the OK button
    class ItemListener implements IUIItemListener
    {
        public void itemStateChanged(UIItemEvent e)
        {
            // The UIItemEvent class has the particular item
            // selected; however, for a list, it's usually
            // easier to query the list for all
            // selected items.
            IUIComponent[] selComps = list.getSelectedItems();

            // Remove anything that's currently in the selected items
            // group.
            selGroup.removeAllChildren();

            // Now add the ASCII representation of the
            // selected items.
```

```
        for (int i = 0; i < selComps.length; i++)
        {
            selGroup.add(
                    new UIText(selComps[i].getName())
                );
        }
    }
}


public void init()
{
    // Populating the list is the same as
    // populating a Choice object.
    FileDescr fileList = new FileDescr("c:/temp");
    fileList.sort(true);
    int nLength = fileList.getChildCount();
    for (int i = 0; i < nLength; i++)
    {
        // For each entry, create a UIRow object using the
        // filename, file length, and full pathname.
        // (Hey, that's all I could think of.)
        FileDescr file =
                    new FileDescr(fileList,
                                    fileList.getChild(i));

        Object[] row = new Object[3];
        row[0] = file.getName();
        row[1] = Integer.toString(file.getChildCount());
        row[2] = file.getFullPath();

        UIRow rowObj = new UIRow(row);

        // Add this row instead of the String object that
        // contains the filename.
        list.add(rowObj);
    }

    // Set the item listener.
    list.addItemListener(new ItemListener());

    // Add the list to the window.
    UIRowLayout rowLayout = new UIRowLayout(2);
    int[] nWidths = new int[2] {350, 150};
    rowLayout.setWidths(nWidths);
    setLayout(rowLayout);
```

>>

```
        // Put the list in a group on the left.
        UIGroup listGroup = new UIGroup("List");
        listGroup.add(list);
        add(listGroup);

        // Display the selected files on the right.
        selGroup = new UIGroup("Selected items");
        selGroup.setLayout(new UIVerticalFlowLayout());
        add(selGroup);
    }
}
```

In principle, this program is similar to the Choice02 example program earlier in this chapter. Just as in Choice02, this program creates an *EXTENDSELECT* list and populates that list with the names of the files contained in my C:\temp directory. Unlike Choice02, however, this program includes the file size and the full pathname along with the filename. The key to the difference is in the *for* loop that populates the list:

```
for (int i = 0; i < nLength; i++)
{
    // For each entry, create a UIRow object using the
    // filename, file length, and full pathname.
    // (Hey, that's all I could think of.)
    FileDescr file =
                new FileDescr(fileList,
                                fileList.getChild(i));

    Object[] row = new Object[3];
    row[0] = file.getName();
    row[1] = Integer.toString(file.getChildCount());
    row[2] = file.getFullPath();

    UIRow rowObj = new UIRow(row);

    // Add this row instead of the String object that
    // contains the filename.
    list.add(rowObj);
}
```

After creating a *FileDescr* object to read the next file in the directory, this applet creates an array of three objects. The first object contains the name, the second object contains the length of the file, and the third object contains the full pathname of the file. This array of objects is used to create a *UIRow* object, which is then added to the list in the same way that the filename might have been added before.

The results of the Row01 applet are shown in Figure 8-6.

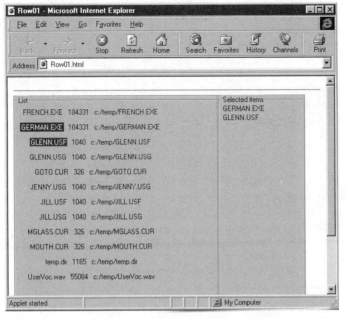

FIGURE 8-6   *A multiple-row list created using the* UIRow *class.*

WHAT'S NEXT

In this chapter, you've seen the different types of lists offered by AFC. Lists allow the user to select from a number of different options. However, the most common of all selection devices is the menu. In Chapter 9, "Menus," we will analyze the various forms of menus, including the relatively new band box. We'll add text and graphics to menu options and work with context menus.

Menus

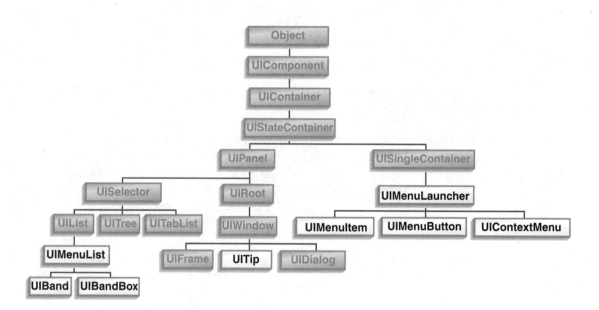

One of the most important features a graphical user interface package can offer is a good set of menus. After all, the menu set is probably the first thing that the user of a program sees. Of course, if the menus are implemented properly, they quickly blend into the background and become just an extension of the tool. In order to make this happen, the programmer must have available in the toolkit the necessary expressive power.

In this chapter, you'll see different forms of AFC menus. The chapter starts with a basic, no-frills menu. It continues by adding graphical widgets to the menu items, by adding cascading menus, and by transforming the conventional menu into one of those menus (a context menu) that pops up out of nowhere when you click the right mouse button. The final menu is a band box menu that Microsoft uses in many of its applications, including Microsoft Internet Explorer.

In the process of discussing menus, I've tried to solve the same problem in more than one way. I haven't done this to confuse you. Rather, I want you to see different types of solutions to a single problem so that you can choose the features you like best when you build your own applications.

SIMPLE AFC MENUS

Menus are created through the collaboration of a number of classes. Showing you a menu program is easier than enumerating the classes and what they do. The following program, Menu01, displays a simple menu at the top of an applet window:

```
// Menu01 - Demonstrates a basic menu.
//          Here strings are used as menu labels and
//          the listener is attached to the menu list.
//          This technique means fewer classes, but it can
//          lead to a nonextensible, non-object-oriented
//          solution.
import java.applet.*;
import java.awt.*;

import com.ms.ui.*;
import com.ms.ui.event.*;

import Application;

public class Menu01 extends AwtUIApplet
{
    Menu01()
    {
        super(new MyApplet());
    }

    public static void main(String[] arg)
    {
        new Application(new MyApplet());
    }
}

class MyApplet extends UIApplet
{
    // showStatus - If MyApplet is being invoked as an
    //              applet, output the message in the status
    //              bar; otherwise, just output.
    public void showStatus(String s)
```

```
    {
        if (getApplet() != null)
        {
            super.showStatus(s);
        }
        else
        {
            System.out.println(s);
        }
    }

    public void init()
    {
        // Create a list of menu items.
        UIMenuList fileList = new FileMenuList(this);
        UIMenuList editList = new EditMenuList(this);

        // Create a button to activate the menu; give it
        // a name and attach the file list to it.
        UIMenuButton fileButton =
                        new UIMenuButton("File", fileList);
        UIMenuButton editButton =
                        new UIMenuButton("Edit", editList);

        // Add the buttons to the menu band.
        UIBand editMenu = new UIBand();
        editMenu.add(fileButton);
        editMenu.add(editButton);

        // Put the menu band in a band box. A band box is
        // a type of group for menu bands (in the same
        // way that UIRadioGroup groups radio buttons).
        UIBandBox menu = new UIBandBox();
        menu.add(editMenu);

        // Now position the band box at the top of the container.
        setLayout(new UIBorderLayout());
        add(menu, "North");
    }
}
```

>>

```
// MyMenuList - Menu list with a built-in event listener
class MyMenuList extends UIMenuList
{
    UIApplet parent;

    class Listener implements IUIActionListener
    {
        public void actionPerformed(UIActionEvent e)
        {
            String s = e.getActionCommand();
            parent.showStatus("User clicked on " + s);
        }
    }

    MyMenuList(UIApplet parent)
    {
        this.parent = parent;

        // Add an action listener to handle selecting
        // the menu.
        addActionListener(new Listener());
    }
}

// FileMenuList - Extends MyMenuList by providing
//                the different file options
class FileMenuList extends MyMenuList
{
    FileMenuList(UIApplet parent)
    {
        // Pass the applet to the parent class.
        super(parent);

        // Add the menu options.
        add("Open");
        add("Save");
        add("Close");
        add(new UILine());
        add("Exit");
    }
}
```

```
// EditMenuList - Extends MyMenuList by providing
//                 the different edit options
class EditMenuList extends MyMenuList
{
    EditMenuList(UIApplet parent)
    {
        super(parent);

        add("Copy");
        add("Cut");
        add("Paste");
    }
}
```

The *MyApplet.init* method demonstrates the classic pattern of steps for building an AFC menu:

1. First create the menu list. This is a list of menu items; each item corresponds to a menu option.

2. Create a menu button, and attach the file list to the button. The menu button launches the menu list.

3. Add the menu button to a menu band. If you are adding more than one, add them in the order in which you want them to appear.

4. Add the menu band to a band box. This step is optional—you can add the menu band directly to the applet window; however, the band box provides the same type of grouping features that a radio group provides for a set of radio buttons. (For details, see Chapter 6, "Buttons.")

The Menu01 example program we just looked at follows this pattern exactly, creating the *UIMenuList* objects *fileList* and *editList* through the subclasses *FileMenuList* and *EditMenuList*.

TIP

As I've mentioned, I find that putting these details in a subclass simplifies the overall program by keeping all the details for a given menu in one place.

Once the menu lists have been built, *init* creates *UIMenuButton* objects, which it then adds to the *UIBand* object *editMenu*. Last the menu band is added to a *UIBandBox* object, which is then positioned at the top of the applet window.

The constructors for the subclasses *FileMenuList* and *EditMenuList* build their respective menu lists by calling *add(String)* for each menu item. The *add(new UILine())* call adds the horizontal divider line, as shown in Figure 9-1.

FIGURE 9-1   *The output of Menu01, showing the File menu dropped down.*

Notice that both menu list subclasses extend *UIMenuList* through the locally defined class *MyMenuList*. This class extends *UIMenuList* by adding an action listener. This listener is invoked when the user selects one of the menu items. The listener provided does nothing more than display the label of the menu item in the applet window's status bar. Obviously, in a real-world application, you would want to take some type of action, depending on which menu item was selected.

You might be tempted to compare the menu item label with all of the possible button labels and take the appropriate action when a match is found. This is not a good approach, as it requires the *MyMenuList* base class to have intimate knowledge of all of the different menu items defined in the program—a maintenance nightmare. In the next example program, we will see an alternative approach, which, while wordier, does not suffer from this problem.

GRAPHICAL MENU ITEM LABELS

In today's graphically oriented world, a simple, no-frills, text-only menu item just doesn't cut it. Today menu items must be decorated like the handwritten books of old, with ornate fonts and descriptive images. The following program, Menu02, demonstrates how this need can be met in an AFC menu:

```
// Menu02 - Extends Menu01 by:
//          1) Adding graphics to the menu items
//             (applies to File menu only)
//          2) Applying different fonts to the menu buttons
//          3) Defining a different subclass for each menu
//             item, thereby providing a more extensible
//             solution to taking action when the user
//             selects a menu item
import java.applet.*;
import java.awt.*;

import com.ms.ui.*;
import com.ms.ui.event.*;
import com.ms.fx.*;

public class Menu02 extends AwtUIApplet
{
    Menu02()
    {
        super(new MyApplet());
    }

    public static void main(String[] arg)
    {
        System.out.println("Cannot execute as an application.");
    }
}

class MyApplet extends UIApplet
{
    public void init()
    {
        // Create a list of menu items.
        UIMenuList fileList = new FileMenuList(this);
        UIMenuList editList = new EditMenuList(this);

        // Create a button to activate the File menu -
        // this time use a UIStatic object for the button label.
        UIText fileLabel = new UIText("File", UIStatic.HOTTRACK);
        fileLabel.setFont(new FxFont("Helvetica",
                                FxFont.ITALIC,
                                14,
                                FxFont.STRIKEOUT));
```

```
                            UIMenuButton fileButton =
                                        new UIMenuButton(fileLabel,
                                                         0,
                                                         fileList);

                    // Do the same for the Edit menu.
                    UIText editLabel = new UIText("Edit", 0);
                    editLabel.setFont(new FxFont("TimesRoman",
                                                 FxFont.PLAIN,
                                                 14,
                                                 FxFont.UNDERLINE));

                    UIMenuButton editButton =
                                        new UIMenuButton(editLabel,
                                                         UIPushButton.RAISED,
                                                         editList);

                    // Same as Menu01 from here on
                    UIBand editMenu = new UIBand();
                    editMenu.add(fileButton);
                    editMenu.add(editButton);

                    UIBandBox menu = new UIBandBox();
                    menu.add(editMenu);

                    setLayout(new UIBorderLayout());
                    add(menu, "North");
            }
    }


    // FileMenuList - Create a menu list by adding
    //                subclasses of menu items, each
    //                with its own listener.
    class FileMenuList extends UIMenuList
    {
        FileMenuList(UIApplet parent)
        {
            // Add the menu options.
            add(new OpenMenuItem(parent));
            add(new SaveMenuItem(parent));
            add(new CloseMenuItem(parent));
            add(new UILine());
            add(new ExitMenuItem(parent));
        }
    }
```

```
// EditMenuList - Normally, you would implement this
//                menu the same way as the FileMenuList menu.
class EditMenuList extends UIMenuList
{
    EditMenuList(UIApplet parent)
    {
        add("Copy");
        add("Cut");
        add("Paste");
    }
}


// MyMenuItem - Extend UIMenuItem by providing code
//              to load the menu item graphics image.
class MyMenuItem extends UIMenuItem
{
    MyMenuItem(UIApplet parent, String sImage, String sText)
    {
        // Go ahead and create a UIItem object with no graphic.
        super(new UIItem(null, sText));

        // Get that UIItem object back...
        UIItem item = (UIItem)getHeader();

        // ...and add an image to it.
        Images images = new Images(parent, sImage);
        images.load();
        Image  image = images.getImage();

        item.setImage(image);
    }
}


// OpenMenuItem - Extend MyMenuItem by overriding
//                the mouseClicked method to provide
//                a listener.
class OpenMenuItem extends MyMenuItem
{
    UIApplet parent;

    OpenMenuItem(UIApplet parent)
    {
        super(parent, "Open.gif", "Open");

        this.parent = parent;
    }
```

>>

>>

```
    public boolean mouseClicked(Event e, int x, int y)
    {
        parent.showStatus("Open!");
        return true;
    }
}
class SaveMenuItem extends MyMenuItem
{
    UIApplet parent;

    SaveMenuItem(UIApplet parent)
    {
        super(parent, "Save.gif", "Save");

        this.parent = parent;
    }

    public boolean mouseClicked(Event e, int x, int y)
    {
        parent.showStatus("Save!");
        return true;
    }
}
class CloseMenuItem extends MyMenuItem
{
    UIApplet parent;

    CloseMenuItem(UIApplet parent)
    {
        super(parent, "Close.gif", "Close");

        this.parent = parent;
    }

    public boolean mouseClicked(Event e, int x, int y)
    {
        parent.showStatus("Close!");
        return true;
    }
}
class ExitMenuItem extends MyMenuItem
{
    UIApplet parent;
```

```
ExitMenuItem(UIApplet parent)
{
    super(parent, "Exit.gif", "Exit");

    this.parent = parent;
}

public boolean mouseClicked(Event e, int x, int y)
{
    parent.showStatus("Exit!");
    return true;
}
}
```

Here a *UIText* object is used to label the top-level menu buttons. I have chosen a completely unreasonable set of graphics just to demonstrate some of the combinations that are possible, even without graphics. The results of Menu02 are shown in Figure 9-2.

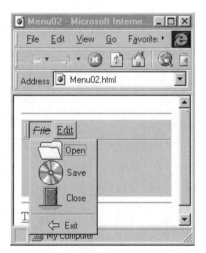

FIGURE 9-2   *The graphical appearance of Menu02.*

Notice that the different menu items in *FileMenuList* are no longer simple strings. Here each menu item is represented by a class of the form *xMenuItem*, where *x* corresponds to what appears on the menu list. (I didn't bother to make this change in *EditMenuList*, although in the real world you would need to do this for all menu lists.)

The *xMenuItem* classes each provide two features. First they extend *MyMenuItem*, which creates a menu item with a *UIItem* object as a label. (The *UIItem* class is used to label elements with both a graphics object and a text string. See Chapter 5, "Canvases," for details.)

MyMenuItem has to be fairly sneaky when creating its label. The label for a menu item is attached by passing the *UIItem* object to the constructor for *UIMenuItem*. The problem is that the *MyMenuItem* constructor cannot execute any statements before this call to the base class constructor; note that at this point, the image hasn't been loaded yet. The function gets around this problem by creating the *UIItem* label using a *null* image value and then substituting an image using the *UIItem.setImage* call after the fact.

The second capability added by the *xMenuItem* classes is a separate mouse click handler for each subclass. These handlers are added by overriding *mouseClicked* in the individual subclasses, which effectively moves the job of handling mouse clicks out to the leaves of the menu hierarchy tree.

You might not be thrilled with this technique. The biggest problem is that this approach results in the generation of a lot of subclasses. In a real-world program, however, you would probably end up having a lot of subclasses anyway for handling the different operations. It's only in small applets, such as those found in programming books, that the overhead becomes so evident.

Keep in mind that this approach is easier to maintain. The code for detecting the menu item is right there with the code for displaying and handling it.

CASCADING MENUS

Most applications embed menus within menus in a cascading fashion. The following example program, Menu03, demonstrates how to create cascading menus. In addition, Menu03 shows a different solution to the *UIMenuItem* constructor problem described earlier.

```
// Menu03 - This applet includes several variations on Menu02.
//          The creation of MyLabel avoids the static
//          function kludge. In addition, this applet
//          provides cascading menus.
import java.applet.*;
import java.awt.*;

import com.ms.ui.*;
import com.ms.ui.event.*;
import com.ms.fx.*;

public class Menu03 extends AwtUIApplet
{
    Menu03()
    {
        super(new MyApplet());
    }

    public static void main(String[] arg)
    {
        System.out.println("Cannot execute as an application.");
    }
}

class MyApplet extends UIApplet
{
    // Font to be used for the top-level menu buttons
    static FxFont font = new FxFont("Courier",
                                    FxFont.PLAIN,
                                    14,
                                    0);
    public void init()
    {
        UIItem label;
        UIMenuList list;

        // Create the File menu list first, letting MyLabel
        // do most of the work of creating the label.
        label = new MyLabel(this,
                            "File.gif",  // Graphic
                            "File",      // Text
                            font);       // Font to use
```

```
        list = new FileMenuList(this);
        UIMenuButton fileButton =
                        new UIMenuButton(label, list);

        // Do the same thing for the Edit menu.
        label = new MyLabel(this,
                            "Edit.gif",
                            "Edit",
                            font);
        list = new EditMenuList(this);
        UIMenuButton editButton =
                        new UIMenuButton(label, list);

        // Same as Menu02 from here on
        UIBand editMenu = new UIBand();
        editMenu.add(fileButton);
        editMenu.add(editButton);

        UIBandBox menu = new UIBandBox();
        menu.add(editMenu);

        setLayout(new UIBorderLayout());
        add(menu, "North");
    }
}


// MyLabel - Returns a UIText object with the
//           specified image, text, and font
class MyLabel extends UIItem
{
    // getImage - Load the image part and return
    //            it; this method should be used only
    //            by the constructor.
    private static Image getImage(UIApplet parent,
                                  String sImage)
    {
        Images images = new Images(parent, sImage);
        images.load();
        return images.getImage();
    }

    // constructor - Load the image and create a UIText
    //               object using it and the text. If a font
    //               is provided, set that as well.
```

```
MyLabel(UIApplet parent,
        String sImage,
        String sText,
        FxFont font)
{
    // Note that it is legal to call a static method
    // of the class when you invoke super - this is
    // the only way to execute code before passing
    // control to the base class constructor.
    super(getImage(parent, sImage),
          sText);

    // If a font was provided,...
    if (font != null)
    {
        // ...set it as well.
        setFont(font);
    }
}
}


// FileMenuList - Create the File menu list.
class FileMenuList extends UIMenuList
{
    FileMenuList(UIApplet parent)
    {
        // Add the menu options.
        add(new OpenMenuItem(parent));
        add(new SaveMenuItem(parent));

        // Add a submenu.
        add(new UIMenuButton(
                    new MyLabel(parent,
                                "Save2.gif",
                                "Save...",
                                null),
                    new SaveAsMenuList(parent)));

        // Continue adding menu options.
        add(new CloseMenuItem(parent));
        add(new UILine());
        add(new ExitMenuItem(parent));
    }
}
```

>>

```
// SaveAsMenuList - Create a submenu that extends
//                  from the Save item on the File menu.
class SaveAsMenuList extends UIMenuList
{
    SaveAsMenuList(UIApplet parent)
    {
        add(new SaveDocumentItem(parent));
        add(new SaveAttachmentItem(parent));
    }
}


// EditMenuList - Once again, I didn't bother to implement
//                the EditMenuList class.
class EditMenuList extends UIMenuList
{
    EditMenuList(UIApplet parent)
    {
        add("Copy");
        add("Cut");
        add("Paste");
    }
}


// MyMenuItem - The MyLabel class makes this a very simple
//              class indeed.
class MyMenuItem extends UIMenuItem
{
    MyMenuItem(UIApplet parent, String sImage, String sText)
    {
        super(new MyLabel(parent, sImage, sText, null));
    }
}


// OpenMenuItem, SaveMenuItem, CloseMenuItem - These
// classes are the same as in Menu02.
class OpenMenuItem extends MyMenuItem
{
    UIApplet parent;

    OpenMenuItem(UIApplet parent)
    {
        super(parent, "Open.gif", "Open");

        this.parent = parent;
    }
```

```java
    public boolean mouseClicked(Event e, int x, int y)
    {
        parent.showStatus("Open!");
        return true;
    }
}
class SaveMenuItem extends MyMenuItem
{
    UIApplet parent;

    SaveMenuItem(UIApplet parent)
    {
        super(parent, "Save.gif", "Save");

        this.parent = parent;
    }

    public boolean mouseClicked(Event e, int x, int y)
    {
        parent.showStatus("Save!");
        return true;
    }
}
class CloseMenuItem extends MyMenuItem
{
    UIApplet parent;

    CloseMenuItem(UIApplet parent)
    {
        super(parent, "Close.gif", "Close");

        this.parent = parent;
    }

    public boolean mouseClicked(Event e, int x, int y)
    {
        parent.showStatus("Close!");
        return true;
    }
}
class ExitMenuItem extends MyMenuItem
{
    UIApplet parent;
```

>>

```
    ExitMenuItem(UIApplet parent)
    {
        super(parent, "Exit.gif", "Exit");

        this.parent = parent;
    }

    public boolean mouseClicked(Event e, int x, int y)
    {
        parent.showStatus("Exit!");
        return true;
    }
}
class SaveDocumentItem extends MyMenuItem
{
    UIApplet parent;

    SaveDocumentItem(UIApplet parent)
    {
        super(parent, "SaveDoc.gif", "Save document");
        this.parent = parent;
    }

    public boolean mouseClicked(Event e, int x, int y)
    {
        parent.showStatus("Save document!");
        return true;
    }
}
class SaveAttachmentItem extends MyMenuItem
{
    UIApplet parent;

    SaveAttachmentItem(UIApplet parent)
    {
        super(parent, "SaveAt.gif", "Save attachment");

        this.parent = parent;
    }

    public boolean mouseClicked(Event e, int x, int y)
    {
        parent.showStatus("Save attachment!");
        return true;
    }
}
```

The initial structure of this program is very much the same as that of its predecessor, Menu02. One difference can be found in the *FileMenuList* class, which adds a *UIMenuButton* object labeled Save along with the menu items. Clicking this button opens a second, cascaded menu, as shown in Figure 9-3.

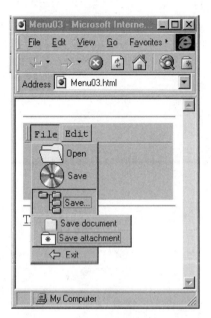

FIGURE 9-3   *The output of Menu03, showing the cascaded menu open.*

One other change is the addition of the *MyLabel* class. This class creates a *UIItem* object from the name of an image file on disk, a string of text, and a font. (The *font* argument is optional and is null if not provided.) As in Menu02, this class cannot load the *Image* object before invoking the base class constructor, but it solves the problem in a different way.

You cannot invoke a normal method before the base class constructor is invoked because no *this* pointer exists until the base class constructor has finished executing. However, you can invoke a static method of the class because static methods do not require a *this* pointer. *MyLabel* takes advantage of this fact by creating a static method *getImage*, which is called as an argument to the base class constructor:

```
super(getImage(parent, sImage), sText);
```

In this way, the code within *getImage* is executed before the *super* call passes control to the base class.

CONTEXT MENUS

A form of menu made popular by Microsoft Windows 95 and Motif is the "right mouse button" pop-up menu, also known as a context menu. This context menu is normally invisible. It can be displayed by clicking the right mouse button over the sensitive area.

Context menus are created using the class *UIContextMenu*, as demonstrated in the following applet, ContextMenu01:

```java
// ContextMenu01 - A basic context menu; pops up when
//                 the user clicks the right mouse button
//                 within the applet window
import java.applet.*;
import java.awt.*;

import com.ms.ui.*;
import com.ms.ui.event.*;

import Application;

public class ContextMenu01 extends AwtUIApplet
{
    ContextMenu01()
    {
        super(new MyApplet());
    }

    public static void main(String[] arg)
    {
        System.out.println("Cannot execute as an application.");
    }
}


class MyApplet extends UIApplet
{
    public void init()
    {
        // The context menu remains hidden until it's
        // opened using the right mouse button.
        new MyContextMenu(this);

        // Tell the user what to do.
        add(new UIDrawText(
                "Click right mouse button to display menu."));
    }
}
```

```
// MyContextMenu - Implements the context menu in question
class MyContextMenu extends UIContextMenu
{
    UIApplet parent;

    // Define button masks for our use:
    // B1 - left button
    // B2 - middle button on three-button mouse or
    //      left and right buttons simultaneously on
    //      two-button mouse
    // B3 - right button
    public static final int B1 = UIInputEvent.BUTTON1_MASK;
    public static final int B2 = UIInputEvent.BUTTON2_MASK;
    public static final int B3 = UIInputEvent.BUTTON3_MASK;
    public static final int BMASK = B1|B2|B3;

    // Listener - The mouse listener is invoked when
    //            mouse events occur.
    class Listener implements IUIMouseListener
    {
        // We're not interested in the following
        // statements, but we have to define them in order to
        // fully implement the mouse listener interface.
        // (Their presence won't hurt anything.)
        public void mouseClicked(UIMouseEvent e){}
        public void mouseReleased(UIMouseEvent e){}
        public void mouseEntered(UIMouseEvent e){}
        public void mouseExited(UIMouseEvent e){}

        // mousePressed - Called when the user presses
        //                the mouse button
        public void mousePressed(UIMouseEvent e)
        {
            // Just to verify that the mouse button
            // was in fact pressed
            parent.showStatus("mousePressed");

            // We are interested only if this is a
            // right mouse click - get the mouse
            // modifiers.
            int nModifiers = e.getModifiers();

            // We're interested only in the buttons.
            nModifiers &= BMASK;
```

>>

>>

```
                    // Now verify that only the right mouse button
                    // was clicked.
                    if (nModifiers == B3)
                    {
                        // The location of the cursor in the
                        // event is relative to the frame -
                        // adjust this position by the location of the
                        // frame on the screen.
                        Point loc = parent.getLocation(null);
                        loc.x += e.getX();
                        loc.y += e.getY();

                        // Now display the pop-up menu at that location.
                        launchAt(loc.x,
                                 loc.y,
                                 parent);
                    }
                }
            }

        MyContextMenu(UIApplet parent)
        {
            // Initialize the context menu using the
            // menu list contained in MyMenuList.
            super(new MyMenuList(parent));

            // Save the parent.
            this.parent = parent;

            // Now add a mouse listener to the parent
            // that will display the pop-up menu when activated
            // by the right mouse button.
            parent.addMouseListener(new Listener());
        }
    }


// MyMenuList - A conventional menu list just
//              like those implemented in Menu01 or
//              Menu02. (This one happens to look more
//              like the menu list in Menu01, but that's
//              arbitrary.)
class MyMenuList extends UIMenuList
{
    UIApplet parent;
```

```
// Listener - Does nothing more than
//             display the menu item
class Listener implements IUIActionList
{
    public void actionPerformed(UIActi
    {
        String s = e.getActionCommand();
        parent.showStatus("User clicked on " + s);
    }
}

MyMenuList(UIApplet parent)
{
    this.parent = parent;

    // Add the menu options.
    add("Open");
    add("Save");
    add("Close");
    add(new UILine());
    add("Exit");

    // Add an action listener to handle selecting
    // a menu option.
    addActionListener(new Listener());
}
}
```

Here the *init* function is straightforward, simply creating a *MyContextMenu* object for the applet window and then attaching a text field telling the user to click the right mouse button somewhere within the applet window.

The *MyContextMenu* constructor creates a menu list that it then passes to the *UIContextMenu* constructor. The menu list used in a context menu is identical to the menu lists used in other types of menus. That done, the *MyContextMenu* constructor goes on to add a mouse listener to the parent applet panel.

NOTE

It is the parent panel that receives the mouse event and not the *MyContextMenu* constructor itself.

It may seem odd that the mouse listener interface defines five methods, one for each type of mouse action. Because the *Listener* class implements this *IUIMouseListener* interface, it must define all five methods; however, because we are interested only in the *mousePressed* action, the other four action methods can be "do-nothing" functions. Since all listeners receive the same mouse event, their presence will not interfere with other mouse listeners that might be defined.

The *mousePressed* method is slightly more complicated than the other action events you have seen. This method is invoked whenever a mouse button is pressed, but for this applet, we're interested in knowing only when the right mouse button has been pressed. To determine which button was clicked, *mousePressed* starts by calling *UIMouseEvent.getModifiers*, which returns such modifier information as the state of the Shift, Ctrl, and Alt keys, along with the state of the mouse buttons. (Note that *UIMouseEvent* actually inherits the *getModifiers* method from its base class, *UIActionEvent*.)

The *mousePressed* method isolates the mouse button information by ANDing the modifier flags using *BMASK*. *BMASK* is a combination of the three flags BUTTON1_MASK, BUTTON2_MASK, and BUTTON3_MASK. Button 1 corresponds to the left mouse button, button 2 corresponds to the center mouse button on a three-button mouse or to both buttons being pressed on a two-button mouse, and button 3 corresponds to the right mouse button. The *mousePressed* method then compares the result of the AND operation with the BUTTON3_MASK flag. If only the right mouse button is pressed, the two values will be equal.

Once the *mousePressed* method has determined that the right mouse button has been pressed, it must determine where to display the context menu. Normally, this position would be next to the mouse pointer. Fortunately, the mouse event passed to *mousePressed* contains the location of the mouse at the time the button was pressed. Unfortunately, this location is relative to the event target—in this case, the applet window. The *UIContextMenu* class wants the location of the menu in screen coordinates. To convert from one to the other, *mousePressed* calls *parent.getLocation(null)*, which returns the location of the parent object (in this case, the applet window) relative to the upper left corner of the screen. Adding the event offset to this location results in the proper screen coordinates at which to display the menu.

The coordinates are passed to *UIContextMenu.launchAt*, which displays the context menu at the specified location. The results are shown in Figure 9-4.

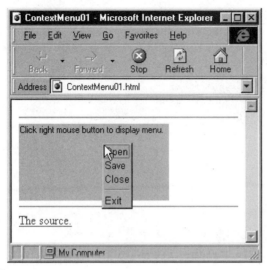

FIGURE 9-4 *The context menu displayed in the applet window.*

Making Your Context Menu Context Sensitive

The context menu is called a context menu because it is context sensitive, meaning that what appears when the user clicks the right mouse button is dependent on what the mouse is pointing at.

The ContextMenu01 program implemented only a single context menu. There are a number of ways to add multiple context menus to an applet such as ContextMenu01. One way would be to perform a *getComponent(x, y)* operation on the container, passing it the location reported in the mouse event. This method returns the coordinates of the component at that location. The applet could then decide which context menu to display depending on which component was discovered.

A more extensible and, in my opinion, a better approach is to define and attach a different context menu to each component as it is added to the applet. When the user clicks the right mouse button over a component within the applet, AFC passes the mouse event to the proper listener automatically for processing. This approach is demonstrated in the following example applet, ContextMenu02:

```java
// ContextMenu02 - Implements multiple components in the
//                 applet window, each with its own
//                 context menu
import java.applet.*;
import java.awt.*;

import com.ms.ui.*;
import com.ms.ui.event.*;

import Application;

public class ContextMenu02 extends AwtUIApplet
{
    ContextMenu02()
    {
        super(new MyApplet());
    }

    public static void main(String[] arg)
    {
        System.out.println("Cannot execute as an application.");
    }
}

class MyApplet extends UIApplet
{
    public void init()
    {
        setLayout(new UIBorderLayout());

        // Provide a context menu for the applet
        // window itself.
        new MyContextMenu(this,        // Applet
                          this,        // Menu anchor
                          new ApMenuList(this)); // Menu list
```

```
        // Position a text field across the top of the window
        // with its own context menu...
        UIDrawText text =
            new UIDrawText("Click right mouse button.");
        add(text, "North");
        new MyContextMenu(this, text, new TextMenuList());

        // ...and position a selection box at the bottom with its
        // own context menu.
        UIChoice choice = new UIChoice();
        choice.addString("Selection 1");
        choice.addString("Selection 2");
        add(choice, "South");
        new MyContextMenu(this, choice, new LabelMenuList());
    }
}

// MyContextMenu - Implements the context menu in question
class MyContextMenu extends UIContextMenu
{
    UIApplet parent,
    IUIComponent target;

    // Define button masks for our use:
    // B1 - left button
    // B2 - middle button on three-button mouse or
    //       left and right buttons simultaneously on
    //       two-button mouse
    // B3 - right button
    public static final int B1 = UIInputEvent.BUTTON1_MASK;
    public static final int B2 = UIInputEvent.BUTTON2_MASK;
    public static final int B3 = UIInputEvent.BUTTON3_MASK;
    public static final int BMASK = B1|B2|B3;

    // Listener - The mouse listener is invoked when
    //            mouse events occur.
    class Listener implements IUIMouseListener
    {
        public void mouseClicked(UIMouseEvent e){}
        public void mouseReleased(UIMouseEvent e){}
        public void mouseEntered(UIMouseEvent e){}
        public void mouseExited(UIMouseEvent e){}
```

>>

>>

```
// mousePressed - Called when the user presses
//                the mouse button
public void mousePressed(UIMouseEvent e)
{
    // Ignore this event if it has already
    // been consumed. (See below.)
    if (e.isConsumed())
    {
        return;
    }

    // Verify that the mouse button
    // was, in fact, pressed.
    parent.showStatus("mousePressed on " +
        target.toString());

    // If this is the right mouse button,...
    int nModifiers = e.getModifiers();
    nModifiers &= BMASK;
    if (nModifiers == B3)
    {
        // ...process the mouse button event as follows:

        // Mark the event as consumed - this
        // won't keep the event from being
        // propagated up to superior objects,
        // but it will allow the superior objects to check
        // using the isConsumed method.
        e.consume();

        // The location reported in the event
        // is relative to the target - adjust
        // this setting by adding the screen location
        // of the target to this location.
        Point loc = target.getLocation(null);
        loc.x += e.getX();
        loc.y += e.getY();

        // Now display the pop-up menu at that location.
        launchAt(loc.x,
                 loc.y,
                 parent);
    }
}
```

```
MyContextMenu(UIApplet      parent, // Parent applet
              IUIComponent target, // Target component
              UIMenuList list)     // Menu list
{
    super(list);

    // Save the parent applet and the target component.
    this.parent = parent;
    this.target = target;

    // Now add a mouse listener to the target.
    target.addMouseListener(new Listener());
}
}


// ApMenuList - Default menu list for the applet window
class ApMenuList extends UIMenuList
{
    UIApplet parent;

    // Listener - This listener does nothing more than
    //            display the menu item.
    class Listener implements IUIActionListener
    {
        public void actionPerformed(UIActionEvent e)
        {
            String s = e.getActionCommand();
            parent.showStatus("User clicked on " + s);
        }
    }


    ApMenuList(UIApplet parent)
    {
        this.parent = parent;

        // Add the menu options.
        add("Open");
        add("Save");
        add("Close");
        add(new UILine());
        add("Exit");

        // Add an action listener to handle selecting
        // menu options.
        addActionListener(new Listener());
    }
}
```

>>

```
// LabelMenuList - Context menu for the choice field
class LabelMenuList extends UIMenuList
{
    LabelMenuList()
    {
        // Add the menu options.
        add("Clear");
        add("Copy");
    }
}

// TextMenuList - Context menu for the text field
class TextMenuList extends UIMenuList
{
    TextMenuList()
    {
        add("What's this?");
    }
}
```

This applet displays a text field across the top of the applet window and a selection box extending across the bottom. Both of these objects are assigned their own context-sensitive help, with a context menu based on *TextMenuList* going to the text field and a context menu based on *LabelMenuList* going to the drop-down selection box *choice*. A default *ApMenuList* menu object is assigned to the applet window to field right button clicks outside of either object. The results are shown in Figure 9-5.

FIGURE 9-5   *The output of the ContextMenu02 applet, showing different context-sensitive menus.*

The first thing you should notice about the ContextMenu02 example program is that the class *MyContextMenu* has been modified slightly by adding the menu list as an argument to the constructor. ContextMenu01 had only one menu list, so embedding this information in *MyContextMenu* made sense. Now that there is more than one menu list, separating the menu lists from their context menus allows the same *MyContextMenu* class to be used for all three context menus, as well as for any future context menus we might want to define.

Another argument, the context menu target, has also been added to the *MyContextMenu* constructor after the parent applet argument. This is the object to which the mouse listener will be attached. This argument wasn't necessary in ContextMenu01 because the target object was the parent applet—that is, the parent applet and the target were the same object. This is still the case for *ApMenuList*, which is reflected in the fact that the first and second arguments are both *this*. These arguments are not the same for the text field and the selection box, however.

Other than these minor changes to the constructor, the class *MyContextMenu* is practically the same as it was in ContextMenu01 except for one small but critical addition: the calls to *consume* and *isConsumed*. To understand these functions, you need to know something about the way events are propagated.

When an event such as a mouse event occurs over an object such as the text field in ContextMenu02, the event is sent to all of the mouse event listeners attached to the object.

NOTE

Remember that the order in which the event is passed to the listeners attached to an object is indeterminate. In particular, it is not necessarily the order in which the listeners were added to the object.

Once the mouse event has been processed by all of the listeners of that component, AFC passes the event up to the parent of that component. There it is processed by the event handlers attached to the parent component and then passed up to that component's parent, and so on until the top-level component is reached.

For our context menu, this process is a problem. Once we have handled the mouse event at the text-field level, for example, we don't want the mouse event passed up to the applet window. If that is allowed to happen, the applet window will display its context menu directly over the text field's context menu.

As it turns out, we can't stop the event from being propagated up the chain; however, we can mark the event as having been processed at some lower level. That is the significance of the *consume* call. Calling *consume* sets a bit within the event that we can then test by calling *isConsumed*.

Thus, when the user clicks the right mouse button over the text field, for example, a mouse event is generated and passed first to the mouse listener attached to the text field component. That listener displays the *TextMenuList* menu and marks the event as consumed. When that same event is then passed to the mouse listener for the applet window, the mouse listener notices that the event has been consumed and returns without taking any further action.

> Try the following experiment. Remove the calls to *consume* and *isConsumed*. Now all you'll ever see is the default menu; however, if you watch the status bar very carefully, you'll see the message for the local context menu displayed and then instantly replaced by the message for the applet context menu.

BAND BOXES

So far, we have used band boxes simply to provide window dressing for a *UIBand* object, but they can do much more than that. In fact, the primary purpose of band boxes is to generate the sliding menu bands introduced in applications such as Internet Explorer.

To use a band box in this way, multiple menu bands are added to a single band box. AFC automatically inserts a thumb (the vertical bars on the left side of the toolbar) between the bands so that the user can slide back and forth in order to view the band in which she is most interested. She can even grab the menu thumb and pull the menu band down onto a row by itself.

Adding Multiple Bands to a Band Box

The following applet, BandBox01, creates a band box containing two menu bands:

```java
// BandBox01 - This applet demonstrates a band box.
//              This band box has two menu bands, one with
//              two menus containing file-type commands and a
//              second with browser-type entries.
import java.applet.*;
import java.awt.*;

import com.ms.ui.*;
import com.ms.ui.event.*;
import com.ms.fx.*;

import Images;
import Application;

public class BandBox01 extends AwtUIApplet
{
    BandBox01()
    {
        super(new MyApplet());
    }

    public static void main(String[] arg)
    {
        System.out.println("Cannot execute as an application.");
    }
}

class MyApplet extends UIApplet
{
    // The following images are used to label the
    // menu buttons.
    String[] sImages = new String[]{"File.gif",
                                    "Edit.gif",
                                    "Go.gif",
                                    "Left.gif",
                                    "Right.gif"};

    static final int FILE = 0;
    static final int EDIT = 1;
    static final int GO   = 2;
    static final int LEFT = 3;
    static final int RIGHT= 4;
```

>>

>>

```
// init - Creates the band box from the menu band
//          classes below
public void init()
{
    // Load the images we'll need.
    Images images = new Images(this, sImages);
    images.load();

    // Now create the band box from the menu band
    // classes defined below.
    UIBandBox menu = new UIBandBox();
    menu.add(new EditBand(this, images));
    menu.add(new NavBand (this, images));

    // Position the band box at the top of the container.
    setLayout(new UIBorderLayout());
    add(menu, "North");
    }
}

// EditBand - Create a menu band that looks like the
//            type of menu an editor program might
//            present.
class EditBand extends UIBand
{
    UIApplet parent;

    EditBand(UIApplet parent, Images images)
    {
        this.parent = parent;

        UIMenuList list;
        UIItem     label;
        UIMenuButton button;

        // Put a File menu in the first menu.
        list   = new FileMenuList(parent);
        label  = new UIItem(images.getImage(MyApplet.FILE),
                        "File");
        button = new UIMenuButton(label, list);
        add(button);
```

```
        // Put an Edit menu in the second menu.
        list   = new EditMenuList(parent);
        label  = new UIItem(images.getImage(MyApplet.EDIT),
                            "Edit");
        button = new UIMenuButton(label, list);
        add(button);
    }
}

// NavBand - Create a menu band like that in a Web browser.
class NavBand extends UIBand
{
    UIApplet parent;

    NavBand(UIApplet parent, Images images)
    {
        this.parent = parent;
        UIMenuList   list;
        UIItem       label;
        UIMenuButton button;

        // Put a Navigation menu in the first menu.
        list   = new NavMenuList(parent);
        label  = new UIItem(images.getImage(MyApplet.GO),
                            "Go",
                            UIItem.CENTERED,
                            UIItem.ABOVE);
        button = new UIMenuButton(label, list);
        add(button);

        // Now add a Back button...
        label  = new UIItem(images.getImage(MyApplet.LEFT),
                            "Back",
                            UIItem.CENTERED,
                            UIItem.ABOVE);
        add(new UIPushButton(label, UIPushButton.RAISED));

        // ...and a Forward button.
        label  = new UIItem(images.getImage(MyApplet.RIGHT),
                            "Forward",
                            UIItem.CENTERED,
                            UIItem.ABOVE);
        add(new UIPushButton(label, UIPushButton.RAISED));
```

>>

```
            // Create a label for the URL window to follow.
            UIDrawText addr = new UIDrawText("URL:");
            addr.setFont(new FxFont("Courier", FxFont.PLAIN, 18));
            add(addr);

            // The choices list takes the place of the URL window.
            // Note that normally the choices list would be
            // populated with previous sites.
            UIEditChoice choice = new MyEditChoice();
            choice.addString("First");
            choice.addString("Second");
            choice.addString("Third");
            add(choice);
        }
    }


// MyEditChoice - This editable drop-down box will be
//                used as a place to enter text.
class MyEditChoice extends UIEditChoice
{
    MyEditChoice()
    {
        // Specify a large-size font.
        setFont(new FxFont("Courier", FxFont.PLAIN, 18));
    }

    // getPreferredSize - Verify that the text entry space
    //                    is long enough.
    Dimension d = new Dimension(300, 15);
    public Dimension getPreferredSize()
    {
        return d;
    }
}


// MyMenuList - Forms the base class for the different
//              menus. See Menu01 for further details.
class MyMenuList extends UIMenuList
{
    UIApplet parent;

    class Listener implements IUIActionListener
    {
        public void actionPerformed(UIActionEvent e)
```

```
        {
            String s = e.getActionCommand();
            parent.showStatus("User clicked on " + s);
        }
    }

    MyMenuList(UIApplet parent)
    {
        this.parent = parent;

        // Add an action listener to handle selecting
        // the menu.
        addActionListener(new Listener());
    }
}

// FileMenuList - Set up a file-type menu.
class FileMenuList extends MyMenuList
{
    FileMenuList(UIApplet parent)
    {
        // Pass the applet to the parent class.
        super(parent);

        // Add the menu options.
        add("Open");
        add("Save");
        add("Close");
        add(new UILine());
        add("Exit");
    }
}

// EditMenuList - Set up an edit-style menu.
class EditMenuList extends MyMenuList
{
    EditMenuList(UIApplet parent)
    {
        super(parent);

        add("Copy");
        add("Cut");
        add("Paste");
    }
}
```

>>

```
// NavMenuList - Set up a navigation-style menu.
class NavMenuList extends MyMenuList
{
    NavMenuList(UIApplet parent)
    {
        super(parent);

        add("Read Mail");
        add("New Mail");
        add("News Group");
    }
}
```

The *init* method of this applet begins by loading the images to be used for the menu items rather than leaving the loading to the menu item itself. It then creates a band box to which it adds two menu bands: the class *EditBand* containing edit operations and the class *NavBand* containing Internet navigation operations. Last the band box is attached to the top of the applet window for display.

The *EditBand* class creates a menu band very similar to those created earlier in this chapter. The menu button is a conventional button with a *UIItem* label. The menu lists used to create the *EditBand*, *FileMenuList*, and *EditMenuList* objects are also completely typical in order to demonstrate that there is nothing unique about the menu bands that make up a band box.

The second menu band of class *NavBand* is different from those seen earlier only to demonstrate the types of features that you can put into a menu. (These features are uncommon in a typical menu, but common in a band box menu.) The first component in *NavBand* is a drop-down menu based on the options contained in *NavMenuList*.

The next two components are simple push buttons, labeled with a left arrow and a right arrow just like the buttons you would find in a Web browser.

Following the Back and Forward buttons is a label created using a *UIDrawText* object followed by a *UIEditChoice* object into which the user can enter a URL destination. Notice that I did not use *UIEditChoice* directly; instead, I used the subclass *MyEditChoice*. Besides setting a larger font, *MyEditChoice* overrides the *getPreferredSize* method to return a dimension that is large enough for the user to enter a reasonably long URL. Otherwise, the *UIEditChoice* object defaults to a size too small for most URLs.

The choice of *UIEditChoice* as what is essentially a text entry field may seem odd at first. After all, why not use a straightforward editable text field such as a *UIEdit* object? *UIEditChoice* lets the user enter an address manually or display a drop-down list of options. Presumably, this list would be managed by the applet to contain the previous Web addresses visited, but it could contain anything the programmer wants. In this case, just to prove the principle, I have hard-coded a set of values.

The three screen shots shown in Figure 9-6 were generated from the same BandBox01 applet by manually manipulating the thumb, or divider, between the two bands. The upper image shows the band box with the navigation band hidden. The central image shows the same applet with the navigation band visible. The lower image shows the navigation band pulled down onto a row by itself.

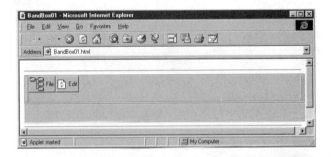

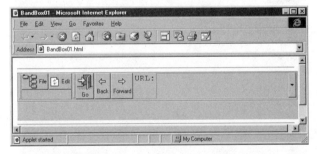

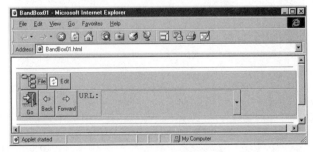

FIGURE 9-6   *A band box with the navigation band hidden (top), with the navigation band fully visible (center), and with the navigation band pulled down onto a row by itself (bottom).*

Implementing ToolTips

While the edit band in example program BandBox01 retained the appearance of a conventional menu, the navigation band looked a lot more like the icon toolbars that appear along the top of the windows of some of the most popular PC tools. One of the problems with such toolbars, however, is that they don't always have a text label displayed with an icon, so it isn't always obvious what a particular icon stands for. To counteract this lack of clarity, toolkits such as that supplied with Visual C++ provide something called ToolTips.

A ToolTip is a small label that appears next to an icon when the user positions the mouse pointer over the icon and leaves it there, motionless, for a second or so. The ToolTip contains a short explanation of the purpose of the icon.

AFC supports ToolTips by overriding the *getHelp* method. The following program, BandBox02, demonstrates the addition of ToolTips:

```
// BandBox02 - To provide ToolTips, simply override the
//             getHelp method by providing subclasses
//             of UIMenuButton, UIPushButton, and
//             UIChoice.
import java.applet.*;
import java.awt.*;

import com.ms.ui.*;
import com.ms.ui.event.*;
import com.ms.fx.*;

import Images;
import Application;

public class BandBox02 extends AwtUIApplet
{
    BandBox02()
    {
        super(new MyApplet());
    }

    public static void main(String[] arg)
    {
        System.out.println("Cannot execute as an application.");
    }
}
```

```
class MyApplet extends UIApplet
{
    // The following images are used to label the
    // menu buttons.
    String[] sImages = new String[]{"File.gif",
                                    "Edit.gif",
                                    "Go.gif",
                                    "Left.gif",
                                    "Right.gif"};

    static final int FILE = 0;
    static final int EDIT = 1;
    static final int GO   = 2;
    static final int LEFT = 3;
    static final int RIGHT= 4;

    // init - Creates the band box from the band
    //        classes below
    public void init()
    {
        // Load the images we'll need.
        Images images = new Images(this, sImages);
        images.load();

        // Now create the band box from the band
        // classes defined below.
        UIBandBox menu = new UIBandBox();
        menu.add(new EditBand(this, images));
        menu.add(new NavBand (this, images));

        // Position the band box at the top of the container.
        setLayout(new UIBorderLayout());
        add(menu, "North");
    }
}

// TipMenuButton - Provide a menu button with
//                 support for a ToolTip.
class TipMenuButton extends UIMenuButton
{
    String sHelp;

    TipMenuButton(UIStatic label,
                  UIMenuList list,
                  String sHelp)
    {
        super(label, list);
```

`>>`

```
        // This is the help string that will appear in
        // the ToolTip.
        this.sHelp = sHelp;
    }

    // getHelp - Return the ToolTip to the caller.
    public String getHelp()
    {
        return sHelp;
    }
}

// TipButton - Provide a push button with support
//             for ToolTips.
class TipButton extends UIPushButton
{
    String sHelp;

    TipButton(UIStatic label,
              int      nStyle,
              String   sHelp)
    {
        super(label, nStyle);
        this.sHelp = sHelp;
    }

    public String getHelp()
    {
        return sHelp;
    }
}

// TipChoice - Provide a drop-down list with support
//             for ToolTips.
class TipChoice extends UIEditChoice
{
    String sHelp;

    TipChoice(String sHelp)
    {
        this.sHelp = sHelp;
    }
```

```
    public String getHelp()
    {
        return sHelp;
    }
}


// EditBand - Create a menu band that looks like the
//            type of menu an editor program might
//            present.
class EditBand extends UIBand
{
    UIApplet parent;

    EditBand(UIApplet parent, Images images)
    {
        this.parent = parent;

        UIMenuList list;
        UIItem     label;
        UIMenuButton button;

        // Put a File menu in the first menu.
        list  = new FileMenuList(parent);
        label = new UIItem(images.getImage(MyApplet.FILE),
                        "File");
        button = new TipMenuButton(label,
                                    list,
                                    "File commands");
        add(button);

        // Put an Edit menu in the second menu.
        list  = new EditMenuList(parent);
        label = new UIItem(images.getImage(MyApplet.EDIT),
                        "Edit");
        button = new TipMenuButton(label,
                                    list,
                                    "Edit commands");
        add(button);
    }
}
```

>>

>>

```
// NavBand - Create a menu band like that in a Web browser.
class NavBand extends UIBand
{
    UIApplet parent;

    NavBand(UIApplet parent, Images images)
    {
        this.parent = parent;
        UIMenuList   list;
        UIItem       label;
        UIMenuButton button;

        // Put a Navigation menu in the first menu.
        list  = new NavMenuList(parent);
        label = new UIItem(images.getImage(MyApplet.GO),
                           "Go",
                           UIItem.CENTERED,
                           UIItem.ABOVE);
        button = new TipMenuButton(label,
                                   list,
                                   "Navigation commands");
        add(button);

        // Now add a Back button...
        label = new UIItem(images.getImage(MyApplet.LEFT),
                           "Back",
                           UIItem.CENTERED,
                           UIItem.ABOVE);
        add(new TipButton(label,
                          UIPushButton.RAISED,
                          "Go to previous"));

        // ...and a Forward button.
        label = new UIItem(images.getImage(MyApplet.RIGHT),
                           "Forward",
                           UIItem.CENTERED,
                           UIItem.ABOVE);
        add(new TipButton(label,
                          UIPushButton.RAISED,
                          "Go to next"));

        // Create a label for the URL window to follow.
        UIDrawText addr = new UIDrawText("URL:");
        addr.setFont(new FxFont("Courier", FxFont.PLAIN, 18));
        add(addr);
```

```
        // Use an editable drop-down list as a space
        // in which to enter a URL.
        UIEditChoice choice = new MyEditChoice();
        add(choice);

        // Here I just add a few elements; normally,
        // this task would be managed dynamically to reflect
        // the most recent commands entered by the user.
        choice.addString("First");
        choice.addString("Second");
        choice.addString("Third");
    }
}

// MyEditChoice - This editable drop-down box will be
//                used as a place to enter text.
class MyEditChoice extends TipChoice
{
    MyEditChoice()
    {
        // Provide a tip string.
        super("Enter URL");

        // Specify a large-size font.
        setFont(new FxFont("Courier", FxFont.PLAIN, 18));
    }

    // getPreferredSize - Verify that the text entry space
    //                    is long enough.
    Dimension d = new Dimension(300, 15);
    public Dimension getPreferredSize()
    {
        return d;
    }
}

// MyMenuList - Forms the base class for the different
//              menus. See Menu01 for further details.
class MyMenuList extends UIMenuList
{
    UIApplet parent;
```

```
class Listener implements IUIActionListener
{
    public void actionPerformed(UIActionEvent e)
    {
        String s = e.getActionCommand();
        parent.showStatus("User clicked on " + s);
    }
}

MyMenuList(UIApplet parent)
{
    this.parent = parent;

    // Add an action listener to handle selecting
    // the menu.
    addActionListener(new Listener());
}
}

// FileMenuList - Set up a file-type menu.
class FileMenuList extends MyMenuList
{
    FileMenuList(UIApplet parent)
    {
        // Pass the applet to the parent class.
        super(parent);

        // Add the menu options.
        add("Open");
        add("Save");
        add("Close");
        add(new UILine());
        add("Exit");
    }
}

// EditMenuList - Set up an edit-style menu.
class EditMenuList extends MyMenuList
{
    EditMenuList(UIApplet parent)
    {
        super(parent);

        add("Copy");
        add("Cut");
        add("Paste");
    }
}
```

```
// NavMenuList - Set up a navigation-style menu.
class NavMenuList extends MyMenuList
{
    NavMenuList(UIApplet parent)
    {
        super(parent);

        add("Read Mail");
        add("New Mail");
        add("News Group");
    }
}
```

This example application creates ToolTip versions of basic menu objects: *Tip-MenuButton*, *TipButton*, and *TipChoice*. Each of these classes extends the basic class by allowing the application to pass a ToolTip string in the constructor. These classes override the *getHelp* method to return whatever string was passed to them in the constructor.

When the user positions the mouse pointer over the object and holds it there, AFC invokes *getHelp* on the object being pointed to. Because a string is returned (rather than the default value of *null* returned by *getHelp* in *UIComponent*), AFC wraps the string in a small yellow box and displays it next to the component. The results are shown in Figure 9-7.

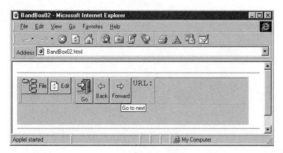

FIGURE 9-7   *The output of the BandBox02 program, showing a ToolTip for the Forward button.*

WHAT'S NEXT

In this chapter, you've seen the various types of menus supported by AFC. You've seen conventional menus, including cascaded menus and menus with cute little graphics icons. In addition, you've seen context-sensitive, "right mouse button" menus of the type made famous by Windows 95 and Motif. Finally, you've seen how easy it is to create the new band boxes used in applications such as Internet Explorer.

NOTE

> The only feature you haven't seen here is the one that allows you to create menus using the Resource Wizard and load them using the *Win32ResourceDecoder* class. You'll see this technique in Chapter 13, "Resource Classes."

In the next chapter, we'll delve into another area of burning interest to interactive applet programmers: dialog boxes. We'll look at how to create and display dialog boxes using the *UIDialog* class and its subclasses—in the process, you'll see similarities to working with other *UIWindow* objects.

Dialog Boxes

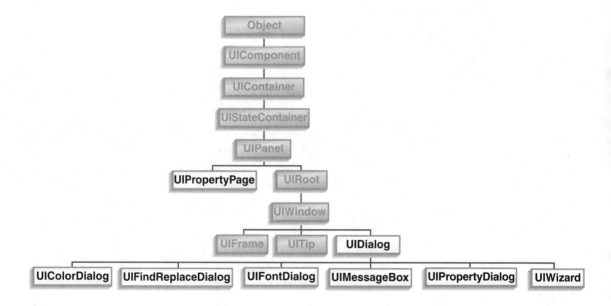

When user input is too involved to be handled by simple menus, the programmer's next step is to resort to dialog boxes. This chapter focuses on the creation and display of dialog boxes using the *UIDialog* class and its subclasses.

In a way, most of the other chapters in Part Two have dealt with dialog boxes. One can make the argument that any window with components such as buttons, text fields, and drop-down selection boxes is a type of dialog box. In fact, we'll see that handling the class *UIDialog* and its subclasses is not a lot different from manipulating any other *UIWindow* object.

MODALITY

Dialog boxes bring an extra feature to the table that windows don't possess: modality. A non-modal dialog box behaves much like any other window—it speaks only when spoken to. In computer terms, this means that it intercepts only those mouse events that occur within its physical boundaries—that is, it sees only mouse clicks that occur when the mouse is within the dialog box window. Other windows are free to continue to receive events regardless of whether the non-modal dialog box is visible.

In contrast, modal dialog boxes intercept all events, whether pointed in their direction or not. Once a modal dialog box gets control, it keeps control until it is closed.

NOTE

Another class of dialog box, *system modal dialog boxes,* takes control from other programs as well. As long as a system modal dialog box is visible, the user cannot communicate with any other application. Because Java is primarily an applet-based language, Java and AFC do not support system modal dialog boxes.

Fortunately, AFC includes considerable support for dialog boxes. The programmer can use the base class *UIDialog* to implement either a modal or nonmodal dialog box of his own design. However, several semispecialized subclasses such as *UIWizard* and *UIPropertyDialog* come with much of the surrounding window dressing already built in. With these classes, about half of the job is already done. And some fully specialized subclasses of *UIDialog* are available, such as *UIColorDialog* and *UIFontDialog*, that do all of the work.

We'll examine the more general case, the *UIDialog* class, before working gradually to more specialized subclasses. Just to get us started, let's take a look at the simple *UIMessageBox* class.

MESSAGE BOXES

The message box is the simplest of all dialog boxes. You probably don't even think of it as a dialog box at all. The message box is primarily an output device, delivering a message when the software detects a problem, such as when the printer is off line or when an invalid floppy disk is in the disk drive. It receives no input (other than from the OK and Cancel buttons at the bottom). Nevertheless, the message box is a dialog box. The class *UIMessageBox* extends the *UIDialog* class. The message box has its own window, and a message box can be modal or nonmodal.

Because a message box is so simple and because there are numerous places that a message box might be needed to display an error message of some sort, the *UIMessageBox* class makes it as easy as possible to generate a message box on the screen. The following example program, MessageBox01, demonstrates the *UIMessageBox* class:

```
// MessageBox01 - Demonstrates the use of the simple
//                  message box
import java.applet.*;
import java.awt.*;

import com.ms.ui.*;
import com.ms.ui.event.*;


import Application;

public class MessageBox01 extends AwtUIApplet
{
    MessageBox01()
    {
        super(new MyApplet());
    }

    public static void main(String[] arg)
    {
        new Application(new MyApplet());
    }
}

class MyApplet extends UIApplet
{
    public void init()
    {
        setLayout(new UIBorderLayout());

        // Adding an empty panel in the center keeps
        // the layout from expanding the button.
        add(new UIPanel(), "Center");

        // Add a push button at the bottom.
        add(new MyPushButton(), "South");
    }
}
```

>>

```
// MyPushButton - Displays the message box
class MyPushButton extends UIPushButton
{
    class PBAction implements IUIActionListener
    {
        public void actionPerformed(UIActionEvent e)
        {
            // Create a message box.
            UIMessageBox box =
                new UIMessageBox(
                        new UIFrame(),
                        "Don't do that!",
                        "I told you not to push that button!",
                        UIMessageBox.EXCLAMATION,
                        UIButtonBar.OK);

            // Now display it modally.
            box.doModal();
        }
    }

    MyPushButton()
    {
        super("Don't push this button!",
            UIPushButton.RAISED);
        addActionListener(new PBAction());
    }
}
```

This program begins in the *init* method by creating a *MyPushbutton* object with the provocative label, "Don't push this button!" This button is positioned at the bottom of the applet window. Positioning an empty *UIPanel* object in the center of the window keeps the *UIBorderLayout* class from expanding the button to fill the entire applet window.

The listener for the *MyPushButton* class is invoked when the user clicks the button, which she most certainly will do regardless of the warning. This listener method responds by creating the message box shown in Figure 10-1. Notice the appearance of the title and the message in the message box. Notice also that the constant EXCLAMATION instructed *UIMessageBox* to display the exclamation point graphic. Other constants exist for different symbols, such as question marks. In addition, the *UIButtonBar.OK* constant instructed *UIMessageBox* to provide only an OK button. Other constants exist for other button combinations, such as OK/Cancel.

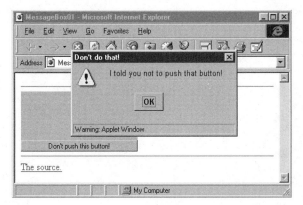

FIGURE 10-1   *The output of the MessageBox01 program, showing the* UIMessageBox *object.*

Last, the call to *box.doModal* displays the dialog box modally. In this mode, control is not returned to the program until the user has closed the message box. The value returned by *doModal* indicates the button selected by the user. This value allows the program to take different actions based on what button was selected. In this case, there is only one button, so the return value is ignored.

Although this program doesn't make use of the *SetTimeout* method, the parent program can call it before invoking *doModal*. In this case, the message box dismisses itself after the specified amount of time (indicated in units of milliseconds) expires.

GENERIC DIALOG BOXES

The class *UIDialog* forms the basis for the generic dialog box. The programmer places components within the generic dialog box in the same way he adds components to any other window. This similarity is hardly surprising because the *UIDialog* class is a subclass of *UIWindow*.

The example program beginning on the next page, Dialog01, builds and displays a crude dialog box using *UIDialog*.

```java
// Dialog01 - Creates a simple dialog box window
import java.applet.*;
import java.awt.*;

import com.ms.ui.*;
import com.ms.ui.event.*;

import Application;

public class Dialog01 extends AwtUIApplet
{
    Dialog01()
    {
        super(new MyApplet());
    }

    public static void main(String[] arg)
    {
        new Application(new MyApplet());
    }
}

class MyApplet extends UIApplet
{
    // dialog - This is the dialog box object we'll
    //          create in this applet.
    MyDialog dialog;

    public void init()
    {
        // Create our dialog box window.
        dialog = new MyDialog();

        // Now create a button in the applet window
        // to open the dialog box. (Put an empty panel
        // in the center of the window to keep the
        // button from being expanded to take up the
        // entire window.)
        setLayout(new UIBorderLayout());
        add(new UIPanel(), "Center");
        add(new MyPushButton(dialog), "South");
    }
}
```

```
// MyPushButton - Displays the dialog box by making it visible
class MyPushButton extends UIPushButton
{
    UIDialog dialog;

    class PBAction implements IUIActionListener
    {
        public void actionPerformed(UIActionEvent e)
        {
            // Make the dialog box visible,...
            dialog.setVisible(true);

            // ...and get rid of any trash left around.
            // (Don't call dispose if the dialog box is
            // nonmodal.)
            dialog.dispose();
        }
    }

    MyPushButton(UIDialog dialog)
    {
        super("View Dialog", UIPushButton.RAISED);
        this.dialog = dialog;
        addActionListener(new PBAction());
    }
}

// MyDialog - Implements a simple dialog box with
//            three example components
class MyDialog extends UIDialog
{
    // The dialog box components
    UICheckButton cb = new UICheckButton("Lowercase");
    UIChoice choice  = new UIChoice();
    UIEdit   text    = new UIEdit("Enter text here");

    MyDialog()
    {
        // Create a modal dialog box with dimensions 100x150
        // pixels.
        super(new UIFrame(), "Dialog01", true);
        setSize(100, 150);
```

>>

307

>>

```
// Add a few items to the list of options.
choice.addString("Option 1");
choice.addString("Option 2");
choice.addString("Option 3");

// Now add components to the dialog box.
UIPanel panel = new UIPanel();
panel.setLayout(new UIGridLayout(3, 1, 0, 10));
panel.add(cb);
panel.add(choice);
panel.add(text);

add(panel, "Center");

// Create a button panel with OK and Cancel buttons.
UIPanel buttons = new UIPanel();
buttons.setLayout(new UIRowLayout(2));
buttons.add(
    new UIPushButton("OK", UIPushButton.RAISED));
buttons.add(
    new UIPushButton("Cancel", UIPushButton.RAISED));

add(buttons, "South");
    }
}
```

Once again, *init* adds an object to the applet window of class *MyPushButton* that is responsible for displaying the dialog box. The *MyPushButton* class does this by calling *UIDialog.setVisible(true)* from within the push button action listener.

NOTE

If the dialog box is modal, control does not return from *setVisible(true)* until the user closes the dialog box. If the dialog box is nonmodal, control returns from *setVisible* immediately.

The constructor for the *MyDialog* class begins by invoking the *UIDialog* constructor and passing it a new frame, the name of the dialog box, and the value *true*, indicating that this is to be a modal dialog box. It then sets its own size to 100 units wide by 150 units high.

That done, the *MyDialog* constructor sets about adding a check box, a selection box with three options, and a text box to an input panel. The input panel is then added to the dialog box above a pair of buttons, OK and Cancel. The results are shown in Figure 10-2.

FIGURE 10-2   *Simple dialog box built using* UIDialog.

Note that this modal dialog box example can be easily converted to a nonmodal dialog box. First change the call to the *UIDialog* constructor to pass a value of *false* as the third argument, as shown here:

```
// Create a nonmodal dialog box.
super(new UIFrame(), "Dialog01", false);
```

Second remove the call to *dialog.dispose* in the push button action listener. The *dispose* method returns memory that the dialog box no longer needs once the dialog box has been closed. However, because control returns immediately from the *dialog.setVisible(true)* call, rather than after the user has closed the dialog box, you shouldn't make this call until the window is closed.

Getting Input from a Dialog Box—Nonmodal Approach

Because dialog boxes behave much like any other window, the techniques you have already seen for getting input from components embedded within panels works fine for dialog boxes. When the user clicks the OK button, a function can read the components that make up the dialog box and store the results directly in the parent applet. This approach is taken in the example program that begins on the next page, Dialog02.

```
// Dialog02 - Adds input to the dialog box created in Dialog01.
//            This version works for both modal and nonmodal
//            dialog boxes, but it's not quite as modular as
//            Dialog03.
import java.applet.*;
import java.awt.*;

import com.ms.ui.*;
import com.ms.ui.event.*;
import com.ms.fx.*;

import Application;

public class Dialog02 extends AwtUIApplet
{
    Dialog02()
    {
        super(new MyApplet());
    }

    public static void main(String[] arg)
    {
        new Application(new MyApplet());
    }
}

class MyApplet extends UIApplet
{
    MyDialog dialog;

    // The following fields are used to hold the
    // data read from the dialog box.
    boolean bChanged = false;
    boolean bLowerCase;
    String sChoice;
    String sText;

    // The following draw text fields are used to
    // display the data read from the dialog box.
    UIDrawText lowerCase = new UIDrawText();
    UIDrawText choice     = new UIDrawText();
    UIDrawText text       = new UIDrawText();
```

```
public void init()
{
    // Create our dialog box window.
    dialog = new MyDialog(this);

    // Create a panel to display the results.
    UIPanel display = new UIPanel();
    display.setLayout(new UIVerticalFlowLayout());
    display.add(lowerCase);
    display.add(choice);
    display.add(text);

    // Now create a button in the applet window
    // to open the dialog box.
    setLayout(new UIBorderLayout());
    add(display, "Center");
    add(new MyPushButton(dialog), "South");
}

// paint - Update the displayed components based
//         on the most recently read data.
public void paint(FxGraphics fg)
{
    // If something has changed,...
    if (bChanged)
    {
        // ...update the fields and note that they've
        // been updated so we don't do it too often.
        bChanged = false;
        lowerCase.setValueText(
            bLowerCase ? "Lowercase set." :
                         "Lowercase not set.");
        choice.setValueText(sChoice);
        text.setValueText(sText);
    }
}
}

// MyPushButton - Displays the dialog box
class MyPushButton extends UIPushButton
{
    UIDialog dialog;
```

```
>>                  class PBAction implements IUIActionListener
                    {
                        public void actionPerformed(UIActionEvent e)
                        {
                            dialog.setVisible(true);
                            dialog.dispose();
                        }
                    }

                    MyPushButton(UIDialog dialog)
                    {
                        super("View Dialog", UIPushButton.RAISED);
                        this.dialog = dialog;
                        addActionListener(new PBAction());
                    }
                }

                // MyDialog - Implements the same dialog box as Dialog01
                //            but now with direct input
                class MyDialog extends UIDialog
                {
                    MyApplet parent;

                    UICheckButton cb = new UICheckButton("Lowercase");
                    UIChoice choice = new UIChoice();
                    UIEdit   text   = new UIEdit("Enter text here");

                    MyDialog(MyApplet parent)
                    {
                        super(new UIFrame(), "Dialog02", true);
                        setSize(100, 150);

                        this.parent = parent;

                        // Add a few items to the options list.
                        choice.addString("Option 1");
                        choice.addString("Option 2");
                        choice.addString("Option 3");

                        // Add components to the dialog box.
                        UIPanel panel = new UIPanel();
                        panel.setLayout(new UIGridLayout(3, 1, 0, 10));
                        panel.add(cb);
                        panel.add(choice);
                        panel.add(text);
```

```
        add(panel, "Center");

        // Now create a button panel.
        UIPanel buttons = new UIPanel();
        buttons.setLayout(new UIRowLayout(2));
        buttons.add(new DButton(this, "OK", true));
        buttons.add(new DButton(this, "Cancel", false));

        add(buttons, "South");
    }

    // read - Read the dialog box information, and store it in
    //        the proper fields within MyApplet.
    void read()
    {
        parent.bLowerCase = cb.isChecked();
        parent.sChoice = choice.getValueText();
        parent.sText    = text.getValueText();
        parent.bChanged = true;
        parent.repaint();
    }
}


// DButton - Implement a common class between the OK
//           and Cancel buttons; the only difference
//           between the two is that the OK button
//           reads the dialog box and the Cancel button
//           doesn't.
class DButton extends UIPushButton
{
    MyDialog parent;

    // bReadDialog - OK = true; CANCEL = false
    boolean  bReadDialog;

    class OKListener implements IUIActionListener
    {
        public void actionPerformed(UIActionEvent e)
        {
            // If we're supposed to,...
            if (bReadDialog)
            {
                // ...read the dialog box information.
                parent.read();
            }
```

```
            // Now hide the dialog box.
            parent.setVisible(false);
            parent.dispose();
        }
    }

    DButton(MyDialog parent,
            String   sLabel,
            boolean  bReadDialog)
    {
        super(sLabel, RAISED);

        this.parent     = parent;
        this.bReadDialog = bReadDialog;

        addActionListener(new OKListener());
    }
}
```

The *MyApplet.init* method for this program adds three text fields—*lowerCase*, *choice*, and *text*—in which to display the selections the user makes in the dialog box. The *MyPushButton* class looks and behaves the same as its Dialog01 cousin. In addition, the *MyDialog* class starts out the same, building the same simple dialog box window. Here *MyDialog* uses a new class, *DButton*, to define the dialog box buttons. This class is instantiated twice: once for the OK button with a *bReadDialog* value of *true* and again for the Cancel button with a *bReadDialog* value of *false*. Both buttons hide the dialog box by calling *setVisible-(false)*. However, the OK button also calls *MyDialog.read*.

MyDialog.read reads the three dialog box components. It stores the results in the variables *bLowerCase*, *sChoice*, and *sText*, all defined within *MyApplet*. Last it sets the *bChanged* flag to *true*, indicating that these variables have changed, before calling repaint to display the new information.

The call to repaint forces the browser to invoke *MyApplet.paint* to refresh the screen. The *paint* method begins by checking to see whether the input data has changed since the last time the output *UIDrawText* objects were updated. If so, *paint* updates these output objects to reflect the most recent input from the dialog box and sets the flag back to *false*.

Nonmodal mode operation

As mentioned, the Dialog02 program supports nonmodal operation. However, in doing so Dialog02 must solve a problem common to all programs that make use of nonmodal dialog boxes: How does the main program know when the dialog box has been closed?

When the user clicks OK, the *DButton* action listener asynchronously reports the data to the variables stored within *MyApplet*. It then sets a flag, *bChanged*, to indicate to the applet that the data is there to be read. Next the OK button action listener must call some function to stimulate the main applet to read the data (unless the main thread is periodically checking the changed flag on its own). The call to *repaint* stimulates *MyApplet* to take note of the change and repaint the display using the new values.

Getting Input from a
Dialog Box—Modal Approach

Although Dialog02 is valuable because it supports both modal and nonmodal execution, it suffers from what is in my mind a serious problem. The main applet, *MyApplet*, and the dialog box class, *MyDialog*, are very tightly coupled. When the user clicks the OK button, the dialog box reaches directly into the applet to set the reporting variables *bLowerCase*, *sText*, and *sChoice*. This means that not only must the dialog box know exactly what the variables are called, but also the applet must deal with the fact that some other class is messing with its data members.

Strictly modal dialog boxes can use a different technique that avoids some of these pitfalls. This technique follows these general steps:

1. Update the dialog box to reflect the applet information. (Write to the dialog box.)

2. Display the dialog box.

3. Update the applet information to reflect what the user selected. (Read the dialog box.)

Notice that the applet reads the information in step 3 and processes it synchronously rather than having the dialog box write into the applet asynchronously. This technique is applicable only for modal dialog boxes, however, because it relies on the fact that step 3 will not be executed until after the user has closed the dialog box opened in step 2.

The following example program, Dialog03, uses this technique plus the introduction of an intermediate information exchange class to minimize the level of coupling:

```
// Dialog03 - Implements input by reading the dialog box modally.
//            This approach uses a much more modular
//            MyDialogInterface communication class rather
//            than the direct approach used in Dialog02.
import java.applet.*;
import java.awt.*;

import com.ms.ui.*;
import com.ms.ui.event.*;
import com.ms.fx.*;

import Application;

public class Dialog03 extends AwtUIApplet
{
    Dialog03()
    {
        super(new MyApplet());
    }

    public static void main(String[] arg)
    {
        new Application(new MyApplet());
    }
}

class MyApplet extends UIApplet
{
    MyDialog dialog;

    // The following structure is used as communication
    // between the applet and the dialog box.
    MyDialogInterface inter =
        new MyDialogInterface(true,
                              "Option 1",
                              "Enter some text");
```

```
// The following draw text fields are used to
// display the data selected in the dialog box.
UIDrawText lowerCase = new UIDrawText();
UIDrawText choice    = new UIDrawText();
UIDrawText text      = new UIDrawText();

public void init()
{
    // Create our dialog box window as before.
    dialog = new MyDialog(this);

    // Create the same panel to display the results.
    UIPanel display = new UIPanel();
    display.setLayout(new UIVerticalFlowLayout());
    display.add(lowerCase);
    display.add(choice);
    display.add(text);

    // Now create a button in the applet window
    // to open the dialog box, just like before.
    setLayout(new UIBorderLayout());
    add(display, "Center");
    add(new MyPushButton(this, dialog), "South");
}

// readDialog - Request an interface object from the
//              dialog box and, if one is received, update
//              the local information with it.
void readDialog()
{
    // Get an interface object from the dialog box.
    MyDialogInterface inter = dialog.read();

    // If we got one,...
    if (inter != null)
    {
        // ...save it. (We will need it for the
        // write operation when the dialog box is opened
        // the next time.)
        this.inter = inter;
```

>>

```
                    // Now update the displayed areas so that the
                    // user can see that the changes were read.
                    lowerCase.setValueText(inter.bLowerCase ?
                                            "Lowercase set." :
                                            "Lowercase not set.");
                    choice.setValueText(inter.sChoice);
                    text.setValueText(inter.sText);

                    repaint();
                }
            }


            // writeDialog - Update the dialog box with the most recent
            //               valid interface information.
            void writeDialog()
            {
                dialog.write(inter);
            }
        }


// MyPushButton - Displays the dialog box
class MyPushButton extends UIPushButton
{
    MyApplet parent;
    UIDialog dialog;

    class PBAction implements IUIActionListener
    {
        public void actionPerformed(UIActionEvent e)
        {
            // Update the dialog box with the applet's stored
            // information. (Synchronize on the way in.)
            parent.writeDialog();

            // Now make the dialog box visible - this won't
            // return until the user clicks either OK or
            // Cancel.
            dialog.setVisible(true);
            dialog.dispose();

            // Now update the applet with the dialog box's
            // new information. (Synchronize on the way out.)
            parent.readDialog();
        }
    }
```

```
    MyPushButton(MyApplet parent, UIDialog dialog)
    {
        super("View Dialog Box", UIPushButton.RAISED);

        this.parent = parent;
        this.dialog = dialog;

        addActionListener(new PBAction());
    }
}


// MyDialogInterface - This class serves as an interface
//                     between the dialog box and the applet,
//                     which reduces the amount of coupling
//                     between the two classes.
class MyDialogInterface
{
    boolean bLowerCase;
    String sChoice;
    String sText;

    MyDialogInterface(boolean bLowerCase,
                      String  sChoice,
                      String  sText)
    {
        this.bLowerCase = bLowerCase;
        this.sChoice    = sChoice;
        this.sText      = sText;
    }
}


// MyDialog - Same dialog box as Dialog01 and Dialog02 but
//            updated to use MyDialogInterface as the
//            communications mechanism
class MyDialog extends UIDialog
{
    MyApplet parent;

    // bValid - True when the user clicks OK, and false
    //          when the user clicks Cancel
    boolean  bValid;

    UICheckButton cb = new UICheckButton("Lowercase");
    UIChoice choice  = new UIChoice();
    UIEdit   text    = new UIEdit("Enter text here");
```

>>

>>

```
MyDialog(MyApplet parent)
{
    super(new UIFrame(), "Dialog03", true);
    setSize(100, 150);

    this.parent = parent;

    // Add a few items to the list of options.
    choice.addString("Option 1");
    choice.addString("Option 2");
    choice.addString("Option 3");

    // Add components to the dialog box.
    UIPanel panel = new UIPanel();
    panel.setLayout(new UIGridLayout(3, 1, 0, 10));
    panel.add(cb);
    panel.add(choice);
    panel.add(text);

    add(panel, "Center");

    // Now create a button panel.
    UIPanel buttons = new UIPanel();
    buttons.setLayout(new UIRowLayout(2));
    buttons.add(new DButton(this, "OK",     true));
    buttons.add(new DButton(this, "Cancel", false));

    add(buttons, "South");
}

// read - Populate a MyDialogInterface object with
//        the contents of the dialog box window.
MyDialogInterface read()
{
    // If the data isn't valid (the user clicks Cancel),...
    if (!bValid)
    {
        // ...just return a null value (no data).
        return null;
    }

    // Otherwise, build a valid interface object.
    return new MyDialogInterface(
                cb.isChecked(),
                choice.getValueText(),
                text.getValueText());
}
```

```
    // write - Populate the dialog box window using the contents
    //          of a MyDialogInterface object.
    void write(MyDialogInterface inter)
    {
        cb.setChecked(inter.bLowerCase);
        choice.setValueText(inter.sChoice);
        text.setValueText(inter.sText);
    }
}


// DButton - Implement a common class between the OK
//           and Cancel buttons; the only difference
//           is that the OK button reads the dialog box
//           and the Cancel button doesn't.
class DButton extends UIPushButton
{
    MyDialog parent;
    boolean  bReadDialog;

    class OKListener implements IUIActionListener
    {
        public void actionPerformed(UIActionEvent e)
        {
            // Set the validity flag in the dialog box
            // based on whether the user clicks OK
            // (bReadDialog == true) or Cancel
            // (bReadDialog == false)...
            parent.bValid = bReadDialog;

            // ...and hide the dialog box.
            parent.setVisible(false);
            parent.dispose();
        }
    }

    DButton(MyDialog parent,
            String    sLabel,
            boolean   bReadDialog)
    {
        super(sLabel, RAISED);

        this.parent     = parent;
        this.bReadDialog = bReadDialog;

        addActionListener(new OKListener());
    }
}
```

The key code segment from this rather lengthy example is embedded in the action listener for *MyPushButton*:

```
// Update the dialog box using the applet's stored
// information. (Synchronize on the way in.)
parent.writeDialog();

// Now make the dialog box visible - this won't
// return until the user clicks either OK or
// Cancel.
dialog.setVisible(true);
dialog.dispose();

// Now update the applet using the dialog box's
// new information. (Synchronize on the way out.)
parent.readDialog();
```

The call to *writeDialog* writes the information to the dialog box. The call to *setVisible(true)* displays the dialog box; the call to *readDialog* reads the information from the dialog box back into the applet's data members and then repaints the screen to display the results.

If you look more closely at how these functions work, you'll notice another trick to further reduce the coupling. The function *readDialog* calls *MyDialog.read*. This function returns an object of class *MyDialogInterface*. This class is nothing more than a set of data members, each member representing a field in the dialog box. The *MyDialog.read* function populates this class from the data on the screen. Similarly, the *writeDialog* function passes a *MyDialogInterface* object to *MyDialog.write*, which uses this object to populate the data fields in the dialog box.

Why bother with *MyDialogInterface*? This class effectively decouples the dialog box class from the applet that uses it. The applet no longer has to worry about some dialog box class writing directly into its data members. In addition, the applet has some flexibility with regard to those data members. The applet knows only about the data members that make up *MyDialogInterface*—it has no intimate knowledge of the make-up of the dialog box display itself.

I can hear it now: "All you've done is transfer the coupling with *MyDialog* from *MyApplet* to *MyDialogInterface*." True, but this is a big step nonetheless. *MyDialogInterface* has no member functions (other than the constructor). That means there are no member functions to trip up. If *MyDialog* sets one of these data members to some invalid value, *MyDialogInterface* won't care. The applet class can (and must) check these values when reading them back out, and it can reject illegal data, which allows the applet to protect itself from what might otherwise be fatal input from the user. The alternative of putting this kind of checking code in the *MyDialog* class is not particularly attractive since it gives that class too much knowledge about the applet.

The examples in the following section, Wizard01 and PropertyDialog01, demonstrate other approaches that lie somewhere between Dialog02 and Dialog03 in terms of coupling.

SEMISPECIALIZED DIALOG BOXES

The *UIDialog* class is a completely nonspecialized class. The upside to this lack of specialization is that *UIDialog* allows the programmer to build whatever dialog box classes he might want. The downside is that *UIDialog* provides little help in doing so.

The two classes *UIWizard* and *UIPropertyDialog* represent what I call semispecialized dialog box classes. These classes don't specify the contents of the dialog box; however, they do specify the format. In so doing, they remove some of the flexibility the programmer has in designing the appearance of the dialog box. But these classes also eliminate much of the work of making a decent-looking dialog box. At the same time, they help standardize the appearance of the dialog box across applets.

Wizards

The *UIWizard* and *UIWizardStep* classes implement the so-called wizard dialog box. This is the type of dialog box presented by applications such as the Visual J++ Applet Wizard. Wizards present a series of steps, each with an image on the left and a series of components—usually check boxes, text entry fields, and selection boxes—on the right. Along the bottom is a series of buttons—Back, Next, Finish, and Cancel—that enable the user to navigate the wizard. The Back and Next buttons allow the user to move back and forth in the sequence of wizard steps.

The following example application, Wizard01, demonstrates a sample wizard applet. I have tried to keep the size of the application to a minimum by implementing only three steps, but wizard applets get rather large. When you follow the program one step at a time, however, you see that it isn't very complicated.

```
// Wizard01 - Demonstrates a fairly capable wizard
//             using the UIWizard class. While the
//             example is somewhat lengthy, the logic
//             is simple.
import java.applet.*;
import java.awt.*;

import com.ms.ui.*;
import com.ms.ui.event.*;
import com.ms.fx.*;

import Application;
import Images;

public class Wizard01 extends AwtUIApplet
{
    Wizard01()
    {
        super(new MyApplet());
    }

    public static void main(String[] arg)
    {
        System.out.println("Cannot execute as an application");
    }
}

class MyApplet extends UIApplet
{
    // Names of the images used for the wizard steps
    String[] sImageNames = new String[3] {"Step1.jpg",
                                          "Step2.jpg",
                                          "Step3.jpg"};

    // wizard - This is the demonstration wizard.
    MyWizard wizard;

    // The following text fields are used to display
    // what was selected in the wizard menus (just to
    // prove that the UIWizard dialog box works).
    UIDrawText t1 = new UIDrawText();
    UIDrawText t2 = new UIDrawText();
    UIDrawText t3 = new UIDrawText();
    UIDrawText t4 = new UIDrawText();
```

```
// init
public void init()
{
    // Load the images we'll need.
    Images images = new Images(this, sImageNames);
    images.load();

    // Use them to create a wizard dialog box.
    wizard = new MyWizard(this, "Trial Wizard", images);

    // Create a group to display the results, and add it
    // at the top.
    UIGroup group = new UIGroup("Results");
    group.add(t1);
    group.add(t2);
    group.add(t3);
    group.add(t4);

    setLayout(new UIBorderLayout());
    add(group, "North");

    // Create a button to display the wizard.
    add(new MyPushButton(this,
                        "Show Wizard",
                        wizard),
        "South");
}

// paint - If the wizard has been modified, set the
//         local text fields based on the contents of
//         the wizard.
public void paint(FxGraphics fg)
{
    // If the wizard has changed,...
    if (wizard.getChanged())
    {
        // ...query the wizard's flags.
        t1.setValueText(wizard.bAFCApplet ?
                        "AFC applet" : "Not AFC applet");
        t2.setValueText(wizard.bIncludeComments ?
                        "Comments"   : "No comments");
        t3.setValueText(wizard.bIncludeAppCommon?
                        "AppCommon" : "No AppCommon");
        t4.setValueText("Path = " + wizard.sHTMLFileName);
    }
}
```

>>

```
// MyPushButton - Displays the wizard and updates the parent
//                MyApplet with the results
class MyPushButton extends UIPushButton
{
    UIApplet parent;
    UIWizard wizard;

    class PBAction implements IUIActionListener
    {
        public void actionPerformed(UIActionEvent e)
        {
            // Read the wizard dialog box.
            wizard.doModal();

            // Verify that the applet reads
            // and displays the results.
            repaint();
        }
    }

    MyPushButton(UIApplet parent,
                 String   sLabel,
                 UIWizard wizard)
    {
        super(sLabel);

        this.parent = parent;
        this.wizard = wizard;

        // Attach the listener.
        addActionListener(new PBAction());
    }
}

//IStep - All of the steps of a MyWizard class must implement the
//        IStep interface. This interface provides a method
//        that allows the steps to update the flags in the
//        MyWizard class.
interface IStep
{
    void setFlags(MyWizard parent);
}
```

```
// MyWizard - A UIWizard class built with a particular set of steps
class MyWizard extends UIWizard
{
    UIApplet parent;

    // This wizard has three steps.
    IStep[] steps = new IStep[3];

    // bChanged - Set if anything has changed since the last
    //            time it was read.
    boolean bChanged = false;

    // These are the flags that the wizard will set:
    // Step 1
    boolean bAFCApplet = true;
    boolean bIncludeComments = false;
    boolean bIncludeAppCommon = false;

    // Step 2
    String sHTMLFileName = new String("<null>");

    // Step 3
    // none

    // constructor - Sets up the wizard steps and attaches
    //               them to the wizard dialog box
    MyWizard(UIApplet parent, String sLabel, Images images)
    {
        super(new UIFrame(), sLabel);
        this.parent = parent;

        // Set the size of the image and the contents.
        setForcedBounds("image", new Dimension(190, 320));
        setForcedBounds("contents", new Dimension(200, 320));

        // This wizard has three steps and a separate class for
        // each.
        steps[0] = new Step1();
        steps[1] = new Step2();
        steps[2] = new Step3();
```

>>

>>

```
            // Create a wizard step from each of these IStep objects.
            // (Notice that each of these IStep objects is a subclass
            // of Panel.)
            int nLast = steps.length - 1;
            for (int i = 0; i <= nLast; i++)
            {
                // Set bLast for the last step.
                boolean bLast = (i == nLast);

                // Create a step from each panel.
                UIWizardStep step = new UIWizardStep(
                            new UIGraphic(images.getImage(i)),
                            (UIPanel)steps[i],
                            bLast);
                addStep(step);
            }
        }

        // getChanged - Get and reset the changed flag.
        boolean getChanged()
        {
            boolean bChanged = this.bChanged;
            this.bChanged = false;
            return bChanged;
        }

        // doFinishAction - Overrides the finish action in order to
        //                  read the wizard steps and allow the applet
        //                  to take action
        public boolean doFinishAction(Event e, Object o)
        {
            // Read each of the wizard steps.
            for (int i = 0; i < steps.length; i++)
            {
                steps[i].setFlags(this);
            }

            // Let's assume that something has changed.
            bChanged = true;

            // Do whatever else AFC wants to do.
            return super.doFinishAction(e, o);
        }
```

```
    // The following methods can be overridden as well;
    // here they don't do anything.
    public void doBackAction(Event e, Object o)
    {
        parent.showStatus("Going back");
        super.doBackAction(e, o);
    }
    public void doNextAction(Event e, Object o)
    {
        parent.showStatus("Going forward");
        super.doNextAction(e, o);
    }
    public boolean doCancelAction(Event e, Object o)
    {
        parent.showStatus("Cancel");
        return super.doCancelAction(e, o);
    }
}


// Step1 - Implement the contents of wizard step 1:
//          a pair of radio buttons and two check buttons.
class Step1 extends UIPanel implements IStep
{
    UIRadioButton rb1 =
        new UIRadioButton("Use AFC to create applet");
    UIRadioButton rb2 =
        new UIRadioButton("Do not use AFC to create applet");

    UICheckButton cb1 = new UICheckButton("Include comments");
    UICheckButton cb2 = new UICheckButton("Include AppCommon");

    // constructor - Put the two radio buttons in a radio
    //               group and the two check buttons in a group
    //               of their own.
    Step1()
    {
        UIRadioGroup rg = new UIRadioGroup();
        rg.add(rb1);
        rg.add(rb2);
        rb1.setChecked(true);

        UIGroup cg = new UIGroup();
        cg.add(cb1);
        cg.add(cb2);
```

>>

```
        // Put the radio group at the top and the check
        // button group at the bottom.
        setLayout(new UIBorderLayout());
        add(rg, "North");
        add(cg, "South");
    }

    // setFlags - Called when the user clicks Finish
    public void setFlags(MyWizard parent)
    {
        // Read the radio button.
        parent.bAFCApplet = rb1.isChecked();

        // Read the two check buttons.
        parent.bIncludeComments = cb1.isChecked();
        parent.bIncludeAppCommon= cb2.isChecked();
    }
}

// Step2 - Implement the contents of wizard step 2:
//         a text entry box.
class Step2 extends UIPanel implements IStep
{
    UIEdit htmlPath = new UIEdit();

    Step2()
    {
        setLayout(new UIVerticalFlowLayout());
        add(new UIDrawText("Enter HTML file name:"));
        add(htmlPath);
    }
    public void setFlags(MyWizard parent)
    {
        parent.sHTMLFileName = htmlPath.getValueText();
    }
}

// Step3 - Implement the contents of wizard step 3:
//         does nothing more than allow the user to click Finish.
class Step3 extends UIPanel implements IStep
{
    Step3()
    {
        setFont(new FxFont("Helvetica", FxFont.BOLD, 14));
        add(new UIDrawText("Click Finish\nto\ncreate applet."));
    }
```

```
// setFlags - This does nothing; the flags
//            have already been set by the previous
//            wizards (not unusual for the final
//            step).
public void setFlags(MyWizard parent)
{
}
}
```

MyApplet begins by defining the names of the images to be used in the wizard steps: Step1.jpg, Step2.jpg, and Step3.jpg. The applet continues by defining four text fields that will be used to display the results of the selections made in the wizard on the applet window. Once again, this is done just to verify that the applet is reading the wizard results correctly.

The *init* function begins by loading the wizard step images defined in *sImageNames*. To do this, *init* uses the class *Images* defined in AppCommon and described in Appendix B, "Utility Classes Used in This Book." It creates the wizard dialog box—an object of class *MyWizard*—by using these images and then creates a display group for the wizard results, as well as a *MyPushButton* object to display the wizard dialog box, before exiting.

When the user clicks on the *MyPushButton* object, the action listener first displays the wizard modally by invoking *doModal*. It then calls *repaint* to ensure that the applet reads the wizard data.

MyApplet.paint reads the display data from the wizard dialog box. If the data in the dialog box has changed, *paint* updates its display text fields to reflect the new data. This approach results in a level of coupling slightly better than that demonstrated in Dialog02 but not as good as that in Dialog03.

The *MyWizard* class performs the actual work of creating and displaying the wizard steps. First *MyWizard* defines data fields for each of the entry components defined in the wizard steps. (This is the data the applet will read once the wizard dialog box is finished.) The constructor for *MyWizard* continues by setting the size of the image area and the contents area, the area devoted to input components, by calling *setForcedBounds* for each. The constructor defines and saves three *Step* classes, each a subclass of *UIPanel*. The *Step* objects represent the contents of the wizard steps. Last the constructor defines a *UIWizardStep* object from each *Step* class and the corresponding image.

The *UIWizard* class contains built-in methods for handling standard buttons, such as forward and backward buttons. These methods can be overridden in the user-defined subclass. Here I have overridden the *doFinishAction* method that is called when the user clicks Finish. This method reads the contents of each of the wizard steps. It then continues by invoking the base class *doFinish-Action*, which allows AFC to perform the normal Finish operations. (This class also overrides some of the other action methods merely to demonstrate the principle.)

Each of the *Step* classes extends *UIPanel* while implementing the *IStep* interface. The constructor for these functions displays a set of components much like any other panel. The *setFlags* method required by the *IStep* interface reads the contents of the step. The results are stored in the parent *MyDialog* object.

The results are fairly impressive. The first step of this wizard dialog box is shown in Figure 10-3.

As you run the Wizard01 example, you might notice that the Finish button is not enabled until the final step. Sometimes, you want to enable the Finish button at some intermediate point. If the user clicks Finish at this intermediate point, she gets default values for all remaining steps.

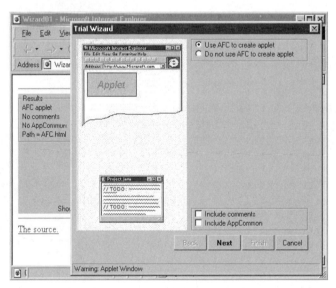

FIGURE 10-3   *The first step in the example wizard, with the results of the previous wizard displayed in the applet window in the background.*

To enable the Finish button earlier, you must create a subclass of *UIWizardStep* as follows:

```
// FinishWizardStep - This class allows the user to specify whether
//                    the Finish button should be enabled.
class FinishWizardStep extends UIWizardStep
{
    // bEnableFinish - true = Enable the Finish flag for this
    //                 step.
    boolean bEnableFinish;

    FinishWizardStep(UIGraphic graphic,
                     UIPanel panel,
                     boolean bFlag,
                     boolean bEnableFinish)
    {
        super(graphic, panel, bFlag);

        this.bEnableFinish = bEnableFinish;
    }
    public boolean isFinishStep()
    {
        return bEnableFinish;
    }
}
```

This subclass overrides the *isFinishStep* method to return a value of *true* if the step should enable the Finish button and a value of *false* if it should not.

Property Pages

Another of the semispecialized dialog boxes is the property page implemented by *UIPropertyDialog*. Superficially, the property page looks nothing like a wizard dialog box. But if you take a closer look, you can see that they are quite similar. Each *UIPropertyDialog* object provides a sequence of separate dialog boxes that collectively make up the entire dialog box "book."

The primary difference between the property page dialog box and the wizard dialog box is that the wizard displays dialog boxes in a sequential manner, leading the user from one step to the next, whereas the property pages have no such sequential relationship. In the property dialog, the user can jump from one property page to the next by clicking on the various property tabs.

Nevertheless, from a coding standpoint the similarities are more apparent than the differences, as the following example program, PropertyDialog01, demonstrates:

```java
// PropertyDialog01 - A property page
//                    that implements the same
//                    properties as the wizard
import java.applet.*;
import java.awt.*;

import com.ms.ui.*;
import com.ms.ui.event.*;
import com.ms.fx.*;

import Application;

public class PropertyDialog01 extends AwtUIApplet
{
    PropertyDialog01()
    {
        super(new MyApplet());
    }

    public static void main(String[] arg)
    {
        System.out.println("Cannot execute as an application");
    }
}

// MyApplet - This is almost the same as in the
//            wizard-based example.
class MyApplet extends UIApplet
{
    // This is the property dialog box.
    MyPropD prop;

    // The following text fields are used to display
    // what was set in the property pages.
    UIDrawText t1 = new UIDrawText();
    UIDrawText t2 = new UIDrawText();
    UIDrawText t3 = new UIDrawText();
    UIDrawText t4 = new UIDrawText();
```

```java
public void init()
{
    // Create a property dialog box.
    prop = new MyPropD(this);

    // Create a group to display the results and add it
    // at the top of the applet window.
    UIGroup group = new UIGroup("Results");
    group.add(t1);
    group.add(t2);
    group.add(t3);
    group.add(t4);

    setLayout(new UIBorderLayout());
    add(group, "North");

    // Now attach a button below that displays the
    // property dialog box.
    add(new MyPushButton("Open Property Dialog Box", prop),
        "South");
}


// paint - If the properties have been changed by the
//         property page, display the changes.
public void paint(FxGraphics fg)
{
    // If the wizard has changed,...
    if (prop.getChanged())
    {
        // ...query the wizard's flags.
        t1.setValueText(prop.bAFCApplet ?
                        "AFC applet" : "Not AFC applet");
        t2.setValueText(prop.bIncludeComments ?
                        "Comments"   : "No comments");
        t3.setValueText(prop.bIncludeAppCommon?
                        "AppCommon" : "No AppCommon");
        t4.setValueText("Path = " + prop.sHTMLFileName);
    }
}
}
```

>>

>>

```
// MyPushButton - Displays the property dialog box
class MyPushButton extends UIPushButton
{
    UIApplet  parent;
    MyPropD prop;

    class PBAction implements IUIActionListener
    {
        public void actionPerformed(UIActionEvent e)
        {
            prop.display();
        }
    }

    MyPushButton(String sLabel, MyPropD prop)
    {
        super(sLabel, UIPushButton.RAISED);
        this.prop = prop;

        // Attach the listener.
        addActionListener(new PBAction());
    }
}

// MyPropD - My property dialog box implements property pages
//           that contain the same fields as the
//           wizard dialog box.
class MyPropD extends UIPropertyDialog
{
    // Parent applet
    UIApplet parent;

    // The currently visible pages
    MyPage[] pages = new MyPage[2];

    // bChanged - Set if anything has changed since
    //            the last time it was read.
    boolean bChanged = true;

    // These are the flags that the property page
    // keeps track of:
    // Page 1
    boolean bAFCApplet = true;
    boolean bIncludeComments = false;
    boolean bIncludeAppCommon = false;
```

```
// Page 2
String sHTMLFileName = new String("<null>");

MyPropD(UIApplet parent)
{
    super(new UIFrame(),
          "Property Dialog Box",
          true,
          SMALL);

    this.parent = parent;

    // Now add two property pages.
    pages[0] = new Page1();
    pages[1] = new Page2();
    addPage(pages[0]);
    addPage(pages[1]);
}


// The following set methods set the corresponding
// property and then set the changed flag.
void setAFCApplet(boolean bFlag)
{
    bAFCApplet = bFlag;
    changed();
}
void setIncludeComments(boolean bFlag)
{
    bIncludeComments = bFlag;
    changed();
}
void setIncludeAppCommon(boolean bFlag)
{
    bIncludeAppCommon = bFlag;
    changed();
}
void setHTMLFileName(String s)
{
    if (s == null)
    {
        s = "<null>";
    }
    sHTMLFileName = s;
    changed();
}
```

>>

```
// changed - Sets the changed flag and prompts the
//           applet to pick up the change by invoking
//           repaint
void changed()
{
    bChanged = true;
    parent.repaint();
}

// getChanged - Returns the value of the changed
//              flag and then resets the flag
boolean getChanged()
{
    boolean bChanged = this.bChanged;
    this.bChanged = false;
    return bChanged;
}

// display - When a property page is made visible by the
//           user clicking on the tab, the doDisplay method
//           is invoked automatically; however, doDisplay
//           is not invoked for the property page that
//           happens to be on top when the Property
//           dialog box is first displayed. I consider this an
//           error, and the following code fixes it.
public Object display()
{
    for (int i = 0; i < pages.length; i++)
    {
        pages[i].reset(this);
    }
    return super.display();
}
}


// MyPage - Extends the UIPropertyPage class by adding the
//          reset method
abstract class MyPage extends UIPropertyPage
{
    abstract void reset(MyPropD propDialog);
}
```

```java
// Page1 - Implement the first property page.
class Page1 extends MyPage
{
    UIRadioButton rb1 =
        new UIRadioButton("Use AFC to create applet");
    UIRadioButton rb2 =
        new UIRadioButton("Do not use AFC to create applet");

    UICheckButton cb1 = new UICheckButton("Include comments");
    UICheckButton cb2 = new UICheckButton("Include AppCommon");

    // constructor - Set the name of the property page.
    Page1()
    {
        setName("Code properties");
    }

    // addContent - Invoked when the property page
    //              is first made visible
    public boolean addContent()
    {
        UIRadioGroup rg = new UIRadioGroup();
        rg.add(rb1);
        rg.add(rb2);
        rb1.setChecked(true);

        UIGroup cg = new UIGroup();
        cg.add(cb1);
        cg.add(cb2);

        // Position the radio group at the top and the check
        // buttons immediately below.
        setLayout(new UIVerticalFlowLayout());
        add(rg);
        add(cg);

        return true;
    }

    // doApplyAction - Called when the user clicks Apply
    //                 or OK
    public boolean doApplyAction()
    {
        MyPropD parent = (MyPropD)getSheet();
```

>>

>>

```
        // Read the radio button.
        parent.setAFCApplet(rb1.isChecked());

        // Read the two check buttons.
        parent.setIncludeComments(cb1.isChecked());
        parent.setIncludeAppCommon(cb2.isChecked());

        return true;
    }

    // reset - Invoked when the dialog box is made visible;
    //         this method resets the property page.
    void reset(MyPropD parent)
    {
        rb1.setChecked(parent.bAFCApplet);
        rb2.setChecked(!parent.bAFCApplet);

        cb1.setChecked(parent.bIncludeComments);
        cb2.setChecked(parent.bIncludeAppCommon);
    }

    // isApplyable   If a value of true is returned, the Apply button
    //               is enabled for the property page.
    public boolean isApplyable()
    {
        return true;
    }
}

// Page2 - Do the same for the second property page.
class Page2 extends MyPage
{
    UIEdit htmlPath = new UIEdit();

    Page2()
    {
        setName("HTML Path");
    }

    public boolean addContent()
    {
        setLayout(new UIVerticalFlowLayout());
        add(new UIDrawText("Enter HTML filename:"));
        add(htmlPath);

        return true;
    }
```

```
public boolean doApplyAction()
{
    MyPropD parent = (MyPropD)getSheet();

    parent.setHTMLFileName(htmlPath.getValueText());

    return true;
}

void reset(MyPropD parent)
{
    htmlPath.setValueText(parent.sHTMLFileName);
}

public boolean isApplyable()
{
    return true;
}
}
```

The *MyApplet* class here is virtually identical to the *MyApplet* class described in Wizard01. Similarly, the *MyPushButton* class is about the same. The primary difference here is that PropertyDialog01 calls *UIPropertyPage.display* to display the dialog box rather than the more conventional *doModal* or *setVisible(true)*. (The reason for the difference is that when it is invoked on a modal property page, *display* returns the value indicating which type of button was clicked to close the page. The most common values are *OK* and *Cancel*.)

The property page dialog box *MyPropD* defines the same fields as the earlier wizard class. The constructor begins by invoking the base class constructor, indicating the title, the fact that it wants to be modal, and the fact that this is a small property page rather than a medium or large one.

MyPropD goes on to define a set of *set* methods, each designed to define a different data member. *MyPropD* provides these methods to allow outside classes such as the property page classes to change their data members. This is in contrast to allowing the pages to write directly into the *MyPropD*'s data members, which slightly reduces the coupling between *MyPropD* and its property pages.

The two *Page* classes implement the actual property pages. The inclusion of the *MyPage* class as an abstract intermediate class lets us define *reset* as a method common to all pages. (Compare this to the interface approach demonstrated in Wizard01.)

Each page overrides *addContent* to add the components to the property page. Returning a value of *true* indicates that the *addContent* method does not need to be called again when the property page is redisplayed.

In addition, each page overrides *doApplyAction* to handle those cases when the user clicks the Apply or OK button. Each such function gets the parent *MyPropD* object and then invokes *set* methods to pass data from its own fields into the property dialog box.

Last each page overrides *isApplyable* to return *true* if the Apply button should be enabled for this page. Returning *false* disables the Apply button.

The *reset* method added by the abstract *MyPage* class allows the dialog box to reset the property page prior to displaying it. This process is the same as writing to the dialog box prior to displaying it, as we saw in Dialog02, and ensures that what is displayed represents the data as stored by the applet and not as was previously displayed. (The two data sets may differ if the user exits the dialog box by clicking Cancel rather than OK.)

The results of the PropertyDialog01 applet are shown in Figure 10-4.

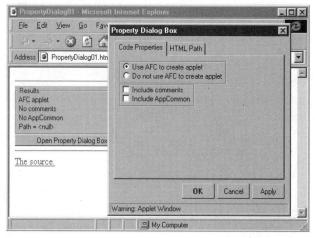

FIGURE 10-4   *One of the property pages of PropertyDialog01, with the currently applied settings displayed in the applet window in the background.*

FULLY SPECIALIZED DIALOG BOXES

In addition to the general *UIDialog* class and the semispecialized *UIWizard* and *UIProperty-Dialog* classes, AFC provides three classes that I call "fully specialized": *UIFind-ReplaceDialog*, *UIColorDialog*, and *UIFontDialog*. These classes are designed to perform one and only one function each. However, in return they are very easy to use, requiring a minimum of coding on the programmer's part.

The Find/Replace Dialog Box

The following example program, FindAndReplace01, demonstrates the care and feeding of the *UIFindReplaceDialog* class:

```java
// FindAndReplace01 - Demonstrates the UIFindReplaceDialog class
import java.applet.*;
import java.awt.*;

import com.ms.ui.*;
import com.ms.ui.event.*;

import Application;

public class FindAndReplace01 extends AwtUIApplet
{
    FindAndReplace01()
    {
        super(new MyApplet());
    }

    public static void main(String[] arg)
    {
        new Application(new MyApplet());
    }
}

class MyApplet extends UIApplet
{
    // fr - A modal Find/Replace dialog box with default title
    UIFindReplaceDialog fr = new UIFindReplaceDialog(
                            new UIFrame(),
                            null,
                            true);
```

>>

>>

```
// sTypes - The strings associated with the type
//           of search returned by display
String[] sTypes = new String[5]{"",
                                "FindNext",
                                "Cancel",
                                "Replace",
                                "ReplaceAll"};

// The following text fields are used to display
// the results.
UIDrawText t1 = new UIDrawText();
UIDrawText t2 = new UIDrawText();
UIDrawText t3 = new UIDrawText();
UIDrawText t4 = new UIDrawText();
UIDrawText t5 = new UIDrawText();

public void init()
{
    // Create a group for the text output fields.
    UIGroup group = new UIGroup();
    group.setLayout(new UIVerticalFlowLayout());
    group.add(t1);
    group.add(t2);
    group.add(t3);
    group.add(t4);
    group.add(t5);

    // Now add a button to display the dialog box.
    setLayout(new UIBorderLayout());
    add(group, "Center");
    add(new MyPushButton(this), "South");
}

// update - Called from the push button listener
void update()
{
    // Display the Find/Replace dialog box - because the
    // dialog box is modal, this call doesn't return until
    // the user selects an action.
    int nSelect = fr.display(UIFindReplaceDialog.REPLACE);

    // Now read the dialog box and display the results in
    // the applet window.
    t1.setValueText(sTypes[nSelect]);
    t2.setValueText("Replace " + fr.getFindText());
    t3.setValueText("With    " + fr.getReplaceText());
    t4.setValueText(fr.isWholeWord() ?
```

```
            "Match whole word" :
            "Do not match whole word");
        t5.setValueText(fr.isCaseSensitive() ?
            "Case sensitive" :
            "Case insensitive");
    }
}

// MyPushButton - Displays the Find/Replace dialog box when
//                selected
class MyPushButton extends UIPushButton
{
    MyApplet parent;

    class PBAction implements IUIActionListener
    {
        public void actionPerformed(UIActionEvent e)
        {
            parent.update();
        }
    }

    MyPushButton(MyApplet parent)
    {
        super("Find/Replace", UIPushButton.RAISED);

        this.parent = parent;

        addActionListener(new PBAction());
    }
}
```

The majority of this example program is dedicated to displaying the results of the Find/Replace dialog box, but it takes only one line to actually display the dialog box:

```
int nSelect = fr.display(UIFindReplaceDialog.REPLACE);
```

The one argument to the *UIFindReplaceDialog.display* method is either RE-PLACE or FIND. REPLACE displays a Find/Replace dialog box, and FIND displays a simple Find dialog box. The value returned from *display* indicates which button in the dialog box the user clicked.

The results of this rather modestly sized applet are shown in Figure 10-5 on the following page.

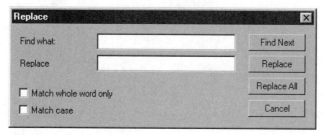

FIGURE 10-5 *The dialog box displayed by the* UIFindReplaceDialog *class.*

The Color Dialog Box

The *UIColorDialog* class allows the user to select colors from a color palette. It is no more difficult to use than the *UIFindReplaceDialog* class, as the following example, ColorDialog01, demonstrates:

```
// ColorDialog01 - Demonstrates the Color dialog box
import java.applet.*;
import java.awt.*;

import com.ms.ui.*;
import com.ms.ui.event.*;
import com.ms.fx.*;

import Application;

public class ColorDialog01 extends AwtUIApplet
{
    ColorDialog01()
    {
        super(new MyApplet());
    }

    public static void main(String[] arg)
    {
        new Application(new MyApplet());
    }
}

class MyApplet extends UIApplet
{
    public void init()
    {
        setLayout(new UIBorderLayout());
```

```
        // Define a text area in which the font name is displayed.
        UIDrawText text = new UIDrawText("Sample Text");
        text.setFont(new FxFont("Arial", FxFont.BOLD, 24));
        add(text, "North");

        // Add a raised dialog box button.
        add(new MyPushButton(text), "South");
    }
}


// MyPushButton - Displays the Color dialog box and displays
//                the results in the text area
class MyPushButton extends UIPushButton
{
    UIDrawText text;

    class PBAction implements IUIActionListener
    {
        public void actionPerformed(UIActionEvent e)
        {
            // Create a Color dialog box.
            UIColorDialog dialog =
                new UIColorDialog(new UIFrame());

            // Displaying the dialog box is all that's required to
            // start processing because this dialog box
            // is always modal.
            dialog.show();

            // Get the color selected by the user.
            FxColor color = dialog.getFxColor();

            // Use the text object to display the selected color.
            text.setForeground(color);
        }
    }

    MyPushButton(UIDrawText text)
    {
        super("Set Color", UIPushButton.RAISED);
        this.text = text;
        addActionListener(new PBAction());
    }
}
```

The key to this program is in the push button action listener.

First the action listener creates the Color dialog box. Next it displays the dialog box by invoking the *show* method. Once control is returned from the modal Color dialog box, the call to *getFxColor* returns the color selected by the user as an object of class *FxColor*. To demonstrate that this is the selected color, the program goes on to display a text string in the selected color in the applet window by calling *setForeground* on the text string.

The Color dialog box is shown in Figure 10-6. Of course, this black-and-white image does not do the dialog box justice. The display on a good multicolor monitor is awesome.

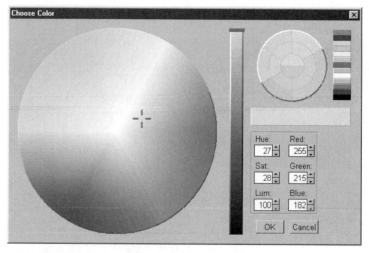

FIGURE 10-6   *The Color dialog box displayed by the* UIColorDialog *class.*

The Font Dialog Box

The last of the fully specialized classes is *UIFontDialog*, which is used to select a font from a list of available fonts. The following example program, FontDialog01, demonstrates how easy this class is to use:

```
// FontDialog01 - Demonstrates the Font dialog box
import java.applet.*;
import java.awt.*;

import com.ms.ui.*;
import com.ms.ui.event.*;
import com.ms.fx.*;

import Application;

public class FontDialog01 extends AwtUIApplet
{
    FontDialog01()
    {
        super(new MyApplet());
    }

    public static void main(String[] arg)
    {
        new Application(new MyApplet());
    }
}

class MyApplet extends UIApplet
{
    public void init()
    {
        setLayout(new UIBorderLayout());

        // Define a text area in which the font name is displayed.
        UIDrawText text = new UIDrawText();
        add(text, "North");

        // Add a raised dialog box button.
        add(new MyPushButton(text), "South");
    }
}

// MyPushButton - Displays the Font dialog box and displays
//                the result in the text area
class MyPushButton extends UIPushButton
{
    UIDrawText text;
```

>>

>>

```
class PBAction implements IUIActionListener
{
    public void actionPerformed(UIActionEvent e)
    {
        // Create a Font dialog box.
        UIFontDialog dialog =
            new UIFontDialog(new UIFrame());

        // Displaying the dialog box is all that's required
        // to start processing because this dialog box
        // is always modal.
        dialog.show();

        // Get the font selected by the user.
        FxFont font = dialog.getFxFont();

        // Use the text object to display the name of the font
        // in that font.
        text.setFont(font);
        text.setValueText(font.getName());
    }
}

MyPushButton(UIDrawText text)
{
    super("Set Font", UIPushButton.RAISED);
    this.text = text;
    addActionListener(new PBAction());
}
}
```

Once again, the actual work is performed in the action listener method of *UIPushButton*. The class creates a *UIFontDialog* object and then displays it by calling *show*. Once the control is returned from the dialog box, the call to *getFxFont* returns an *FxFont* object containing the font selected by the user. The name of this selected font is then displayed in the applet window in the style of that font.

The result of selecting Dialog Italics as the font is shown in Figure 10-7.

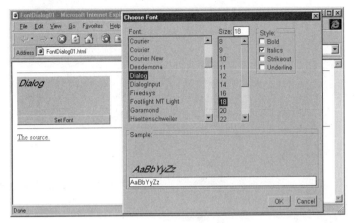

FIGURE 10-7 *The Font dialog box displayed by the* UIFontDialog *class, with the result of the previous selection displayed in the applet window in the background.*

WHAT'S NEXT

This chapter has demonstrated how to use the various dialog box classes to produce some impressive dialog boxes. In addition, this chapter has examined some of the problems inherent in communicating between the applet and the dialog box and presented several solutions to this problem.

It turns out that tabbed property pages can appear apart from any dialog box. In the next chapter, we will examine how to use property pages in window classes that are not based on *UIDialog*. In so doing, we'll have an opportunity to compare the windowed approach to property pages with the dialog-based approach discussed in this chapter.

Tabs

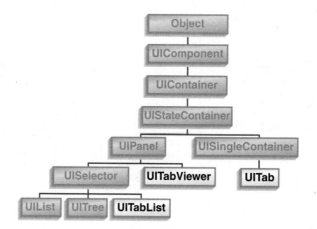

It's difficult to beat a well laid out window for displaying data to the user; however, the dimensions of a window limit the amount of data the window can display. You can make the components smaller to crowd more of them into the window. But after a point, the components are too small to see easily. Even before that, the window starts to become crowded and confusing.

Another approach to displaying large amounts of information is to utilize the z-dimension (in addition to the x- and y-dimensions inherent in the window itself) by stacking frames on top of each other, much like the pages in a notebook. A small, labeled tab at the top of each page orients the user in the stack of windows and gives an indication of what other windows might be available. The tabs also provide a convenient means for navigating among pages—clicking on a tab brings that tab to the top of the stack.

In this chapter, we'll see how the tabbed viewer represented by the *UITabViewer* class uses this approach and how the tabbed viewer differs from the property pages discussed in Chapter 10, "Dialog Boxes."

THE TABBED VIEWER

The *UITabViewer* class works much like the other viewer panels. The basic steps for creating a tabbed viewer are outlined in the following code snippet:

```
public void init()
{
    // Step 1 - Create an empty viewer.
    UITabViewer viewer = new UITabViewer();

    // Step 2 - Add a page to the UITabViewer object.
    //          The first argument is the String object, and the
    //          second is a UIPanel object of some type that
    //          will be added to the tabbed viewer page.
    viewer.add(sSomeString, panel);

    // Repeat for each page.
    ⋮

    // Step 3 - Add the viewer to the applet window.
    add(viewer);
}
```

First the program creates a *UITabViewer* object. The tabbed viewer begins life without any pages in it. Second the program adds a page by calling *UITab-Viewer.add(String, UIPanel)* or *UITabViewer.add(IUIComponent, UIPanel)*. The contents of the page are contained in the *UIPanel* object, whereas the *String* or *IUIComponent* object is used as a label for the tab.

NOTE

One of the parameters for the *UIStatic* constructor, like most class constructors that make up AFC, is an object that implements the *IUIComponent* interface. This parameter allows for the inclusion of text and/or a graphical image in the *UIStatic* object. In addition, the *UIStatic* class allows the programmer to control hot-tracking. For more information about the use of *UIStatic* and hot-tracking, see Chapter 5, "Canvases."

The *UITabViewer.add* step is repeated for each page that will be added to the tabbed viewer. Last the viewer is added to the component in which it is to be visible—in this case, the applet window.

A Simple Example

The example program in this section, Tab01, uses the tabbed viewer to give the user a much broader set of selections than would be possible in a single panel or a set of menus. This tabbed viewer allows the user to view samples of all Arial font types that *FxFont* supports, in all sizes from 8-point to 35-point. Each font size is displayed in a separate tabbed viewer window, with the point size indicated on the tab, as shown in Figure 11-1.

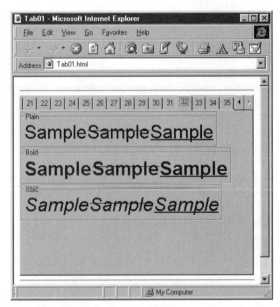

FIGURE 11-1   *The output of the Tab01 program, showing the types of fonts available on tab page 32.*

This output was created using the Tab01 program:

```
// Tab01 - Creates a simple tabbed viewer. This viewer displays
//         samples of the different types of the FxFont object.
import java.applet.*;
import java.awt.*;

import com.ms.ui.*;
import com.ms.fx.*;

import Application;
```

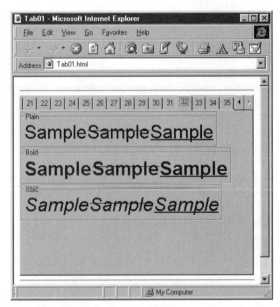

```
>>        public class Tab01 extends AwtUIApplet
          {
              Tab01()
              {
                  super(new MyApplet());
              }

              public static void main(String[] arg)
              {
                  new Application(new MyApplet());
              }
          }

          class MyApplet extends UIApplet
          {
              // init - Creates the tabbed viewer and then
              //          populates the pages
              public void init()
              {
                  // Create an empty viewer.
                  UITabViewer viewer = new UITabViewer();

                  for (int i = 8; i < 36; i++)
                  {
                      // Now add pages to it: the first argument is the
                      // label for the tab, the second argument is the
                      // contents of the page.
                      viewer.add(Integer.toString(i), new MyPage(i));
                  }

                  // Last add the viewer to the applet window.
                  add(viewer);
              }
          }

          // MyPage - Display sample text in the Arial font, showing all
          //          combinations of available properties.
          class MyPage extends UIPanel
          {
              // nNames - Used as the label for the three groups;
              //          these are the types of font.
              String[] nNames = new String[3] {"Plain",
                                               "Bold",
                                               "Italic"};
```

```
// nStyles - These are the types of font available
//           when you are creating an FxFont object.
int[] nStyles = new int[3]{FxFont.PLAIN,
                           FxFont.BOLD,
                           FxFont.ITALIC};

// nFlags - These are the possible flags when you are creating
//          an FxFont object.
int[] nFlags = new int[3]{0,
                          FxFont.STRIKEOUT,
                          FxFont.UNDERLINE};

// MyPage - Create a page consisting of three groups.
MyPage(int nFontSize)
{
    // Use a vertical layout for the three groups.
    setLayout(new UIVerticalFlowLayout());
    for (int i = 0; i < nStyles.length; i++)
    {

        // Create a group for each font type.
        UIGroup group = new UIGroup(nNames[i]);
        group.setLayout(new UIRowLayout(nFlags.length));

        // Put a sample of each flag type in the group.
        for (int j = 0; j < nFlags.length; j++)
        {

            // Create the font using the indicated type and
            // flags - use a different size for each page.
            FxFont font = new FxFont("Arial",
                                     nStyles[i],
                                     nFontSize,
                                     nFlags[j]);

            // Now create a sample using that font,...
            UIDrawText text = new UIDrawText("Sample");
            text.setFont(font);

            // ...and add it to the group.
            group.add(text);
        }

        // Add the group to the page.
        add(group);
    }
}
```

The *init* function follows the classic steps given at the beginning of this chapter. First it creates an empty *UITabViewer* object named *viewer*. Next it begins adding pages of class *MyPage*, one for each font size from 8-point up to but not including 36-point. The call to *Integer.toString(int)* converts the integer point-size value to a *String* object. This string is used as the label on the *MyPage* tab. Last *init* adds the *viewer* object to the applet window.

The constructor for the *MyPage* class combines the *PLAIN*, *BOLD*, and *ITALIC* properties with *Normal (0)*, *STRIKEOUT*, and *UNDERLINE* to create nine font styles. The text string *"Sample"* is displayed in each of these font styles, giving the user an example of what each style looks like.

The program arranges these samples in a column of three groups. The *UIVertical-FlowLayout* layout manager ensures that the groups are placed one above the other. Each group contains three samples, arranged from left to right using the *UIRowLayout* layout manager.

Adding an Image to a Tab

The Tab02 sample program modifies Tab01 in three ways. First, it demonstrates how the *UIItem* class can be used to add a graphic to accompany the text. Second, Tab02 encapsulates the details of creating the tabbed viewer in the class *MyTabViewer*. Third, the tab creation process has been moved into the *MyPage* class. These moves pull the details of creating the tabbed viewer out of the *init* function, which in a normal applet might be performing multiple operations in addition to creating a tabbed viewer. In this way, the *init* function is completely uncoupled from the details of the tabbed viewer itself.

The Tab02 program is shown here:

```
// Tab02 - This applet is similar to Tab01, except it
//         loads an image for the tab and rearranges
//         some of the functions by uncoupling the
//         tabbed viewer maintenance from the main
//         applet code.
import java.applet.*;
import java.awt.*;

import com.ms.ui.*;
import com.ms.ui.event.*;
import com.ms.fx.*;

import Application;
import Images;
```

```java
public class Tab02 extends AwtUIApplet
{
    Tab02()
    {
        super(new MyApplet());
    }

    public static void main(String[] arg)
    {
        System.out.println("Cannot execute as an application.");
    }
}


class MyApplet extends UIApplet
{
    // init - Add a MyTabViewer object to the applet window.
    public void init()
    {
        add(new MyTabViewer(this));
    }
}


// MyTabViewer   Put tabbed viewer stuff into a separate
//               subclass.
class MyTabViewer extends UITabViewer
{
    MyTabViewer(MyApplet parent)
    {
        // Load the image that will appear next to the tab text.
        Images images = new Images(parent, "ball.gif");
        images.load();

        // Pass this image to the tab pages to use in creating
        // the tabs.
        for (int i = 8; i < 36; i++)
        {
            // Create the page as before.
            MyPage page = new MyPage(images, i);

            // Load the UIItem object containing the graphic
            // and text for the tab.
            UIItem tab = page.getTab();

            // Now use the page contents and the tab label to
            // create the tab page and add it to the tabbed viewer.
            // (Use addTab instead of add for UIItem objects.)
            addTab(tab, page);
        }
```

>>

>>

```
                        // Set the background color of the applet to match
                        // that of the image.
                        setBackground(new FxColor(0xbf, 0xbf, 0xbf));
            }
        }

// MyPage - This class is similar to that in Tab01 except
//             for the creation of the tab label object.
class MyPage extends UIPanel
{
        // tab - The tab to be used for this page
        UIItem tab = null;

        // nNames - Used as the label for the three groups,
        //             these are the types of font.
        static String[] nNames = new String[3] {"Plain",
                                                "Bold",
                                                "Italic"};

        // nStyles - These are the types of fonts available when you
        //             are creating an FxFont object.
        static int[] nStyles = new int[3]{FxFont.PLAIN,
                                          FxFont.BOLD,
                                          FxFont.ITALIC};

        // nFlags - These are the possible flags when you are creating
        //             an FxFont object.
        static int[] nFlags  = new int[3]{0,
                                          FxFont.STRIKEOUT,
                                          FxFont.UNDERLINE};

        // MyPage - Create tab pages using a fancier tab.
        MyPage(Images images, int nFontSize)
        {
            // Create the tab first:
            // get the image to use.
            Image image = images.getImage();

            // Convert the font size to a String object.
            String label = Integer.toString(nFontSize);

            // Now create a UIItem object using that image and
            // that string.
            tab = new UIItem(image, label);
```

```
        // Just for effect, set the font of the tab
        // label to match the page setting.
        FxFont tabFont = new FxFont("Arial",
                                    FxFont.PLAIN,
                                    nFontSize);
        tab.setFont(tabFont);

        // From here on, Tab02 is the same as Tab01.
        setLayout(new UIVerticalFlowLayout());
        for (int i = 0; i < nStyles.length; i++)
        {

            UIGroup group = new UIGroup(nNames[i]);
            group.setLayout(new UIRowLayout(nFlags.length));

            for (int j = 0; j < nFlags.length; j++)
            {
                UIDrawText text = new UIDrawText("Sample");
                FxFont font = new FxFont("Arial",
                                         nStyles[i],
                                         nFontSize,
                                         nFlags[j]);
                text.setFont(font);
                group.add(text);
            }

            add(group);
        }
    }

    // getTab - Return the tab created by the constructor.
    UIItem getTab()
    {
        return tab;
    }
}
```

Since all of the tabbed viewer maintenance code is now in the *MyTabViewer* and *MyPage* classes, Tab02's *init* method need do nothing more than add an object of class *MyTabViewer* to the applet window. The *MyTabViewer* constructor begins by creating an object of class *Images* to load the image ball.gif. The call to *images.load* performs the actual load operation. The constructor then enters the same loop as in Tab01, creating pages for each font size from 8-point to 35-point.

When each *MyPage* object is created, it not only creates the font page, using basically the same steps as in Tab01, but also creates the tab label of class *UIItem*. The *MyTabViewer* constructor reads this label by calling *page.getTab* and then adds both the label and the page itself to the tabbed viewer by calling *add(tab, page)*.

The results of Tab02 are shown in Figure 11-2.

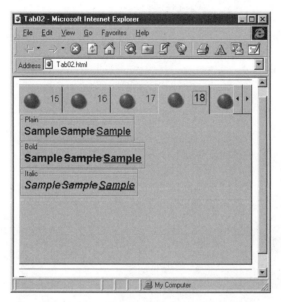

FIGURE 11-2   *The output of the Tab02 applet, showing small image objects on the tabs.*

ADDING ACTION TO THE TABBED VIEWER

The previous example programs used the tabbed viewer as an output device. The following example applet, Tab03, demonstrates how to use the tabbed viewer as an input device as well. This version of the tabbed applet reads the user selection and displays a sample string in that font.

```
// Tab03 - This version of the Tab applet adds the ability to
//         read user selections from
//         the tab pages.
import java.applet.*;
import java.awt.*;
```

```
import com.ms.ui.*;
import com.ms.ui.event.*;
import com.ms.fx.*;

import Application;
import Images;

public class Tab03 extends AwtUIApplet
{
    Tab03()
    {
        super(new MyApplet());
    }

    public static void main(String[] arg)
    {
        System.out.println("Cannot execute as an application.");
    }
}

class MyApplet extends UIApplet
{
    // text - The following text field is used to display
    //        the user's font selection.
    UIDrawText text = new MyDrawText();

    // init - Add a MyTabViewer object to the applet window.
    public void init()
    {
        setLayout(new UIBorderLayout());
        add(text, "North");
        add(new MyTabViewer(this), "Center");
    }

    // setSampleFont - Report the font selected by the user to
    //                 the applet.
    public void setSampleFont(FxFont font)
    {
        // If we get a font...
        if (font != null)
        {
            // ...and if it's really a font,...
            if (font instanceof FxFont)
            {
                // ...stuff it into the text field.
                text.setFont(font);
            }
        }
    }
}
```

```
// MyDrawText - Set up a fixed-size text field.
class MyDrawText extends UIDrawText
{
    MyDrawText()
    {
        super("Sample");
    }

    static Dimension d = new Dimension(100, 60);
    public Dimension getPreferredSize()
    {
        return d;
    }
}

// MyTabViewer - Put tabbed viewer stuff into a separate
//               subclass.
class MyTabViewer extends UITabViewer
{
    MyApplet parent;

    MyTabViewer(MyApplet parent)
    {
        this.parent = parent;

        Images images = new Images(parent, "ball.gif");
        images.load();

        for (int i = 8; i < 36; i++)
        {
            MyPage page = new MyPage(images, i);
            UIItem tab = page.getTab();
            addTab(tab, page);
        }

        setBackground(new FxColor(0xbf, 0xbf, 0xbf));
    }
}

// MyPage - Display sample text in the Arial font, showing all
//          combinations of available properties.
class MyPage extends UIPanel
{
    MyTabViewer parent = null;

    // tab - The tab to be used for this page
    UIItem tab = null;
```

```
// nNames - Used as the label for the three groups,
//          these are the types of font.
static String[] nNames = new String[3] {"Plain",
                                         "Bold",
                                         "Italic"};


// nStyles - These are the types of font available when you
//           are creating an FxFont object.
static int[] nStyles = new int[3]{FxFont.PLAIN,
                                  FxFont.BOLD,
                                  FxFont.ITALIC};


// nFlags - These are the possible flags when you are creating
//          an FxFont object.
static int[] nFlags  = new int[3]{0,
                                  FxFont.STRIKEOUT,
                                  FxFont.UNDERLINE};


// MyPage - Create a page consisting of three groups.
MyPage(Images images, int nFontSize)
{
    // Create the tab first.
    Image Image = Images.getImage();
    String label = Integer.toString(nFontSize);
    FxFont tabFont = new FxFont("Arial",
                                FxFont.PLAIN,
                                nFontSize);
    tab = new UIItem(image, label);
    tab.setFont(tabFont);

    // Use a vertical layout for the three groups.
    setLayout(new UIVerticalFlowLayout());
    for (int i = 0; i < nStyles.length; i++)
    {

        // Create a group for each font type.
        UIGroup group = new UIGroup(nNames[i]);
        group.setLayout(new UIRowLayout(nFlags.length));

        // Put a sample of each flag type in the group.
        for (int j = 0; j < nFlags.length; j++)
        {
            group.add(new MyFontText(nStyles[i],
                                     nFontSize,
                                     nFlags[j]));
        }
    }
```

>>

```
                // Add the group to the page.
                add(group);
            }
        }

        UIItem getTab()
        {
            return tab;
        }
    }


    // MyFontText - These are the draw text fields that are
    //              added to the tab pages, but they have
    //              a listener defined.
    class MyFontText extends UIDrawText
    {
        FxFont font = null;

        // MFTListener - This is our mouse listener class.
        class MFTListener implements IUIMouseListener
        {
            // mouseClicked - Called when the user
            //                clicks on this text field
            public void mouseClicked(UIMouseEvent e)
            {
                // Work our way up the chain of items,
                // starting with the parent MyFontText
                // object.
                IUIComponent comp = MyFontText.this;
                while ((comp = comp.getParent()) != null)
                {
                    // When we hit the applet,...
                    if (comp instanceof MyApplet)
                    {
                        // ...pass the font information.
                        MyApplet parent = (MyApplet)comp;
                        parent.setSampleFont(font);
                    }
                }
            }
```

```
        // We don't care about the following methods.
        public void mouseEntered(UIMouseEvent e){}
        public void mouseExited(UIMouseEvent e){}
        public void mousePressed(UIMouseEvent e){}
        public void mouseReleased(UIMouseEvent e){}
    }

    MyFontText(int nStyle, int nFontSize, int nFlag)
    {
        super("Sample");

        // Set us up with the indicated font,...
        font = new FxFont("Arial",
                          nStyle,
                          nFontSize,
                          nFlag);
        setFont(font);

        // ...and establish our mouse listener.
        addMouseListener(new MFTListener());
    }
}
```

The *init* method of this applet adds a text field to the top of the applet window and the *MyTabViewer* object to the center. The text field, of class *MyTextField*, contains the text string *"Sample"*.

The *MyTextField* class also overrides the *getPreferredSize* method in order to allocate sufficient space for the text field to handle even the largest font. Otherwise, the layout manager will allocate only enough space for the text field to display a string 10 points high (the size of the string with which the text field was created).

In addition to the required *init* method, the *MyApplet* class also implements the *setSampleFont(FxFont)* method. This method sets the sample text string to the font specified. The checks at the beginning of the function merely verify that the font provided is not *null* and that it is a valid instance of *FxFont*. If either of these tests fail, the function call has no effect.

A more conservative approach would be to use an illegal argument exception because no function should be calling *setSampleFont* with a font other than a valid *FxFont*.

The *MyTabViewer* class is unchanged from its Tab02 equivalent. The *MyPage* class also is the same except that it uses *MyFontText* in place of *UIDrawText* to display the various sample strings.

MyFontText extends the *UIDrawText* class in two ways: First, it saves the font created to display the "Sample" string. Second, as you might have guessed, *MyFontText* adds a mouse listener.

The mouse listener, named *MFTListener*, implements the *IUIMouseListener* interface. To do so, it must include the five methods *mouseClicked*, *mouse-Entered*, *mouseExited*, *mousePressed*, and *mouseReleased*. Because we aren't interested in the last four methods, the functions provided for these operations don't actually do anything. Nevertheless, they must be included or the interface will not be completely implemented.

The *mouseClicked* function, which is called when the user clicks on the *MyFont-Text* object, passes the font associated with this object to the parent applet. To find the parent applet, *mouseClicked* works its way up the chain from parent to parent until it finds an object of class *MyApplet*.

NOTE

This is a different approach from that taken in most of the examples in this book. Personally, I prefer passing the parent applet to the different subordinate objects explicitly. However, climbing the tree from parent to parent by calling *getParent* until we arrive at the parent applet is another valid approach. A third possible approach, calling *getParent* some fixed number of times based on our knowledge of the number of levels between *MyFontText* and *MyApplet*, is *not* valid. The problem with this approach is that it relies too heavily on the details of how the applet is constructed. Trivial changes to the applet in the future can cause the applet to stop working for reasons not obvious to the hapless maintenance programmer.

The results of the Tab03 program are shown in Figure 11-3.

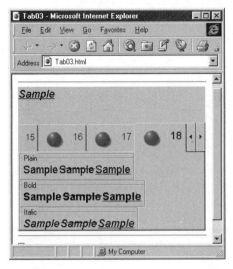

FIGURE 11-3 *The output of the Tab03 program, showing the 18-point, italic, underlined font selected.*

THE TABBED VIEWER VS. THE PROPERTY PAGE DIALOG BOX

After examining the preceding tab examples, you will undoubtedly have noticed the similarity between the tabbed viewer and the property page dialog box (demonstrated in Chapter 10, "Dialog Boxes"). In fact, the tabbed viewer can be used to implement a property page dialog box of sorts. The following sample program, Tab04, demonstrates a tabbed viewer version of the property page dialog box from Chapter 10:

```
// Tab04 - This is a UITabViewer version of the UIPropertyPage
//         object in the PropertyPage01 program. Notice how
//         similar the two programs are. The biggest differences
//         are:
//         1) The tabbed viewer cannot be modal.
//         2) The tabbed viewer does not have built-in
//            OK, Cancel, and Apply buttons.
import java.applet.*;
import java.awt.*;

import com.ms.ui.*;
import com.ms.ui.event.*;
import com.ms.fx.*;
```

>>

```
>>          import Application;

            public class Tab04 extends AwtUIApplet
            {
                Tab04()
                {
                    super(new MyApplet());
                }

                public static void main(String[] arg)
                {
                    System.out.println("Cannot execute as an application.");
                }
            }

            // MyApplet - This class is almost the same as in the property
            //            page-based example in Chapter 10.
            class MyApplet extends UIApplet
            {
                // This is the tabbed viewer.
                MyPropT prop;

                // The following text fields are used to display
                // what was set in the property pages.
                UIDrawText t1 = new UIDrawText();
                UIDrawText t2 = new UIDrawText();
                UIDrawText t3 = new UIDrawText();
                UIDrawText t4 = new UIDrawText();

                public void init()
                {
                    // Create a tabbed viewer.
                    prop = new MyPropT();

                    // Create a group to display the results, and add it
                    // to the top of the applet window.
                    UIGroup group = new UIGroup("Results");
                    group.add(t1);
                    group.add(t2);
                    group.add(t3);
                    group.add(t4);

                    setLayout(new UIBorderLayout());
                    add(group, "North");
```

```
        // Now attach the following three buttons to the viewer:
        // one to open the viewer,
        // a second to read and close the viewer, and
        // a third to close and cancel the viewer.
        UIPanel buttonPanel = new UIPanel();
        buttonPanel.setLayout(new UIRowLayout(3));
        buttonPanel.add(new MyPushButton(this,
                                         prop,
                                         MyPushButton.OPEN));
        buttonPanel.add(new MyPushButton(this,
                                         prop,
                                         MyPushButton.CLOSE));
        buttonPanel.add(new MyPushButton(this,
                                         prop,
                                         MyPushButton.CANCEL));
        add(buttonPanel, "South");
    }


    // paint - If the properties have been changed by the
    //         property page, displays the changes
    public void paint(FxGraphics fg)
    {
        // If properties have changed,...
        if (prop.getChanged())
        {
            // ...query the wizard's flags.
            t1.setValueText(prop.bAFCApplet ?
                            "AFC applet" : "Not AFC applet");
            t2.setValueText(prop.bIncludeComments ?
                            "Comments"   : "No comments");
            t3.setValueText(prop.bIncludeAppCommon?
                            "AppCommon" : "No AppCommon");
            t4.setValueText("Path = " + prop.sHTMLFileName);
        }
    }
}


// MyPushButton - A generic class for the property buttons
//                along the bottom of the applet window
class MyPushButton extends UIPushButton
{
    // The various classes of button...
    public static final int OPEN  = 0;
    public static final int CLOSE = 1;
    public static final int CANCEL = 2;
```

>>

>>

```
// ...and the corresponding labels
static final String[] sLabels = new String[2]
                                        {"Open",
                                         "Close",
                                         "Cancel"};


// parent - The parent applet
UIApplet parent;

// prop - The tabbed viewer to open, close, or cancel
MyPropT prop;

// nType - The type of button this is
int nType;

// PBAction - Either OPEN, CLOSE, or CANCEL
class PBAction implements IUIActionListener
{
    public void actionPerformed(UIActionEvent e)
    {
        // As long as this isn't CANCEL,...
        if (nType != CANCEL)
        {
            // ...update the tabbed viewer from the
            // stored data for an OPEN action, or the
            // other way around for a CLOSE.
            prop.update(nType == OPEN);
        }

        // For an OPEN, make the window visible;
        // for a CLOSE or CANCEL, make the window
        // invisible.
        prop.setVisible(nType == OPEN);

        // Now repaint the applet to force it to
        // display any changes.
        parent.repaint();
    }
}

MyPushButton(UIApplet parent, MyPropT prop, int nType)
{
    // Create a raised button with the appropriate label.
    super(sLabels[nType], UIPushButton.RAISED);
```

```
        // Save the constructor arguments.
        this.parent = parent;
        this.prop = prop;
        this.nType = nType;

        // Attach the listener.
        addActionListener(new PBAction());
    }
}

// MyPropT - A tabbed viewer as much like the PropertyPage01
//          dialog box as possible
class MyPropT extends UIFrame
{
    // This frame contains a single UITabViewer object.
    UITabViewer tabViewer;

    // The currently visible pages
    MyPage[] pages = new MyPage[2];

    // bChanged - true = Something has changed.
    boolean bChanged = false;

    // These are the flags to keep track of:
    // Page 1
    boolean bAFCApplet = true;
    boolean bIncludeComments = false;
    boolean bIncludeAppCommon = false;

    // Page 2
    String sHTMLFileName = new String("<null>");

    MyPropT()
    {
        // Create a frame to hold the tabbed viewer.
        super("Property Viewer");
        setSize(200, 150);

        // Now add a tabbed viewer with two pages.
        tabViewer = new UITabViewer();
        pages[0] = new Page1();
        pages[1] = new Page2();
        tabViewer.addTab(pages[0].getTab(), pages[0]);
        tabViewer.addTab(pages[1].getTab(), pages[1]);

        add(tabViewer);
    }
```

>>

```
// The following set methods set the corresponding
// properties.
void setAFCApplet(boolean bFlag)
{
    bAFCApplet = bFlag;
}
void setIncludeComments(boolean bFlag)
{
    bIncludeComments = bFlag;
}
void setIncludeAppCommon(boolean bFlag)
{
    bIncludeAppCommon = bFlag;
}
void setHTMLFileName(String s)
{
    if (s == null)
    {
        s = "<null>";
    }
    sHTMLFileName = s;
}

// update - Update the tabbed viewer from the stored
//          data (if bWrite is true), or the other
//          way around.
public void update(boolean bWrite)
{
    for (int i = 0; i < pages.length; i++)
    {
        if (bWrite)
        {
            pages[i].reset(this);
        }
        else
        {
            pages[i].doApplyAction(this);
            bChanged = true;
        }
    }
}

// getChanged - Returns the value of the changed
//              flag and then resets the flag
boolean getChanged()
```

```
        {
            boolean bChanged = this.bChanged;
            this.bChanged = false;
            return bChanged;
        }
    }


// MyPage - The base class for pages to be added to this
//          tabbed viewer
abstract class MyPage extends UIPanel
{
    // label - Label to be used for the tab
    UIItem label;

    // Constructor
    MyPage(Image image, String text)
    {
        // Create the tab label.
        label = new UIItem(image, text);
    }

    // getTab - Return a reference to the tab label.
    UIItem getTab()
    {
        return label;
    }

    // reset - Write from the data to the tabbed viewer.
    abstract void reset(MyPropT parent);

    // doApplyAction - Read from the tabbed viewer to the data.
    abstract void doApplyAction(MyPropT parent);
}

// Page1 - Implement the first tab page.
class Page1 extends MyPage
{
    UIItem label;

    UIRadioButton rb1 =
        new UIRadioButton("Use AFC to create applet");
    UIRadioButton rb2 =
        new UIRadioButton("Do not use AFC to create applet");
```

>>

```
UICheckButton cb1 = new UICheckButton("Include comments");
UICheckButton cb2 = new UICheckButton("Include AppCommon");

// Constructor
Page1()
{
    super(null, "Code Properties");

    addContent();
}

// addContent - This method is invoked from the constructor.
boolean addContent()
{
    UIRadioGroup rg = new UIRadioGroup();
    rg.add(rb1);
    rg.add(rb2);
    rb1.setChecked(true);

    UIGroup cg = new UIGroup();
    cg.add(cb1);
    cg.add(cb2);

    // Position the radio group at the top and the check
    // buttons immediately below.
    setLayout(new UIVerticalFlowLayout());
    add(rg);
    add(cg);

    return true;
}

// doApplyAction - Read from the tab page to the stored
//                 data.
void doApplyAction(MyPropT parent)
{
    // Read the radio button.
    parent.setAFCApplet(rb1.isChecked());

    // Read the two check buttons.
    parent.setIncludeComments(cb1.isChecked());
    parent.setIncludeAppCommon(cb2.isChecked());
}
```

```
    // reset - Invoked when the frame is made visible,
    //          this method resets the tab page.
    void reset(MyPropT parent)
    {
        rb1.setChecked(parent.bAFCApplet);
        rb2.setChecked(!parent.bAFCApplet);

        cb1.setChecked(parent.bIncludeComments);
        cb2.setChecked(parent.bIncludeAppCommon);
    }
}


// Page2
class Page2 extends MyPage
{
    UIEdit htmlPath = new UIEdit();

    Page2()
    {
        super(null, "HTML Path");

        addContent();
    }

    boolean addContent()
    {
        setLayout(new UIVerticalFlowLayout());
        add(new UIDrawText("Enter HTML file name:"));
        add(htmlPath);

        return true;
    }

    void doApplyAction(MyPropT parent)
    {
        parent.setHTMLFileName(htmlPath.getValueText());
    }

    void reset(MyPropT parent)
    {
        htmlPath.setValueText(parent.sHTMLFileName);
    }
}
```

NOTE

I have purposely kept the code here as close as possible to that of Property-Dialog01 in order to highlight the similarities.

In this program, *init* begins by creating a tabbed viewer of class *MyPropT*. This object is not added to the applet window since *MyPropT* is based on *UIFrame* and, hence, is designed to stand alone.

The *init* function continues by creating a group in which to display the results read from the tabbed viewer. This group consists of a series of four text fields, *t1* through *t4*. The group is added at the top of the window, just above the button panel.

The button panel contains three buttons, arranged from left to right using the *UIRowLayout* layout manager. Each button is an instance of *MyPushButton*. The third argument to the *MyPushButton* constructor indicates the button's function. The constructor starts by creating a raised button with a label corresponding to the type of button. Thus, an *OPEN*-type button is labeled *Open*, a *CLOSE*-type button is labeled *Close*, and a *CANCEL*-type button is labeled *Cancel*. The constructor then saves the button type as well as a reference to the parent applet and the tabbed viewer object. Before exiting, the constructor attaches an action listener.

When the user clicks one of the *MyPushButton* buttons, Java sends an event to *actionPerformed*. If the button clicked is not the Cancel button, this method calls *MyPropT.update*, passing it a value of *true* for the Open button or *false* for the Close button.

The *update* function loops through the pages attached to the tabbed viewer. If *update* is passed a *true* value (corresponding to the Open button), *update* calls *MyPage.reset*, which resets the contents of the page using the data stored in the tabbed viewer (that is, it writes to the viewer). If *update* is passed a *false* value (corresponding to the Close button), it calls *MyPage.doApplyAction*, which reads the data from the page and stores it back into the data fields of the tabbed viewer (that is, it reads from the viewer).

Once *update* has completed, the *actionPerformed* method continues by making the tabbed viewer visible if the button is of type *OPEN* and invisible otherwise. Finally, *actionPerformed* repaints the applet window to display any changes to the stored data. (This is actually necessary only for the *CLOSE* operation, but it doesn't hurt in the other cases.)

When the applet repaints the window, *MyApplet.paint* begins by checking whether any of the data within the *MyPropT* object *prop* has changed. The *MyPropT.getChanged* method returns a value of *true* if something has changed. This call resets the changed flag to *false*. If something has changed, *paint* reads the data out of *prop* and displays it in the text fields *t1* through *t4*.

The constructor for the *MyPropT* class begins by creating a *UIFrame* object named "Property Viewer" that measures 200 by 150 pixels. It then adds a *UITab-Viewer* object containing two pages, one of class *Page1* and the other of class *Page2*. The *MyPropT* class also defines numerous methods for setting internal data fields corresponding to the fields the user can input in the tab pages. (The other methods of *MyPropT* were discussed in earlier chapters.)

The classes *Page1* and *Page2* both extend the class *MyPage*. This abstract class extends *UIPanel* by building a tab label in the constructor and providing a *getTab* method with which to access it. In addition, *MyPage* defines two abstract methods that both *Page1* and *Page2* must implement: the write function *reset* and the read function *doApplyAction*.

The *Page1* and *Page2* classes are implemented here in much the same way the *Page* classes were defined in *PropertyPage01* (see Chapter 10, "Dialog Boxes"), even down to the inclusion of the *addContent* method. Of course, here the *addContent* method is invoked "manually" from the constructor when the object is constructed rather than being automatically called from AFC when the page is first displayed.

The *Page1* constructor begins by invoking the *MyPage* constructor, passing it a *null* value as the tab image and the string "*Code Properties*" as the tab text. (A *UIItem* object created using a *null* image acts for all intents and purposes like a *UIText* object.) The constructor continues by calling *addContent* to add the components to the page.

The *addContent* method first creates a radio button group to which it adds two radio buttons. It then creates a second group with two check buttons. Last *addContent* adds the radio button group to the page immediately above the check button group, using the *UIVerticalFlowLayout* layout manager.

The results of the Tab04 sample applet are shown in Figure 11-4 on the next page. This tabbed viewer looks very similar to the property page dialog box shown in Figure 10-4 (on page 342).

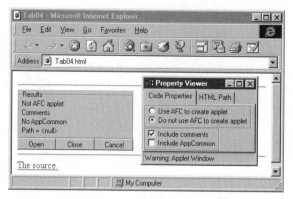

FIGURE 11-4   *The output of the Tab04 sample program.*

What Are the Differences?

So what are the differences between the property page dialog box and this tabbed viewer implementation? First, the property page dialog box can be either modal or nonmodal. The tabbed viewer can be only nonmodal. Second, the OK, Cancel, and Apply buttons are not intrinsic to the tabbed viewer. They could be added to the tabbed viewer, but in this example I put them in the applet window instead to demonstrate the point. Finally, since the tabbed viewer version is based on the *UIFrame* class, it can be moved, resized, and minimized without actually closing the "dialog box." The same is not true of the property page dialog box.

Nevertheless, in the majority of cases you will find yourself using the property page dialog box for tabbed input/output if for no other reason than for the standard look and feel it provides.

WHAT'S NEXT

In this chapter, we've examined how to use the tabbed viewer both for output and as a flexible replacement for the property page dialog box. The components in this chapter resemble the others that we have seen so far in that they are digital. A digital component has a specific value: a check box is on or off; a text field contains individual characters.

Whereas a digital component has a specific value, an analog component has an unspecified value: a slider indicates a range of data; a progress bar indicates a percentage of an overall processing time. In Chapter 12, "Analog Components," we'll examine such analog controls as the scrollbar for input and the progress bar for output. We'll also implement spinner controls and slider controls and discuss the typical uses of each.

Analog Components

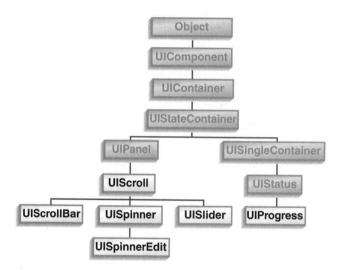

Most of the components we have seen so far have been discrete in nature. Check buttons are binary—they're either selected or not selected. Only one radio button can be enabled in a set. Text fields either input or output a finite number of characters.

The components described in this chapter are of the analog variety. Rather than being turned on or off, or being populated or unpopulated, analog components can indicate less specific conditions, such as "a whole lot" and "not too much," in addition to all and none.

USER INPUT CONTROLS: SCROLLBARS, SPINNERS, AND SLIDERS

Most of the analog components are user input controls. The classes that make up this group of components, *UIScrollBar*, *UISpinner*, *UISpinnerEdit*, and *UISlider*, all extend the class *UIScroll*.

The *UIScrollBar* Class

The *UIScrollBar* class is the basic workhorse of the analog controls. Scrollbars appear in a number of different applications, yet the programmer doesn't normally deal with the scrollbar directly. The most common use for scrollbars is to affect which part of an object is displayed when the object exceeds the size of the display window, and viewers such as *UIScrollViewer* automatically manage the scrollbars for you.

Scrollbars can also be used to accept input from the user, however. The following example applet, Scroll01, demonstrates how an application might use three scrollbars to allow the user to select a color. (This version of the applet doesn't actually read the scrollbar settings, but a later version will.)

```
// Scroll01 - Demonstrates the use of a
//            UIScrollBar object
import Application;

import java.awt.*;

import com.ms.ui.*;
import com.ms.ui.event.*;
import com.ms.fx.*;

public class Scroll01 extends AwtUIApplet
{
    Scroll01()
    {
        super(new MyApplet());
    }

    public static void main(String[] arg)
    {
        new Application(new MyApplet());
    }
}

class MyApplet extends UIApplet
{
    public void init()
    {
        // Put a label at the top,....
        setLayout(new UIBorderLayout());
        add(new MyLabelPanel(), "North");
```

```
        // ...the scroll panel in the middle,...
        add(new MyScrollPanel(), "Center");

        // ...and a small empty space at the
        // bottom.
        add(new UIText(" "), "South");
    }
}


// MyLabelPanel - Builds a set of labels
//                for the scrollbars
class MyLabelPanel extends UIPanel
{
    MyLabelPanel()
    {
        setLayout(new UIRowLayout(3));
        add(new UIText("Red"));
        add(new UIText("Green"));
        add(new UIText("Blue"));
    }
}


// MyScrollPanel - Builds a panel of three scrollbars,
//                 one for each color
class MyScrollPanel extends UIPanel
{
    MyScrollPanel()
    {
        setLayout(new UIRowLayout(3));

        // Build the group, and position the scrollbar
        // in the middle.
        UIGroup red = new MyGroup();
        red.setLayout(new UIBorderLayout());
        red.add(new UIScrollBar(UIScrollBar.VERTICAL,
                                0,
                                0xff,
                                0x0f,
                                1,
                                0x80), "Center");
```

```
                       // Repeat for green...
                       UIGroup green = new MyGroup();
                       green.setLayout(new UIBorderLayout());
                       green.add(new UIScrollBar(UIScrollBar.VERTICAL,
                                                 0,
                                                 0xff,
                                                 0x0f,
                                                 1,
                                                 0x80), "Center");

                       // ...and blue.
                       UIGroup blue = new MyGroup();
                       blue.setLayout(new UIBorderLayout());
                       blue.add(new UIScrollBar(UIScrollBar.VERTICAL,
                                                0,
                                                0xff,
                                                0x0f,
                                                1,
                                                0x80), "Center");

                   add(red);
                   add(green);
                   add(blue);
               }
       }


       // MyGroup - The default insets for a UIGroup object are 0;
       //           override that setting to provide a little room
       //           around the scrollbars.
       class MyGroup extends UIGroup
       {
           Insets insets = new Insets(3, 3, 3, 3);
           public Insets getInsets()
           {
               return insets;
           }
       }
```

The *init* function in this example creates the following three components:

- A panel of class *MyLabelPanel*, which is added at the top of the applet window to contain the Red, Green, and Blue labels

- A panel of class *MyScrollPanel*, which is added at the center of the applet window to contain the color controls

- A blank line, which is added at the bottom for aesthetic reasons

Adding the scroll panel at the center ensures that the scrollbars get whatever room is left over in the applet window after space has been allocated for the labels.

The *MyLabelPanel* constructor is straightforward. First it sets the layout, using the *UIRowLayout* layout manager to ensure that the labels are evenly spaced. Next it adds the three text fields that will serve as the scrollbar labels.

The class *MyScrollPanel* displays the actual scrollbars. It too begins by establishing a *UIRowLayout* layout manager to match the layout of the labels. It then creates a group to which it adds the red scrollbar. The arguments to the *UIScrollBar* constructor have the following significance:

- *VERTICAL* indicates that the scrollbar is to be oriented vertically.

- The next two arguments set the range of the scrollbar, from *0* through *0xff* (255). The values *0* and *0xff* were chosen because they represent the range of the color value.

- The next two arguments specify that the scrollbar steps by a value of *0x0f* when the user clicks in the trough (the area of the scrollbar to either side of the scrollbar slider) and by a value of *1* when she clicks the arrows.

- The final argument, *0x80*, sets the initial position of the scrollbar slider to the middle of its range.

The *MyGroup* container serves two purposes. First, it extends *UIGroup*, which provides an attractive border around the otherwise somewhat plain scrollbar. Second, *MyGroup* overrides the *getInsets* method to further enhance the appearance of the scrollbar.

MyScrollPanel creates three scrollbars, one each for red, green, and blue. These scrollbars are added to the panel in the same order as the labels. Although the application doesn't do anything yet, the appearance of the scrollbars, as shown in Figure 12-1 on the following page, is what we would expect for a color control.

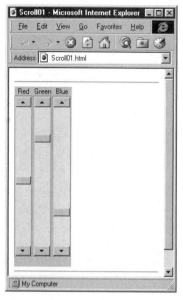

FIGURE 12-1   *The output of Scroll01, showing three vertical scrollbars combined into a color control.*

The *UISpinner* Class

I consider the *UISpinner* class misnamed. To me, the name implies a circular control similar to the knob on a radio. But the spinner control isn't like that at all. Instead, the spinner control has an arrow at each end just like a scrollbar but with nothing in between. I suppose the name derives from the fact that once the spinner gets to the maximum value in its range, it starts over again at the bottom—that is, it wraps around. (This wrapping is optional, by the way.)

In use, the spinner control is similar to its scrollbar cousin, as the following example applet, Spinner01, demonstrates:

```
// Spinner01 - Demonstrates the use of a UISpinner object.
//             This example creates horizontal spinners.
import Application;

import java.awt.*;

import com.ms.ui.*;
import com.ms.ui.event.*;
import com.ms.fx.*;
```

```
public class Spinner01 extends AwtUIApplet
{
    Spinner01()
    {
        super(new MyApplet());
    }

    public static void main(String[] arg)
    {
        new Application(new MyApplet());
    }
}

class MyApplet extends UIApplet
{
    public void init()
    {
        setLayout(new UIBorderLayout());

        // Position the label panel on the left,...
        add(new MyLabelPanel(), "West");

        // ...position the spinner panel in the middle,...
        add(new MySpinnerPanel(), "Center");

        // ...and position a small empty space on the right.
        add(new UIText(" "), "East");
    }
}

// MyLabelPanel - Builds a set of vertically oriented
//                labels
class MyLabelPanel extends UIPanel
{
    MyLabelPanel()
    {
        // Set up a grid of four rows and one column.
        setLayout(new UIGridLayout(4, 1, 0, 2));

        // Leave one row empty; this is where the text field goes.
        add(new UIText(" "));

        // Now add the labels.
        add(new UIText("Red"));
        add(new UIText("Green"));
        add(new UIText("Blue"));
    }
}
```

>>

```
// MySpinnerPanel - Create a set of three spinner controls,
//                  oriented horizontally.
class MySpinnerPanel extends UIPanel
{
    MySpinnerPanel()
    {
        // Build a group around the red spinner control.
        UIGroup red = new MyGroup();
        red.setLayout(new UIBorderLayout());
        red.add(new UISpinner(0,
                              0,
                              0xff,
                              0x0f,
                              1,
                              0x80), "Center");

        // Do it again for the green...
        UIGroup green = new MyGroup();
        green.setLayout(new UIBorderLayout());
        green.add(new UISpinner(0,
                                0,
                                0xff,
                                0x0f,
                                1,
                                0x80), "Center");

        // ...and again for the blue.
        UIGroup blue = new MyGroup();
        blue.setLayout(new UIBorderLayout());
        blue.add(new UISpinner(0,
                               0,
                               0xff,
                               0x0f,
                               1,
                               0x80), "Center");

        // Arrange the spinners in four rows by one column,
        // with a label in the first row.
        setLayout(new UIGridLayout(4, 1, 0, 2));
        add(new UIDrawText("Red/Green/Blue Spinner Controls"));
        add(red);
        add(green);
        add(blue);
    }
}
```

```
// MyGroup - Overrides the default insets of 0
class MyGroup extends UIGroup
{
    Insets insets = new Insets(3, 3, 3, 3);
    public Insets getInsets()
    {
        return insets;
    }
}
```

This example differs from Scroll01 primarily because it has a horizontal layout, not because the spinner control is spinner based as opposed to scrollbar based.

Because the spinner control is laid out horizontally, the labels now go on the left rather than at the top, with the blank space on the right. To achieve the proper effect for the labels, I used a grid layout that specified one column of four rows. The first row is blank because I intend to use this row for a label. The next three rows contain the names of the primary colors.

The *MySpinnerPanel* class starts out the same as *MyScrollPanel* in Scroll01 by building three color controls. Specifying a *0* as the first argument to the *UISpinner* constructor ensures that the controls are laid out horizontally. Once the controls have been built, they are added to the panel using the same one-column, four-row grid layout as was used for the labels. Once again, *MyGroup* provides a small inset to offset the spinner from its surrounding group border.

The results of the Spinner01 applet are shown in Figure 12-2.

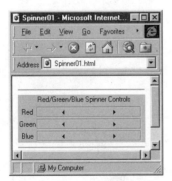

FIGURE 12-2   *The output of Spinner01.*

The *UISpinnerEdit* Class

Except for small controls involving a limited range, the spinner control is less than optimum. Even for our color application, it would take a long time to scroll from one end of the color spectrum to the other. The spinner/edit control addresses this problem by allowing the user to control the value either by using the analog spinner control or by entering the desired value directly into an edit control. The following example applet, Spinner02, demonstrates the spinner/edit control:

```
// Spinner02 - Similar to Spinner01, except here we use the
//              spinner/edit control
import java.awt.*;

import com.ms.ui.*;
import com.ms.ui.event.*;
import com.ms.fx.*;

import Application;

public class Spinner02 extends AwtUIApplet
{
    Spinner02()
    {
        super(new MyApplet());
    }

    public static void main(String[] arg)
    {
        new Application(new MyApplet());
    }
}

class MyApplet extends UIApplet
{
    public void init()
    {
        // Set up the same horizontal spinner panels as
        // in Spinner01.
        setLayout(new UIBorderLayout());
        add(new MyLabelPanel(), "West");
        add(new MySpinnerPanel(), "Center");
        add(new UIText(" "), "East");
    }
}
```

```
// MyLabelPanel - Same as in Spinner01
class MyLabelPanel extends UIPanel
{
    MyLabelPanel()
    {
        setLayout(new UIGridLayout(4, 1, 0, 2));
        add(new UIText(" "));
        add(new UIText("Red"));
        add(new UIText("Green"));
        add(new UIText("Blue"));
    }
}


// MySpinnerPanel - Same panel as in Spinner01, except
//                  this one is based on UISpinnerEdit and
//                  the logic is largely in MyGroup
class MySpinnerPanel extends UIPanel
{
    MySpinnerPanel()
    {
        UIGroup red   = new MyGroup();
        UIGroup green = new MyGroup();
        UIGroup bluc  = ncw MyGroup(),

        setLayout(new UIGridLayout(4, 1, 0, 2));
        add(new UIDrawText
                ("  Red/Green/Blue\nSpinner/Edit Controls"));
        add(red);
        add(green);
        add(blue);
    }
}


// MyGroup - Create a group around a UISpinnerEdit object.
class MyGroup extends UIGroup
{
    // EDITSTYLE - The edit style to use for our spinner/edit
    //             controls
    static final int EDITSTYLE =
        UISpinnerEdit.BORDER|UISpinnerEdit.CENTER;

    MyGroup()
    {
        setLayout(new UIBorderLayout());
```

>>

>>

```
// Create a spinner/edit control - this looks a lot like
// the UISpinner constructor call.
UISpinnerEdit spinner =
    new UISpinnerEdit(0,
                      EDITSTYLE,
                      0,
                      0xff,
                      0x0f,
                      1,
                      0x80);

// Position the control in the middle of the group.
add(spinner, "Center");

// Fetch the UIEdit component of the spinner/edit control.
// (This test is just for safety's sake - what
// we get back is always a UIEdit object.)
IUIComponent comp =
    spinner.getLayoutComponent(UISpinnerEdit.BUDDY);
if (comp instanceof UIEdit)
{
    UIEdit text = (UIEdit)comp;

    // Specify a large font.
    text.setFont(new FxFont("Arial", FxFont.PLAIN, 14));
}
}

// getInsets - Override the default UIGroup insets of 0.
Insets insets = new Insets(3, 3, 3, 3);
public Insets getInsets()
{
    return insets;
}
}
```

This example begins the same as Spinner01 by adding a *MyLabelPanel* object on the left and a *MySpinnerPanel* object in the middle of the applet window. The *MySpinnerPanel* object is much smaller here because the majority of the work of setting up the spinner control has been moved into the *MyGroup* subclass.

The *MyGroup* constructor begins by creating a spinner/edit control. The constructor for the *UISpinnerEdit* class takes the same arguments as the *UISpinner* class plus one more: the second argument defines the style of the edit portion of the control. I defined the EDITSTYLE constant to indicate that the edit field should have a border and that the text should be centered within the box. ("Centered" here does not mean that the text field is between the arrows of the spinner—the edit field is always on the left of the spinner control.)

Once the spinner/edit control has been added to the applet, *MyGroup* needs to change the font used to display the numeric value. This change is necessary because the default font for the *UISpinnerEdit* object is quite small. The *UISpinnerEdit* object labels its *UIEdit* component using a special index, somewhat curiously named *BUDDY* (as in "buddy component," I suppose). Calling *getLayoutComponent(UISpinnerEdit.BUDDY)* returns this component. I then set the font to 14-point plain Arial using the *setFont* method.

The results of the Spinner02 applet are shown in Figure 12-3. Now the user can either click the arrows of the spinner control or type directly into the edit text field to select a value.

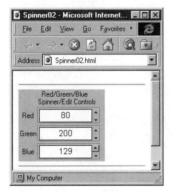

FIGURE 12-3   *The output of Spinner02.*

The *UISlider* Class

Another analog control is the slider represented by the class *UISlider*. This slider is designed to resemble the level controls common on the front of stereo equipment. In practice, the slider works the same as the other analog controls, which the following example applet, Slider01, demonstrates:

```
// Slider01 - Slider version of the Scroll01 example
import Application;

import java.awt.*;
```

>>

```
import com.ms.ui.*;
import com.ms.ui.event.*;
import com.ms.fx.*;

public class Slider01 extends AwtUIApplet
{
    Slider01()
    {
        super(new MyApplet());
    }

    public static void main(String[] arg)
    {
        new Application(new MyApplet());
    }
}

class MyApplet extends UIApplet
{
    public void init()
    {
        // Set up a label panel at the top, a
        // slider panel in the middle, and a small
        // blank line on the bottom (just for spacing).
        setLayout(new UIBorderLayout());
        add(new MyLabelPanel(), "North");
        add(new MySliderPanel(), "Center");
        add(new UIText(" "), "South");
    }
}

// MyLabelPanel - Create a panel consisting of the three
//                primary colors.
class MyLabelPanel extends UIPanel
{
    MyLabelPanel()
    {
        setLayout(new UIRowLayout(3));
        add(new UIText("Red"));
        add(new UIText("Green"));
        add(new UIText("Blue"));
    }
}
```

```
// MySliderPanel - Create a panel consisting of three
//                 vertical slider objects.
class MySliderPanel extends UIPanel
{
    MySliderPanel()
    {
        setLayout(new UIRowLayout(3));

        // Create a slider for each color.
        UISlider red = new UISlider(UISlider.VERTICAL,
                                    0,
                                    0xff,
                                    0x0f,
                                    1,
                                    0x80,
                                    UISlider.DEFAULTSPACING);
        UISlider green=new UISlider(UISlider.VERTICAL,
                                    0,
                                    0xff,
                                    0x0f,
                                    1,
                                    0x80,
                                    UISlider.DEFAULTSPACING);
        UISlider blue= new UISlider(UISlider.VERTICAL,
                                    0,
                                    0xff,
                                    0x0f,
                                    1,
                                    0x80,
                                    UISlider.DEFAULTSPACING);

        add(red);
        add(green);
        add(blue);
    }
}
```

This example is very similar to Scroll01. The *init* function begins by attaching a label panel to the top and the slider panel to the middle of the vertically oriented applet window. The blank line at the bottom enhances the appearance of the display.

The *MyLabelPanel* class uses a *UIRowLayout* layout manager to evenly space the red, green, and blue labels. The *MySliderPanel* class creates three vertically oriented sliders with the range *0* through *0xff* (255).

The results of the Slider01 applet are shown in Figure 12-4 on the following page.

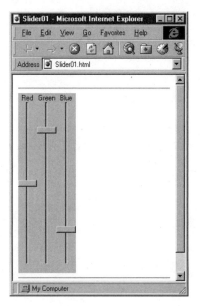

FIGURE 12-4   *The output of Slider01, showing the slider version of the three color controls.*

Adding Action to the Slider

So far, none of our analog controls have actually done anything. Let's convert Slider01 to a complete color control example program, Slider02. The lessons learned here apply directly to the other subclasses of *UIScroll*.

```
// Slider02 - Version of Slider01 that actually
//            reads the sliders and uses them to
//            set the color of an empty panel
import Application;

import java.awt.*;

import com.ms.ui.*;
import com.ms.ui.event.*;
import com.ms.fx.*;

public class Slider02 extends AwtUIApplet
{
    Slider02()
    {
        super(new MyApplet());
    }
```

```
    public static void main(String[] arg)
    {
        new Application(new MyApplet());
    }
}

class MyApplet extends UIApplet
{
    // control - This will be the slider control.
    UIFrame control;

    public void init()
    {
        // Create a field for the slider to adjust.
        UIPanel target = new UIPanel();

        // Add the target field and an explanatory message
        // to the applet window. (The target changes color
        // as we move the slider controls.)
        setLayout(new UIBorderLayout());
        add(new UIDrawText("  Move sliders\nto change color"),
            "North");
        add(target, "Center");

        // Now create the control slider.
        control = new MyControl(target);
        control.setVisible(true);
    }
}

// MyControl - Create a control containing three
//             sliders and a label.
class MyControl extends UIFrame
{
    MyControl(IUIComponent target)
    {
        // Give our frame a label.
        super("Color Control");

        // Set the correct size.
        setSize(100, 300);

        // Position the labels at the top, the sliders in the
        // middle, and a blank line at the bottom.
        add(new MyLabelPanel(), "North");
        add(new MySliderPanel(target), "Center");
        add(new UIDrawText(" "), "South");
    }
```

>>

```
         // handleEvent - When the user clicks the
         //                Close button,
         //                hide the frame.
         public boolean handleEvent(Event e)
         {
             if (e.id == Event.WINDOW_DESTROY)
             {
                 setVisible(false);
             }
             return super.handleEvent(e);
         }
     }


// MyLabelPanel - Create a label for the three
//                slider controls.
class MyLabelPanel extends UIPanel
{
     MyLabelPanel()
     {
         setLayout(new UIRowLayout(3));
         add(new UIText("Red"));
         add(new UIText("Green"));
         add(new UIText("Blue"));
     }
}


// MySliderPanel - Create a panel consisting of
//                 three sliders, one for each
//                 primary color.
class MySliderPanel extends UIPanel
{
     MySliderPanel(IUIComponent target)
     {
         setLayout(new UIRowLayout(3));

         // Set the initial color to match the slider settings.
         // (0x808080 is half of all colors, medium gray.)
         Color color = new Color(0x808080);
         target.setBackground(color);

         // Now create the three sliders,...
         UISlider red   = new MySlider(target, MySlider.RED);
         UISlider green = new MySlider(target, MySlider.GREEN);
         UISlider blue  = new MySlider(target, MySlider.BLUE);
```

```
            // ...and then add them to our panel.
            add(red);
            add(green);
            add(blue);
        }
    }

// MySlider - Implements a single color control slider
class MySlider extends UISlider
{
    // The three primary colors: for documentation
    // refer to primary school.
    public static final int RED   = 0;
    public static final int GREEN = 1;
    public static final int BLUE  = 2;

    // target - The object that will change color
    IUIComponent target;

    // nColor - This variable will have a value of
    //          RED, GREEN, or BLUE.
    int nColor;

    // nMasks - A set of bitmasks indicating where the
    //          red, green, and blue components of the
    //          color are located in the RGB color word
    static int[] nMasks = new int[3]
                            {0xff0000,
                             0x00ff00,
                             0x0000ff};

    // nShifts - These shifts indicate the position of
    //           the red, green, and blue components of
    //           the color in the RGB color word.
    static int[] nShifts= new int[3]
                            {16,
                              8,
                              0};

    // SliderListener - Called when the user moves the slider
    class SliderListener implements IUIAdjustmentListener
    {
        public void adjustmentValueChanged(UIAdjustmentEvent e)
        {
            // Read the slider. (Be sure it's in range.)
            int nValue = getYPosition();
            nValue &= 0xff;
```

```
            // Invert the sense. (We want the top
            // to be "full on" and not "full off.")
            nValue = 0xff - nValue;

            // Adjust the background color using this information.
            // First read the background color.
            Color color = target.getBackground();
            int nRGB = color.getRGB();

            // Now update "our" part of that color.
            nRGB &= ~nMasks[nColor];// Mask out our color,...
            nValue <<= nShifts[nColor];// ...position our value,...
            nRGB |= nValue;         // ...and put our new color in.

            // Update the background using the result.
            target.setBackground(new Color(nRGB));

            // Now force the background to be visible.
            target.repaint();
        }
    }

    // MySlider - Create the slider object.
    MySlider(IUIComponent target,     // Component to adjust.
             int nColor)              // This property specifies
                                      // the color according to
                                      // the internal RED,
                                      // GREEN, or BLUE value.
    {
        // Create a vertical slider that scales in increments of 1,
        // from 0 through 255.
        super(UISlider.VERTICAL,
              0,
              0xff,
              0x0f,
              1,
              0x80,
              UISlider.DEFAULTSPACING);

        // Save the input parameters.
        this.target = target;
        this.nColor = nColor;
```

```
// Verify that the color is in range.
switch (nColor)
{
    case RED:
    case GREEN:
    case BLUE:
        break;
    default:
        throw new IllegalArgumentException(
                "Invalid Slider Color");
}

// Attach the listener.
addAdjustmentListener(new SliderListener());
    }
}
```

Normally, the color control for a real-world application would be contained in a separate dialog box or frame. Therefore, this version of *init* creates a separate frame of class *MyFrame* to contain the color controls. The *UIPanel* field *target* is placed in the center of the applet window—this is the component that will change color as the user drags the color controls.

The constructor for *MyControl* begins much like the *init* function in Slider01. After setting the size of the *MyControl* frame object, the constructor adds a label panel at the top and a slider panel in the middle of the frame. (The HTML file set the size of the applet window in Slider01.) The *handleEvent* method is provided to handle the WINDOW_DESTROY event triggered when the user clicks the Close button in the upper right corner of the frame. The *handleEvent* method responds by hiding the frame.

The *MyLabelPanel* class in Slider02 is identical to its predecessors. *MySlider-Panel* starts by initializing the target's background color to half bright. The value *0x808080* corresponds, in order, to a red value of *0x80*, halfway between *0x0* and *0xff* (the full range for the red color); a green value of *0x80*; and a blue value of *0x80*. *MySliderPanel* continues by adding three *MySlider* objects, each devoted to a different primary color.

The class *MySlider* extends the *UISlider* class by adding the color controls. The constructor for the class *MySlider* begins by initializing the *UISlider* object as vertically oriented with a range from *0* through *0xff* and an initial value of *0x80*. The *MySlider* constructor goes on to save the target component (the component whose color will change when the user drags the slider) and the color value for this slider (*RED, GREEN,* or *BLUE*). The *switch* statement here demonstrates how the arguments to the constructor should be tested to generate a reasonable error message—in this case, the constructor throws an *Illegal-ArgumentException* error if the color value is not one of the expected values of *RED*, *GREEN*, and *BLUE*. Last the *MySlider* constructor attaches the adjustment listener.

The adjustment listener, *SliderListener.adjustmentValueChanged*, is invoked when the user drags the slider bar. It responds by first reading the value of the slider by calling *getYPosition*. (It would call *getXPosition* if the slider were horizontally oriented.) This function returns a value that should be from *0* through *0xff*, the range of the slider; however, ANDing *nValue* using *0xff* ensures this. The default condition is for the top of the slider to represent the minimum value and the bottom to represent the maximum value. The following statement inverts this condition, making the top *0xff* and the bottom *0x0*:

```
nValue = 0xff - nValue
```

At this point, *adjustmentValueChanged* has the desired intensity for the current color hue. What it needs to do is find the current background color of the target component and adjust its value to match this desired intensity. To do this, *adjustmentValueChanged* reads the background color of the target by calling *getBackground*. It converts this color to an RGB value by calling *getRGB*. This RGB value consists of a number in the form *0xrrggbb*, where *rr* is equal to the red setting, *gg* the green setting, and *bb* the blue setting.

The next three statements in *adjustmentValueChanged* match the corresponding color with the value read from the slider. The following table demonstrates how the RGB color values are manipulated using the *adjustValueChanged* function—in this case, for the green slider.

Expression	nValue	nRGB	Explanation
`<initial>`	*0x0000GG*	*0xrrggbb*	Initial value.
`nRGB &= ~nMasks[nColor]`	*0x0000GG*	*0xrr00bb*	Remove the old green value from the RGB value.
`nValue <<= nShifts[nColor]`	*0x00GG00*	*0xrr00bb*	Position the value read from the slider to go into the green slot in the *nValue* value.
`nRGB |= nValue`	*0x00GG00*	*0xrrGGbb*	Put the new green value into the green slot in the RGB value.

The newly recalculated *nRGB* value is used to set the background color of the target component. Calling *target.repaint* forces the target to be repainted in order to make the change visible.

Figure 12-5 shows the Slider02 applet with two very different colors selected. (It's a bit difficult to discern in a black-and-white reproduction, but in the image on the left the target panel is light blue and in the image on the right the target panel is a dark violet.)

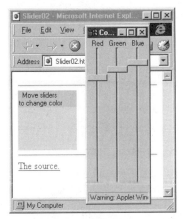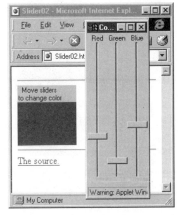

FIGURE 12-5   *The output of Slider02, showing the sample panel with two very different background colors.*

THE PROGRESS OUTPUT INDICATOR

So far, we have looked at controls primarily of the input variety. Now we'll examine an output-only device, the progress indicator component, which is used to demonstrate to the not-always-so-patient user how far along the application is in what could be a lengthy process.

The *UIProgress* class is easy to use. But before you start, you must decide how to divide the processing that your program is doing in order to know when to update the progress indicator. If you are performing a series of calculations, for example, you might be able to use the number of calculations performed vs. the total number of calculations as an indication of progress. Only you can decide what fits best.

The following example applet, Progress01, demonstrates a progress indicator that keeps track of the number of images loaded. This is a reasonable use for the progress indicator since the loading of large image files, especially over a modem connection, is a lengthy process. Knowing the state of this operation is helpful to the user.

```java
// Progress01 - Demonstrates the progress indicator by
//               using it to show the progress of loading
//               several JPG files
import java.applet.*;
import java.awt.*;

import com.ms.ui.*;
import com.ms.ui.event.*;
import com.ms.fx.*;

import Application;
import Images;

public class Progress01 extends AwtUIApplet
{
    Progress01()
    {
        super(new MyApplet());
    }

    public static void main(String[] arg)
    {
        System.out.println("Cannot execute as an application.");
    }
}


class MyApplet extends UIApplet
{
    // The names of six images. (Here we use six copies of a single
    // image, but that doesn't matter.)
    String[] sImageNames = new String[6]
        {"Image1.jpg", "Image2.jpg", "Image3.jpg",
         "Image4.jpg", "Image5.jpg", "Image6.jpg"};
```

```
        /* // You could use the default GIF files generated
           // by the Applet Wizard, but these images load too fast
           // when the files are local.
        {"img0001.gif", "img0002.gif", "img0003.gif",
         "img0004.gif", "img0005.gif", "img0006.gif",
         "img0007.gif", "img0008.gif", "img0009.gif",
         "img0010.gif", "img0011.gif", "img0012.gif",
         "img0013.gif", "img0014.gif", "img0015.gif",
         "img0016.gif", "img0017.gif", "img0018.gif"};
        */

    public void init()
    {
        // Create the Images object, BUT DON'T LOAD IT.
        Images images = new Images(this, sImageNames);

        // Put a text string at the top,...
        setLayout(new UIGridLayout(3, 1, 0, 10));
        UIDrawText text =
            new UIDrawText("Load progress indicator:");
        add(text);

        // ...the progress bar in the middle,...
        MyProgress progress = new MyProgress(images);
        add(progress);

        // ...and the push button to start loading the
        // images at the bottom.
        add(new MyPushButton(images, progress, text));
    }
}

// MyPushButton - Loads the Images object when the button
//                is clicked
class MyPushButton extends UIPushButton
{
    // images - The Images object to load
    Images images;

    // progress - The progress object that is
    //            monitoring the image load
    MyProgress progress;

    // text - Indicate the status in this text field.
    UIDrawText text;
```

>>

```
// PBListener - Invoked when the user clicks the
//             button
class PBListener implements IUIActionListener
{
    public void actionPerformed(UIActionEvent e)
    {
        // Start the progress indicator so that
        // it can begin checking how well the
        // image load process is going.
        progress.start();

        // Change the text to indicate that
        // we've started.
        text.setValueText("Loading...");

        // Go ahead and start the load process.
        images.load();

        // Done!
        text.setValueText("Complete!");
    }
}

// constructor - Typical push button constructor
MyPushButton(Images images,
            MyProgress progress,
            UIDrawText text)
{
    super(new UIText("Load Images"), RAISED);

    this.images = images;
    this.progress = progress;
    this.text    = text;

    addActionListener(new PBListener());
}
}

// MyProgress - Progress indicator to monitor the
//              loading of images
class MyProgress extends UIGroup implements Runnable
{
    // images - Images object on which to monitor progress
    Images images;
```

```
// thread - The load process is monitored from a
//          separate thread.
Thread thread;

// progress - The progress indicator object to use to display
//            progress
UIProgress progress;

MyProgress(Images images)
{
    // Save the Images object.
    this.images = images;

    // Lay out the progress panel.
    setLayout(new UIBorderLayout());

    // Position a legend at the bottom...
    UIPanel legend = new UIPanel();
    legend.setLayout(new UIBorderLayout());
    legend.setFont(new FxFont("Arial", FxFont.PLAIN, 8));
    legend.add(new UIText("0%"), "West");
    legend.add(new UIText("100%"), "East");
    add(legend, "South");

    // ...and a progress display over the rest of the
    // progress panel.
    progress = new UIProgress(images.getTargetProgress());
    progress.setBackground(new FxColor(0xffffff));
    add(progress, "Center");
}

// start - Begin monitoring the Images object.
public void start()
{
    Thread thread = new Thread(this);
    thread.start();
}

// run - This method will be called from the browser when
//       the thread is started in the start method above.
public void run()
{
    // getTargetProgress returns the target value
    // (that is, the value that represents 100%).
    int nTargetProgress = images.getTargetProgress();
    int nProgress;
```

>>

>>

```
    try
    {
        // Keep monitoring the images until the load
        // process is complete.
        do
        {
            // Load the progress so far.
            nProgress = images.getLoadProgress();

            // Update the progress bar using that number.
            progress.setPos(nProgress);

            // Now pause a bit before checking again.
            thread.sleep(50);

        } while (nProgress < nTargetProgress);
    }
    catch (InterruptedException e)
    {
        progress.setPos(0);
    }
    }
}
```

The *init* method begins by creating an *Images* object containing a set of images to be loaded. By default, I have specified six different files all containing the same Hubble Space Telescope image of Jupiter. (I chose this image because it is big and takes a certain amount of time to load even from a local hard disk.) Notice that once the *Images* object has been created, *init* does not call *load* to load the images. It is the load operation that we want to monitor.

The *init* function continues by adding a status text field at the top of the applet window, a progress indicator of class *MyProgress* in the middle of the window, and a push button of class *MyPushButton* at the bottom of the window. When the user clicks the push button, its action listener method *actionPerformed* starts the progress indicator, updates the applet's status text field to "*Loading...*", and begins the load operation. Once the image loading is complete, *actionPerformed* changes the text field to "*Complete!*".

The constructor for the class *MyProgress* begins by establishing a group containing a legend panel at the bottom. This legend puts a 0% on the far left and a 100% on the far right below the *UIProgress* indicator. The argument to the *UIProgress* constructor indicates the value that represents 100%—in this case, the value returned from *Images.getTargetProgress*.

Notice that the *MyProgress* class is designed to execute in a separate thread. When the user clicks the push button that initiates the image load process, *actionPerformed* calls *MyProgress.start*. *MyProgress.start* begins execution of *MyProgress.run* in a separate thread. The *run* method sits in a loop, calling *images.getLoadProgress*, updating the progress bar by calling *setPos* with the value returned, and then sleeping for 50 milliseconds. Executing in a separate process allows the *MyProgress* class to monitor the load process without interfering with it.

Once the progress as reported by *getLoadProgress* reaches the target value as reported by *getTargetProgress*, *run* returns, thereby terminating the task. The entire *Images* class is described in Appendix B, "Utility Classes Used in This Book"; the progress section is repeated here:

```
class Images
{
    MediaTracker tracker;

    // Other methods...

    // Load progress functions:
    // getTargetProgress - Returns the maximum load
    //                     progress score
    public int getTargetProgress()
    {
        return getChildCount();
    }

    // getLoadProgress - Returns the current load progress
    public int getLoadProgress()
    {
        int nScore = 0;

        // If there is no tracker,...
        if (tracker == null)
        {
            // ...we haven't started yet, so the score
            // must be 0.
            return 0;
        }

        // Loop through each image added to the MediaTracker.
        for (int i = 0; i < img.length; i++)
        {
            // Get the status.
            int nStatus = tracker.statusID(i, false);
```

>>

>>

```
        // If the status is COMPLETE,...
        if (nStatus == MediaTracker.COMPLETE)
        {
            // ...score a point.
            nScore += 1;
        }
    }

    // Return the accumulated score.
    return nScore;
    }
}
```

The progress indicator scheme used by the *Image* class is to assign one point for each completely loaded image. The method *getTargetProgress* simply returns the number of children—that is, the number of images to be loaded. This number will be the value of *getLoadProgress* when all of the images have been loaded.

The *getLoadProgress* method first checks to see whether a *MediaTracker* class *tracker* object has been assigned. If not, the application still has to call *Image.load*, so the progress must be *0* (no progress). If there is a *tracker* object, *getLoadProgress* loops through the images attached to it and checks the status of each. The overall progress score, *nScore*, is incremented by 1 for every image whose status is COMPLETE. The final progress is the value of *nScore* once the loop has terminated.

Figure 12-6 shows Progress01 halfway through the load process. (This static image doesn't really do the application justice, however, as it is quite dynamic.) When loading images from a local hard disk, the progress indicator moves rapidly from left to right. When loading images over a phone line, the progress is a good bit slower.

FIGURE 12-6   *The output of Progress01, showing the images about halfway loaded.*

WHAT'S NEXT

In this chapter, we have examined analog controls such as scrollbars, sliders, and progress indicators. This is the last chapter devoted directly to AFC components.

In Chapter 13, "Resource Files," we will deal with a unique class within the AFC—the *ResourceDecoder* class. Using this class, the programmer can generate large, complex windows by using an editing tool much like Microsoft Paint. The *ResourceDecoder* class automatically converts these programmer-created resource windows to AFC objects.

Resource Files

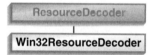

All the examples in this book thus far have been Microsoft Windows–independent. Now we will look at a Windows-specific class—the *Win32ResourceDecoder* class—that is based on *Resource-Decoder*, an abstract AFC class that contains all of the properties described in this chapter. Although, as of this writing, *Win32ResourceDecoder* is the only nonabstract resource decoder class, the techniques discussed here can be applied to non-Windows systems.

This chapter also differs from previous chapters in that all the techniques demonstrated up to now display components by creating instances of AFC classes and combining them in code. Here we'll look at another way to approach displaying components: the resource editor.

THE RESOURCE EDITOR

The resource editor built into the Microsoft Visual J++ Integrated Development Environment (IDE) is much like a graphical drawing program. The programmer edits an image by selecting items from a palette of objects and placing them on the image. Once the objects are placed, the programmer can describe a particular object in more detail by double-clicking it and filling out the dialog box that appears. Resource editors increase programmer productivity by allowing programmers to define GUI-intensive features such as menus and dialog boxes quickly and easily.

Earlier versions of Visual J++ provided a Resource Wizard that could convert the RES resource files created by the resource editor to Java source files. AFC goes one step further by providing the *Win32ResourceDecoder* class, which can read the resource file directly during execution of the application or applet. In this chapter, you'll see how to use *Win32ResourceDecoder* to create menus and dialog boxes more quickly and more flexibly.

MENU RESOURCES

The *Win32ResourceDecoder* class loads menus from the resource file using the *getMenu* method. Menus can be referenced either by name or by ID. (The ID is assigned in the resource editor.) The following sample program, Resource01, demonstrates how easy it is to load and display a resource-created menu:

```
// Resource01 - Opens a menu described in a resource
//               file
import java.applet.*;
import java.awt.*;
import java.io.FileNotFoundException;
import java.net.URL;

import com.ms.ui.*;
import com.ms.ui.resource.*;
import com.ms.security.*;

import Application;

public class Resource01 extends AwtUIApplet
{
    Resource01()
    {
        super(new MyApplet());
    }

    public static void main(String[] arg)
    {
        new Application(new MyApplet());
    }
}
```

```
class MyApplet extends UIApplet
{
    // MENU_ID - The ID of the menu within the resource file
    public static final int MENU_ID = 101;

    public void init()
    {
        // Create a resource object.
        try
        {
            // Enable file I/O so that we can read the resource
            // file.
            // (This statement is defined only for the
            // Microsoft Virtual Machine [Microsoft VM] -
            // if the class is undefined, we are not
            // executing on a Microsoft VM; ignore the error.)
            try
            {
                PolicyEngine.assertPermission(
                                        PermissionID.FILEIO);
            }
            catch(Throwable e)
            {
            }

            // The resource file is in the same directory as
            // the class file.
            URL url = getCodeBase();
            String sResourceFileName = url.getFile();
            sResourceFileName += "Script1.res";

            // Open the resource file.
            Win32ResourceDecoder decoder
                = new Win32ResourceDecoder(sResourceFileName);

            // Now load the menu from that resource.
            UIBand band = decoder.getMenu(MENU_ID);

            // Put it into a band box.
            UIBandBox box = new UIBandBox();
            box.add(band);

            // Attach the band box to the applet window.
            setLayout(new UIBorderLayout());
            add(box, "North");
        }
```

>>

```
>>          // This exception occurs if the resource file
            // has a formatting problem. (The program can't
            // decode the file.)
            catch(ResourceFormattingException e)
            {
                showStatus("Resource formatting exception");
            }

            // This exception occurs if the file doesn't exist.
            catch(FileNotFoundException e)
            {
                showStatus("Can't find resource file.");
            }
        }
    }
```

The first change in this program, compared to the programs we've already examined, is in the *import com.ms.ui.resource.** statement, which is necessary to give the program access to the resource classes. The *init* method begins by giving the program file I/O permission. (For more information about permissions, see the sidebar titled "File Permissions" below.)

FILE PERMISSIONS

File I/O permission is necessary for an applet to perform any type of file I/O under the Microsoft Java Virtual Machine (VM). A trusted applet or an applet executing from the debugger (which is always a trusted applet) can give itself file I/O permission by calling *PolicyEngine.assertPermission*. (See Appendix A, "Signing Applets," for instructions on how to mark an applet trusted.)

This call creates problems for the AFC programmer, however, because the *PolicyEngine* class is a Microsoft-specific class. When executing under some other VM, this class might not be present. To counter this eventuality, I have enclosed the call in a *try* block. The *catch* statement grabs any "class not present"–type exception that might be thrown from this call, and the program continues in the hope that setting file I/O permission is not necessary.

In our other applets, file I/O permission has been handled by the AppCommon class, such as *FileDescr* or *Images*, actually performing the operation. These AppCommon classes are described in Appendix B, "Utility Classes Used in This Book."

Once the permissions have been set to allow file I/O, the program constructs the name of the resource file by appending the string "*Script1.res*" to the URL path of the Resource01.class file returned by *getCodeBase*. This program assumes that the resource file is in the same location as the Java class files. For example, if the applet were being executed from http://www.topher.net/srdavis, the resource filename would become http://www.topher.net/srdavis/Script1.res.

The constructor for the *Win32ResourceDecoder* class actually opens and reads the resource filename. This constructor throws an exception of *FileNotFound-Exception* in the event that the file is not present.

Once the resource file has been opened, *init* reads the menu by calling *get-Menu(MENU_ID)*. MENU_ID is a constant with a value of *101*, which is the value assigned to the menu in the resource editor. (See Figure 13-1.) If the *getMenu* method cannot read the resource file, probably because the file format is incorrect, *getMenu* throws an exception of *ResourceFormattingException*. If nothing goes wrong, the *getMenu* method returns a *UIBand* object containing the menu. The *init* function adds this *UIBand* object to a band box that it displays at the top of the applet window.

The *init* function includes a *catch* block for both resource exceptions. If either occurs, *init* outputs an error message to the status bar and then exits.

Figure 13-1 shows the resource file as it is being created in the resource editor. Figure 13-2 on the following page shows the Resource01 applet with the menu displayed.

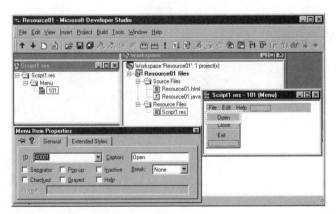

FIGURE 13-1   *The resource editor window, showing the menu being built, including the File/ Open menu item.*

FIGURE 13-2 *The resulting Resource01 applet, displaying the menu stored in the resource file shown in Figure 13-1.*

Adding Action to a Resource Menu

The menu shown in Figure 13-2 is very nice, but the applet doesn't take any action when the user selects a menu item. The following example program, Resource02, adds action to the resource by detecting the menu item selection:

```
// Resource02 - Adds action to the menu by identifying the
//              menu buttons by their IDs
import java.applet.*;
import java.awt.*;
import java.io.FileNotFoundException;
import java.net.URL;

import com.ms.ui.*;
import com.ms.ui.event.*;
import com.ms.ui.resource.*;
import com.ms.security.*;


import Application;

public class Resource02 extends AwtUIApplet
{
    Resource02()
    {
        super(new MyApplet());
    }
```

```java
    public static void main(String[] arg)
    {
        new Application(new MyApplet());
    }
}

class MyApplet extends UIApplet
{
// MENU_ID - The ID of the menu within the resource file
    public static final int MENU_ID = 101;

    // showStatus - If MyApplet is being invoked as an
    //              applet, output message in status
    //              bar; otherwise, just output.
    public void showStatus(String s)
    {
        if (getApplet() != null)
        {
            super.showStatus(s);
        }
        else
        {
            System.out.println(s);
        }
    }

    public void init()
    {
        // Create a resource object.
        try
        {
            try
            {
                PolicyEngine.assertPermission(
                                    PermissionID.FILEIO);
            }
            catch(Throwable e)
            {
            }

            // Open the resource file.
            URL url = getCodeBase();
            String sResourceFileName = url.getFile();
            sResourceFileName += "Script1.res";

            Win32ResourceDecoder decoder
                = new Win32ResourceDecoder(sResourceFileName);
```

>>

```
            // Now load the menu from that resource.
            UIBand band = decoder.getMenu(MENU_ID);

            // Attach an action listener that is invoked
            // when an item is selected from this menu.
            band.addActionListener(
                        new MenuActionListener(this));

            // Put the menu into a band box.
            UIBandBox box = new UIBandBox();
            box.add(band);

            // Attach the band box to the applet window.
            setLayout(new UIBorderLayout());
            add(box, "North");
        }
        catch(ResourceFormattingException e)
        {
            showStatus("Resource formatting exception");
        }
        catch(FileNotFoundException e)
        {
            showStatus("Can't find resource file.");
        }
    }
}

class MenuActionListener implements IUIActionListener
{
    UIApplet parent;

    // The following IDs identify the menu items.
    public static final int MENU_FILE_OPEN = 1001;
    public static final int MENU_FILE_CLOSE= 1002;
    public static final int MENU_FILE_EXIT = 1003;
    public static final int MENU_EDIT_COPY = 1101;
    public static final int MENU_EDIT_CUT  = 1102;
    public static final int MENU_EDIT_PASTE= 1103;
    public static final int MENU_HELP      = 1200;

    // actionPerformed - Invoked when the user selects
    //                   a menu item
    public void actionPerformed(UIActionEvent e)
    {
        // Get the item selected.
        Object o = e.getActionItem();
        UIMenuItem mi = (UIMenuItem)o;
```

```
    // Now fetch its ID...
    int nID = mi.getID();

    // ...and then look it up.
    switch (nID)
    {
    case MENU_FILE_OPEN:
        parent.showStatus("File|Open");
        break;
    case MENU_FILE_CLOSE:
        parent.showStatus("File|Close");
        break;
    case MENU_FILE_EXIT:
        parent.showStatus("File|Exit");
        System.exit(0);
        break;
    case MENU_EDIT_COPY:
        parent.showStatus("Edit|Copy");
        break;
    case MENU_EDIT_CUT:
        parent.showStatus("Edit|Cut");
        break;
    case MENU_EDIT_PASTE:
        parent.showStatus("Edit|Paste");
        break;
    case MENU_HELP:
        parent.showStatus("Help");
        break;
    }
}
MenuActionListener(UIApplet parent)
{
    this.parent = parent;
}
}
```

The *init* function starts out like the nonresponsive Resource01 version. Once the *UIBand* object has been loaded, however, an action listener is attached using the *addActionListener* call. This listener is the locally defined *Menu-ActionListener* class.

The constructor for *MenuActionListener* does nothing more than save a reference to the parent applet. The *actionPerformed* method of the *MenuActionListener* class is invoked when the user selects a menu item. A reference to the selected menu item is contained in the *UIActionEvent* object. This item is returned from the *getActionItem* method.

In earlier example programs, we might have created a subclass of *UIMenuItem* in which to store ID information. When we are loading a menu from the resource file, we don't have that option. Fortunately, each *UIComponent* object carries an ID field that can be fetched from the object using the *getID* method. This ID is set in the resource editor. A set of constants that include constants such as MENU_FILE_OPEN have been defined within *MenuActionListener* to match the value set in the resource editor. The *switch* statement within *actionPerformed* performs an action based on which menu item was selected. Of course, in this simplistic applet, there isn't much to be done other than output a message indicating that control was successfully passed to the appropriate branch.

Multiple Resource Menus

Because each menu carries its own ID, you can store multiple menus in a single resource file. The following example applet, Resource03, demonstrates this process by loading two menus and attaching them to the same band box. (The large sections of code that this applet shares with its predecessors have been left out here for the sake of brevity, but the version on the companion CD is complete.)

```
// Resource03 - Loads multiple menus into a single band
//              box from the same resource file

// This section the same as in Resource01 and Resource02...

class MyApplet extends UIApplet
{
    // *_MENU_ID - The IDs of the two menus within
    //             the resource file
    public static final int FILE_MENU_ID    = 101;
    public static final int PROJECT_MENU_ID = 102;

    public void init()
    {
        try
        {
            // Same as before...

            // Open the resource file.
            Win32ResourceDecoder decoder
                = new Win32ResourceDecoder(sResourceFileName);

            // Create a band box.
            UIBandBox box = new UIBandBox();
```

```
    // Now load the menu from that resource.
    UIBand band1 = decoder.getMenu(FILE_MENU_ID);
    band1.addActionListener(
                new FileMenuActionListener(this));
    box.add(band1);

    // Add a second menu.
    UIBand band2 = decoder.getMenu(PROJECT_MENU_ID);
    band2.addActionListener(
                new ProjectMenuActionListener(this));
    box.add(band2);

    // Attach the band box to the applet window.
    setLayout(new UIBorderLayout());
    add(box, "North");
}
catch(ResourceFormattingException e)
{
    showStatus("Resource formatting exception");
}
catch(FileNotFoundException e)
{
    showStatus("Can't find resource file.");
}
}
}
```

This applet defines two IDs, one for each menu. Once the *Win32Resource-Decoder* object has been created, *getMenu* is invoked separately for each menu. In addition, each menu receives a different action listener.

Figure 13-3 shows the resource file open under the editor; both menus are visible in the lower right quadrant of the IDE window. Figure 13-4 on the following page shows the window displayed by the resulting Resource03 applet.

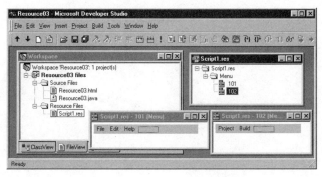

FIGURE 13-3   *The resource file, containing multiple menus.*

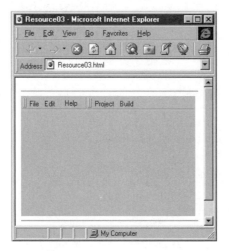

FIGURE 13-4   *The output of Resource03, showing multiple menus added to a single band box.*

DIALOG BOX RESOURCES

The resource editor also supports the inclusion of dialog boxes. Such automatically generated dialog boxes simultaneously reduce the amount of work needed to create an applet while improving the applet's appearance. The following example program, Resource04, demonstrates the loading of dialog boxes from a resource file:

```java
// Resource04 - Loads both a menu and a dialog box from
//               the resource file
import java.applet.*;
import java.awt.*;
import java.io.FileNotFoundException;
import java.net.URL;

import com.ms.ui.*;
import com.ms.ui.event.*;
import com.ms.ui.resource.*;
import com.ms.security.*;

import Application;

public class Resource04 extends AwtUIApplet
{
    Resource04()
    {
        super(new MyApplet());
    }
```

```java
    public static void main(String[] arg)
    {
        new Application(new MyApplet());
    }
}

class MyApplet extends UIApplet
{
    // MENU_ID - The ID of the menu object within
    //           the resource file
    public static final int MENU_ID   = 101;

    // DIALOG_ID - The ID of the dialog box object
    public static final int DIALOG_ID = 201;

    // dialog - Reference to the dialog box object loaded
    //          from the resource file
    UIDialog dialog = null;

    // showStatus - If MyApplet is being invoked as an
    //              applet, output message in status
    //              bar; otherwise, just output.
    public void showStatus(String s)
    {
        if (getApplet() != null)
        {
            super.showStatus(s);
        }
        else
        {
            System.out.println(s);
        }
    }

    public void init()
    {
        try
        {
            try
            {
                PolicyEngine.assertPermission(PermissionID.FILEIO);
            }
            catch(Throwable e)
            {
            }
```

>>

```
                                 // Open the resource file.
         >>                      URL url = getCodeBase();
                                 String sResourceFileName = url.getFile();
                                 sResourceFileName += "Script1.res";

                                 Win32ResourceDecoder decoder
                                     = new Win32ResourceDecoder(sResourceFileName);

                                 // Load the dialog box.
                                 dialog = decoder.getDialog(DIALOG_ID);

                                 // Create the menu.
                                 UIBandBox box = new UIBandBox();
                                 UIBand band = decoder.getMenu(MENU_ID);
                                 band.addActionListener(
                                             new MenuActionListener(this));
                                 box.add(band);

                                 // Attach the band box to the applet window.
                                 setLayout(new UIBorderLayout());
                                 add(box, "North");
                             }
                         catch(ResourceFormattingException e)
                         {
                             showStatus("Resource formatting exception");
                         }
                         catch(FileNotFoundException e)
                         {
                             showStatus("Can't find resource file.");
                         }
                     }
                 }

        // MenuActionListener - Invoked when user selects either
        //                      the Open or the Exit menu option
        class MenuActionListener implements IUIActionListener
        {
            MyApplet parent;

            public static final int MENU_OPEN = 1001;
            public static final int MENU_EXIT = 1002;

            public void actionPerformed(UIActionEvent e)
            {
                Object o = e.getActionItem();
                UIMenuItem mi = (UIMenuItem)o;
```

```
    // If this is the Open button,...
    if (mi.getID() == MENU_OPEN)
    {
        // ...open the dialog box.
        parent.dialog.setVisible(true);
    }

    // If this is the Exit button,...
    if (mi.getID() == MENU_EXIT)
    {
        // ...scram!
        System.exit(0);
    }
}

MenuActionListener(MyApplet parent)
{
    this.parent = parent;
}
}
```

The *init* function of this program begins the same as its predecessor in the way it creates the *Win32ResourceDecoder* object; *init* then loads the dialog box by calling *getDialog*. Dialog box resources carry the same types of IDs as other *UIComponent* objects. Thus, the constant DIALOG_ID is initialized to the same ID assigned to the dialog box in the resource editor.

The menu in this case contains only two menu items. The *actionPerformed* method opens the dialog box by calling *setVisible(true)* when the user clicks on the MENU_OPEN menu item. (See Chapter 10, "Dialog Boxes," for further details on manipulating dialog boxes.) The MENU_EXIT button terminates the applet by calling *System.exit*.

Figure 13-5 on the following page shows the resource editor while the dialog box is being edited. The menu window is open on the left. The dialog box (object *201*) is the largish window on the right in the IDE window. Notice that the dialog box currently has the rather uninspired name Dialog. Also notice that the Edit field has been selected. The property page dialog box visible in the lower left is where the programmer would change the properties of the Edit field. The only property currently set is the *ID* property, which has been set to *1000*.

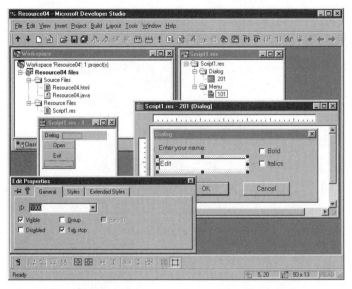

FIGURE 13-5 *The resource file, containing a menu and a dialog box.*

Figure 13-6 shows the Resource04 program in action.

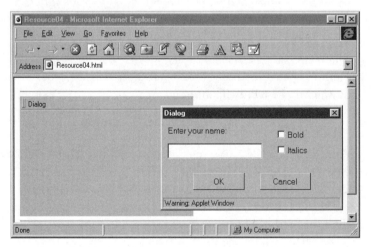

FIGURE 13-6 *The output from the example program Resource04 using the resource file shown in Figure 13-5.*

Adding Action to a Resource Dialog Box

As always, adding action to a resource dialog box involves attaching an event listener to the dialog box class. In contrast to the way it processes menus, AFC supports subclassing of dialog boxes to allow for a more compartmentalized solution, as demonstrated in the following example program, Resource05:

```java
// Resource05 - Opens the dialog box from the menu and
//              then reads the dialog box back into the
//              applet/application
import java.applet.*;
import java.awt.*;
import java.io.FileNotFoundException;
import java.net.URL;

import com.ms.ui.*;
import com.ms.ui.event.*;
import com.ms.fx.*;
import com.ms.ui.resource.*;
import com.ms.security.*;


import Application;

public class Resource05 extends AwtUIApplet
{
    Resource05()
    {
        super(new MyApplet());
    }

    public static void main(String[] arg)
    {
        new Application(new MyApplet());
    }
}

class MyApplet extends UIApplet
{
    // The objects maintained in the resource file
    public static final int MENU_ID   = 101;
    public static final int DIALOG_ID = 201;
    public static final int STRING_ID = 301;

    // dialog - The I/O dialog box
    MyDialog dialog;
```

>>

431

```
// text - Used to display the data entered in the dialog box
UIDrawText text;

// showStatus - If MyApplet is being invoked as an
//              applet, output message in status
//              bar; otherwise, just output.
public void showStatus(String s)
{
    if (getApplet() != null)
    {
        super.showStatus(s);
    }
    else
    {
        System.out.println(s);
    }
}

public void init()
{
    try
    {
        try
        {
            PolicyEngine.assertPermission(PermissionID.FILEIO);
        }
        catch(Throwable e)
        {
        }

        // Open the resource file.
        URL url = getCodeBase();
        String sResourceFileName = url.getFile();
        sResourceFileName += "Script1.res";

        Win32ResourceDecoder decoder
            = new Win32ResourceDecoder(sResourceFileName);

        // Create the dialog box using the decoder.
        dialog = new MyDialog(this, decoder);

        // Open the menu.
        UIBandBox box = new UIBandBox();
        UIBand band = decoder.getMenu(MENU_ID);
        band.addActionListener(
                new MenuActionListener(this));
        box.add(band);
```

```
        setLayout(new UIBorderLayout());
        add(box, "North");

        // Create a text field to output the dialog box results;
        // get the default contents from the resource file.
        String s = decoder.getString(STRING_ID);
        text = new UIDrawText(s);
        text.setFont(new FxFont("Arial", FxFont.PLAIN, 18));
        add(text, "Center");
    }
    catch(ResourceFormattingException e)
    {
        showStatus("Resource formatting exception");
    }
    catch(FileNotFoundException e)
    {
        showStatus("Can't find resource file.");
    }
}

// reportDialog - Reads the dialog box after the user
//                clicks OK or Cancel
public void reportDialog()
{
    // First read the dialog box into an interface object.
    MyDialogInterface inter = dialog.readDialog();

    // If the user clicked OK,...
    if (inter.bOKButton)
    {
        // ...update the text field's contents...
        text.setValueText(inter.sText);

        // ...and font style to match the dialog box
        // selections.
        int nStyle = 0;
        if (inter.bBold)
        {
            nStyle |= FxFont.BOLD;
        }
        if (inter.bItalics)
        {
            nStyle |= FxFont.ITALIC;
        }
        text.setFont(new FxFont("Arial", nStyle, 18));
    }
}
}
```

>>

```
// MenuActionListener - Invoked when the user selects one
//                      of the menu items
class MenuActionListener implements IUIActionListener
{
    MyApplet parent;

    public static final int MENU_OPEN = 1001;
    public static final int MENU_EXIT = 1002;

    public void actionPerformed(UIActionEvent e)
    {
        Object o = e.getActionItem();
        UIMenuItem mi = (UIMenuItem)o;

        // If the user clicks Open,...
        if (mi.getID() == MENU_OPEN)
        {
            // ...open the modal dialog box...
            parent.dialog.setVisible(true);

            // ...and then read its contents.
            parent.reportDialog();
        }

        // If the user clicks Exit,...
        if (mi.getID() == MENU_EXIT)
        {
            // ...exit the application.
            System.exit(0);
        }
    }

    MenuActionListener(MyApplet parent)
    {
        this.parent = parent;
    }
}

// MyDialogInterface - Interface class containing the
//                     raw data from the dialog box
class MyDialogInterface
{
    boolean    bOKButton;
    String     sText;
    boolean    bBold;
    boolean    bItalics;
```

```
MyDialogInterface(boolean bOKButton,
                  String   sText,
                  boolean bBold,
                  boolean bItalics)
{
    this.bOKButton = bOKButton;
    this.sText = sText;
    this.bBold = bBold;
    this.bItalics = bItalics;
}
}


// MyDialog - The dialog box from the resource file
class MyDialog extends UIDialog
{
    MyApplet parent;

    // The IDs of the dialog box components
    public final static int OK     = 2001;
    public final static int CANCEL = 2002;
    public final static int TEXT   = 2003;
    public final static int BOLD   = 2004;
    public final static int ITALICS= 2005;

    // bOKButton - If true, the user exited by clicking OK.
    boolean bOKButton;

    class PBAction implements IUIActionListener
    {
        boolean bOK;  // True - This is the OK button.

        public void actionPerformed(UIActionEvent e)
        {
            setVisible(false);

            bOKButton = bOK;
        }

        PBAction(boolean bOK)
        {
            this.bOK = bOK;
        }
    }


    MyDialog(MyApplet parent, Win32ResourceDecoder decoder)
                throws ResourceFormattingException
```

>>

>>

```
    {
        super(new UIFrame(), "Test Dialog Box", true);

        this.parent = parent;

        // Populate the dialog box from the resource file.
        decoder.populateDialog(this, MyApplet.DIALOG_ID);

        // Attach an action listener to the OK button...
        UIPushButton okButton
                    = (UIPushButton)getChildByID(OK);
        okButton.addActionListener(new PBAction(true));

        // ...and an action listener to the Cancel button.
        UIPushButton cancelButton
                    = (UIPushButton)getChildByID(CANCEL);
        cancelButton.addActionListener(new PBAction(false));
    }

    // readDialog - Read the contents of the dialog box into a
    //              DialogInterface object.
    MyDialogInterface readDialog()
    {
        UIScrollViewer viewer
                    = (UIScrollViewer)getChildByID(TEXT);
        UIEdit         text
                    = (UIEdit)viewer.getContent();

        UICheckButton  bold
                    = (UICheckButton)getChildByID(BOLD);
        UICheckButton  italics
                    = (UICheckButton)getChildByID(ITALICS);

        return new MyDialogInterface(bOKButton,
                            text.getValueText(),
                            bold.isChecked(),
                            italics.isChecked());
    }


    // getChildByID - Given the ID of a component attached
    //                to the dialog box, find that component and
    //                return a reference to it.
    IUIComponent getChildByID(int nID)
```

```
    {
        // Loop through the components attached to the dialog box.
        int nNoChildren = getChildCount();
        for (int i = 0; i < nNoChildren; i++)
        {
            // Compare each one until the IDs match.
            IUIComponent comp = getChild(i);
            if (nID == comp.getID())
            {
                // Found it!
                return comp;
            }
        }

        // Didn't find it - return a null value.
        return null;
    }
}
```

The *init* function of this program begins like its predecessors, but once it has created the *Win32ResourceDecoder* object, it creates a *MyDialog* object, passing the constructor both a reference to itself and a reference to the decoder object.

At first, *MyDialog* looks a lot like the dialog box classes you saw back in Chapter 10, "Dialog Boxes." It extends the class *UIDialog*. The constructor builds a named, modal dialog box object around a newly created frame before attaching a listener to the OK and Cancel buttons to handle mouse clicks originating from either of those buttons in the dialog box. The difference between this *MyDialog* class and its predecessors is that this constructor uses the resource *decoder* object to add the constituent components to the dialog box. Where *getDialog* constructs a dialog box from the components defined in a resource file, *populateDialog* populates an already existing dialog box with the components defined in the resource file.

As mentioned, the constructor completes by adding a push button–style action listener to the OK and Cancel buttons in the dialog box. The function *getChildByID* is used to find these components among those attached to the dialog box.

The locally added *getChildByID* method searches the components attached to the dialog box (the dialog box's children) until it finds the component with the specified ID. If it cannot find a matching component, the function returns a *null* value.

The dialog box is displayed when the user selects the Dialog/Open menu option in the main applet window. The event listener for this option enables the dialog box by calling *setVisible(true)*. Since the dialog box is modal, control does not return from the *setVisible* call until the user closes the dialog box, either by clicking OK or by clicking Cancel. Once control returns, the listener calls *MyApplet.reportDialog*.

The *reportDialog* method first reads the data from the dialog box by calling *MyDialog.readDialog*. The *readDialog* method calls *getChildByID* to fetch a reference to each of the dialog box components it is interested in. It then returns a *MyDialogInterface* object containing the data read from these components. The *MyDialogInterface* class is nothing more than an intermediary that serves to communicate the dialog box information back to the applet.

If the *MyDialogInterface* object returned to *MyApplet.reportDialog* indicates that the user clicked the OK button and not the Cancel button (that is, *bOKButton* is *true*), *MyApplet.reportDialog* updates the locally displayed text field.

The results of the Resource05 applet are shown in Figure 13-7.

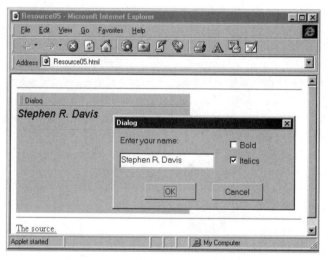

FIGURE 13-7   *The output from the fully functional resource-driven dialog box example.*

RESOURCEFUL LANGUAGE INDEPENDENCE

Although they both process resource files, there is a critical difference in the ways that the Resource Wizard and the *Win32ResourceDecoder* class handle resource files: the Resource Wizard reads the resource file at compile time, whereas the *Win32ResourceDecoder* class doesn't process the resource file until the applet or application is being loaded.

Delaying the resource file load operation makes the *Win32ResourceDecoder* class much more flexible. For example, the *Win32ResourceDecoder*-based applet can decide at run time which among several resources to load. Of course, the different resource files must be basically alike since the applet is expecting certain fields with given component IDs to be present. However, the different resource files could represent the same strings, menus, and dialog boxes in different languages or different character sets. This gives Java applets a level of language independence that is not possible with conventional AFC or AWT programming.

Language independence is great, but how do we know which language the user speaks? We don't, really; however, the *Locale* class can tell us what the default language is. The *Locale* class contains fields for the object's country and language. The static method *Locale.getDefault* returns the default *Locale* object. The method *getLanguage* returns a two-letter indicator for the language specified by this default *Locale* object.

The following *getResource* method, taken from the Resource06 example program, demonstrates how this works. Note that except for *getResource*, the code for Resource06 is the same as for Resource05.

```
// getResource - Gets the resource decoder for the current
//                local language
public Win32ResourceDecoder getResource()
                throws FileNotFoundException
{
    // Get the path to the resource file.
    URL url = getCodeBase();
    String sResourceFileName = url.getFile();

    // From that path, build a default resource filename
    // to be used in the event that the language-specific
    // version is not present.
    String sDefaultResourceFileName
            = sResourceFileName + "Script1.res";
```

>>

>>

```
    // Attach the prefix part of the resource filename
    // to the path.
    sResourceFileName += "Script1_";

    // Now get the language indicator - this will be
    // a two-letter combination, such as "en" for English,
    // "es" for Spanish, or "de" for German.
    Locale locale = Locale.getDefault();
    String suffix = locale.getLanguage();

    // Tack the language indicator onto the resource filename...
    sResourceFileName += suffix;

    // ...and then append the type suffix onto that (for example,
    // "Script1_en.res" for the English version,
    // "Script1_es.res" for the Spanish version, or
    // "Script1_de.res" for the German version).
    sResourceFileName += ".res";

    // Now try to load that resource file.
    Win32ResourceDecoder decoder;
    try
    {
        decoder = new Win32ResourceDecoder(
                            sResourceFileName);
    }
    // If we don't succeed in loading that resource file,
    // just load the default resource file.
    catch(Throwable t)
    {
        decoder
            = new Win32ResourceDecoder(
                            sDefaultResourceFileName);
    }
    return decoder;
}
```

The *getResource* method here starts the same as its predecessor with the path
to the Resource06.class file. To that it attaches the string "*Script1_*", followed by
the two-letter language indicator returned from the default *Locale* object. Last,
the program attaches the suffix *.res*. The *getResource* method calculates the name
Script1_en.res for English-speaking locations, *Script1_de.res* for German-
speaking locations, and so on. Note that the two-letter language indicator derives
from the name of the language in that language —for example, the indicator for
Español (Spanish) is "es," the indicator for Deutsch (German) is "de."

Of course, the developer can't anticipate all the different languages that are defined in *Locale*. If the *Win32ResourceDecoder* object can't find a particular language-specific resource file, *getResource* loads a default resource file (in this case, carrying the old name, Script1.res).

Figure 13-8 shows my project file for Resource06, including three different resource files: one for English, one for German, and one for the default. Figure 13-9 shows the Resource06 program executing using the German-language resource file.

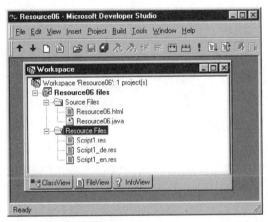

FIGURE 13-8   *The project file, showing a default resource file as well as resource files for German and English.*

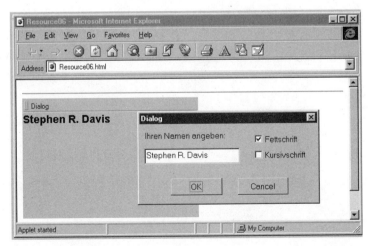

FIGURE 13-9   *The same dialog box applet executed in a German-language environment.*

WHAT'S NEXT

In this chapter, you've seen how the use of resource files can simplify the creation of menus and dialog boxes while simultaneously improving the appearance of the results.

There's nothing left for you to do now except take a look at the two appendixes and then start using AFC in your own applications. I'm hopeful this book will make that task more rewarding and enjoyable.

Many of the example applets contained in Part Two perform functions that the security features built into browsers do not allow in a non-trusted applet. The Interactive Development Environment (IDE) makes special provisions to allow such trusted functions when executing locally. However, before such an applet can be executed over the Web, it must be signed and certified as a trusted applet. Appendix A, "Signing Applets," describes the building and signing of a trusted applet.

Appendix B, "Utility Classes Used in This Book," describes a series of versatile non-AFC classes that are used throughout this book to simplify the code examples.

APPENDIXES

Signing Applets

Executing applets over the Web is a little more involved than executing them from within a development environment such as the Microsoft Visual J++ IDE. One of the main hurdles the applet developer must overcome is applet security. In this appendix, we'll look at how to sign an applet and thereby assign it the security privileges it needs in order to get its job done without compromising the user's machine.

APPLET SECURITY ISSUES AND MODELS

Before we get into the details of signing applets, let's consider applet security. Security is all a matter of trust. When I execute a program, I am trusting that program not to destroy some asset on my machine. Since there really isn't much that a program can do to the hardware, when I say "destroy some asset" I generally mean "destroy some data"—that is, wipe out the hard disk.

Applets executing from the local machine are assumed to be trusted programs. For the most part, these programs originate from large, established software firms. Because these companies base their business on creating and selling software, it is very much in their interest to ensure that their software packages do not inadvertently destroy data. I am willing to trust that they have done their duty in that regard. (But that trust extends only so far—I do maintain a backup.)

Software that I download off the Web is a bit more problematic. Here I must consider the source. If I point my browser to www.realaudio.com, and I am assured that this is the actual site for Real Audio, I feel reasonably comfortable that any program I download from that site is safe. With a public domain site, I have to exercise more judgment. Of course, if I'm downloading from a site run by a reputable company, such as the Ziff-Davis public domain site (ZDNet) at www.hotfiles.com, I assume that a modicum of testing has been performed to ensure that the company's programs are not infected with a data-consuming virus of some type. I can look at the number of previous downloads, consider how long the program has been on the site, and proceed with caution.

Applets that execute as part of a Web page are much more difficult to assess. Java applets are fundamentally different from any other programs I download and execute. As I surf from one Web page to the next, I have no idea whether the page I am about to go to contains a Java applet, so I'm never given the opportunity to decide whether or not to run the applet. Even once I'm viewing the page, I still don't know—Java applets are designed to execute together with the browser page to form a seamless whole, and unless the browser tells me, I don't even know that a Java program is executing. A browser that automatically gives the Java applet security privileges without my consent is unsafe.

Even if I did know that a Java applet was about to run, I would need more information before I could make an informed decision as to whether I would be willing to let this applet execute on my machine. I would want to know who wrote the applet and exactly what types of things the applet wants to do.

The Sandbox Security Model

In the early days of Java, no good solution to the Java applet security problem existed. Rather than hold up development of the language while a solution was worked out, the browser developers adopted what is known as the "sandbox" approach to Java applet security. Under this security model, the browser builds a wall around the applet that the applet cannot penetrate. The applet is not allowed to do anything that might endanger the host machine.

The sandbox model was good for the user's disk, which was fully protected by the browser. Unfortunately, the sandbox model prevented Java applets from doing much of anything useful. For example, it was all right to read data from the Web server machine, but it was not all right to read data from the user's disk, much less write to it. No active exchange with the host machine was possible except through the user. No printing. No updating the database. Nothing. This model severely restricted the usefulness of applets. Clearly, the sandbox security model was only an interim solution.

The Trusted Applet Security Model

The next phase of the security wars was the trusted applet, which is still being used by many browsers. Under this security model, the programmer can sign her applet, indicating who she is, before putting the applet on the Web. Before the applet developer can sign an applet, she has to get a Software Publisher Certificate (SPC) verifying that she is indeed who she claims to be. SPCs are doled out by companies whose job it is to verify people's identities and are encrypted so that they cannot be faked. Of course, corporate SPCs are available for software houses such as Microsoft, Netscape, and Sun Microsystems.

When I link to a Web site containing a signed applet, the browser displays a pop-up window indicating that the applet is asking to be trusted. Contained in that window is the name of the individual or company that wrote the applet. Since I know who wrote the applet, I can consider the source and make a decision from there.

I am not convinced that because an applet is signed, it's not belligerent. No security model can ensure that. But people are much less likely to create data-destructive programs when their names, addresses, and phone numbers are attached to their applets. And they would get the chance to upload a nasty applet only once. The SPC-issuing agency would be sure to revoke the miscreant's license after that.

Most browsers allow trusted SPCs to be stored so that, in the future, when a browser encounters an applet written by the same trusted developer, the browser can extend the applet trusted privileges without bothering to ask the user.

This security model is much better than the sandbox model it replaces because it allows truly useful applets to be written. It is still a blunt instrument, however. Once I decide to let the applet continue, I am giving it carte blanche. Anything that the applet wants to do is allowed.

The Permission-Based Security Model

While the trusted applet security model is a big improvement over the sandbox model, it is still an imprecise, all-or-nothing affair. To address this issue, with Internet Explorer 4.0, Microsoft introduced the permission-based security model. Under this model, a trusted applet indicates not only who wrote it but also exactly what types of permission it is requesting from the user. For example, an applet might need access to the hard disk simply as a scratch pad area. Such an applet would not need access to the entire disk but just to a specially set-aside directory, perhaps the browser cache directory. Under the permission-based model, such an applet would ask for Client Storage Permission. Granting an applet Client Storage Permission is much safer than granting the more general File I/O Permission since File I/O Permission would allow the applet to read any directory or file on the disk. (This File I/O Permission is the same as that asserted by the *FileDescr* class; see Appendix B, "Utility Classes Used in This Book.")

It is left up to the *SecurityManager* class to enforce these permissions. For example, suppose the user granted the applet File I/O Permission with read privilege only. Each file I/O operation is passed through the security manager. If the applet attempts to perform a write operation on the disk, the security manager generates a security exception, thereby protecting the user's disk.

NOTE

> The applet can catch a security exception. It may decide to proceed in some reduced capacity without the requested capability. For example, a word processor without write access might continue operating with the File/Save menu item disabled.

With this information in hand, the user can make a more informed decision as to whether to trust the applet. Not only does he know who the originator of the applet is, he also knows what the applet wants to do. He might be fairly generous with applets requesting relatively benign permissions but be much more circumspect about granting more dangerous permissions.

Permission-based security gives the applet developer the freedom she needs to create truly useful applets while extending the user the information he needs to protect himself from malicious applets. For a detailed discussion of the permission-based security model, see the documentation for the Microsoft SDK for Java version 2.0 or later.

SIGNING AN APPLET

This section guides you through the process of signing an applet as trusted in order to execute it over the Web. These instructions generate a CAB file suitable for loading under Internet Explorer versions 3 and 4. (You might need to experiment if you are attempting to create JAR files or if you are using a browser other than Internet Explorer.) Any applet would work as an example—here we'll use the Choice02 applet from Chapter 8, "Choices."

NOTE

To prevent the signed version of Choice02 from interfering with the unsigned version, the companion CD includes a second subfolder under the Choices folder, named Choice02 Signed, containing the signed Choice02 applet.

The following technique assumes that you have the Microsoft SDK for Java version 2.0 loaded and installed. (Presumably, later versions will also work.) If not, you can install this SDK from the companion CD or you can download it free from Microsoft's Web site at www.microsoft.com/java. You will also need to open an MS-DOS window and specify the SDK-Java.20\bin\PackSign directory as part of the PATH.

For most of the commands shown here, I provided batch (BAT) files in the Signing directory on the companion CD. If you would like to use these files, be sure to also include this directory in your PATH.

Creating the CAB File

Before the applet security issue was ever broached, people realized that it would be helpful to be able to combine a number of CLASS files into a compressed library, much like a ZIP file, in order to reduce download times. This realization led to the creation of two different standards: Sun Microsystems introduced the Java Archive (JAR) format with version 1.1 of the JDK; Microsoft chose to adopt its already standard Cabinet (CAB) format because it can result in significantly enhanced compression rates.

With the introduction of code signing, both the JAR and CAB standards have been expanded to create a block type to hold the signature information. This expansion is fortunate because there is no place in the CLASS file generated during compilation of Java source code to hold the signature.

Execute the following command from the Choice02 directory to create the Choice02.cab file:

```
cabarc -s 6144 N Choice02.cab *.class ..\..\AppCommon\*.class
```

This command tells the cabarc utility to create a new (indicated by the *N*) CAB file, named Choice02.cab, consisting of all the CLASS files contained in the current directory plus all of those contained in the AppCommon directory. The -*s* command tells cabarc to reserve 6 KB of space for the signature, which we will add later. If all works well, this command responds with "Completed successfully."

 NOTE

The preceding command has been bundled in the mkcab.bat file in the Signing subdirectory on the companion CD. To execute this batch file, be sure that Signing is in your PATH and from the Choice02 directory enter *mkcab Choice02*.

The HTML file must also be edited to load the CAB file instead of the CLASS files. The updated HTML file is shown here:

```
<html>
<head>
<title>Choice02</title>
</head>
<body>
<hr>
<applet
    code=Choice02.class
    name=Choice02
    width=100
    height=300 >
  <PARAM NAME="cabbase" VALUE="Choice2.cab">
</applet>
<hr>
<a href="Choice02.java">The source</a>
</body>
</html>
```

Notice the addition of the PARAM NAME value *cabbase*, which tells the browser the name of the CAB file to load instead of the CLASS file.

NOTE

The PARAM NAME value *cabbase* approach applies only to CAB files. You can use the *ARCHIVE* parameter to load a JAR file, or you can use the more universal OBJECT keyword. Refer to the HTML documentation included with your SDK for further details.

Before continuing, test this configuration by executing the HTML locally from the hard disk. The applet should execute; however, it will generate a security exception since it still hasn't been signed.

Creating an SPC

If you already have an SPC, skip this step. If you do not have an SPC, you can apply for one through various vendors such as VeriSign at www.verisign.com. The company will require you to fill out a form and pay a fee (roughly $20 per year plus an initial setup fee) for the creation and maintenance of your SPC.

The following steps use tools that come with the Microsoft SDK for Java version 2.0. These tools enable you to create a make-believe SPC that you can use for testing purposes.

First you will need to make a matching key and certificate. To do so, execute the following command from within the Signing directory on your hard disk:

```
makecert -sk AFC.pvk -n "CN= AFC Programmer's Guide" AFC.cer
```

This command does two things. First, it creates a Personal Verification Key (PVK)—in this case, named AFC.pvk, although you can call it whatever you want. (Notice that no AFC.pvk file is created—an AFC.pvk entry is added to the Registry instead.) When you are issued a real PVK, it should normally be kept on a safe floppy disk somewhere, as the SPC is worthless without it. Second, makecert creates a certificate, here named AFC.cer. The *"CN=AFC Programmer's Guide"* string provides the name of the software publisher to whom the SPC belongs. (To use the batch file equivalent, from within the Signing directory on your hard disk enter *mkcert*.)

Multiple certificates can be combined into a single SPC; however, in this case we have only one. The following command bundles our single certificate into an SPC (to use the batch file equivalent, from within the Signing directory on your hard disk enter *mkspc*):

```
cert2spc AFC.cer AFC.spc
```

This command should create a file AFC.spc in the Signing directory that contains our SPC. This file will be used in conjunction with the PVK issued earlier to sign our CAB files into a trusted applet.

NOTE

> Everyone must generate their own AFC.spc file since this file is matched to the AFC.pvk contained in your Registry and both are created based on the configuration of your computer. Once you have created this SPC, you will not need to re-create it each time you add a certificate to an applet.

Signing the CAB File

All we have left to do is use the SPC file we created to sign the CAB file created earlier. To do so, from the Choice02 directory enter the following command:

```
signcode -j javasign.dll -jp low -spc ..\..\signing\AFC.spc -k
AFC.pvk Choice02.cab
```

This command specifies that you want to sign the file Choice02.cab with the SPC AFC.spc contained in the Signing directory using the AFC.pvk key. The *-j javasign.dll* argument indicates that we are using Internet Explorer 4.0–compatible permissions, and *-jp low* indicates that we are using low security. Low security gives the applet the right to do just about whatever it wants to do.

If all goes well, the command should return with the following message:

```
Warning: This file is signed, but not timestamped.
Succeeded.
```

(To use the batch file version, from the Choice02 directory enter *sign Choice02*.)

NOTE

> Other, more complex, permissions are possible; however, they are not necessary for a test-only applet. If you are considering posting a "real" applet on the Web, you should check out the Microsoft SDK for Java version 2.0 documentation for a complete description of how to set up exactly the security permissions your applet needs.

Testing the Results

You can verify that the CAB file is signed by executing the following command from within the Choice02 directory:

```
chkjava Choice02.cab
```

If the signature has been properly installed, chkjava will respond with the window shown in Figure A-1.

FIGURE A-1   *The output from the chkjava application when executed on Choice02 with a valid debug SPC.*

In the dialog box shown in Figure A-1, you can see that the publisher of this applet is AFC Programmer's Guide. You can also see that this applet is trying to garner full privileges for itself—the result of our setting security to low in the sign step. Had we indicated more detailed, less global permissions in that step, the exact permissions requested would be outlined here. A warning at the top of this dialog box indicates that the holder of this SPC has not been verified by any agency and that, therefore, this applet should not be trusted. This applet is fine for testing, even for testing over the Web, but it should not be attached to a public Web page until it has been signed by a verified SPC.

To execute this applet, double-click on the HTML file as usual. The browser will display the dialog box shown in Figure A-1. If you click Yes, the applet runs just as it did when it was executed from within the IDE. If you click No, the applet executes as an untrusted applet, which will result in a security exception being thrown just as if we had not signed the applet at all.

Utility Classes
Used in This Book

The AppCommon package (all files contained in the AppCommon directory on the companion CD) is a collection of utility classes that simplify the job of writing many AFC programs. The classes that make up the AppCommon package are common to all example programs in this book, and they both simplify the example programs and avoid unnecessary redundancy by providing frequently needed functions. Only one of these classes (*Application*) accesses AFC directly. In this appendix, we'll examine some of the utility classes we've discussed in the book. Feel free to use, adapt, and add to the AppCommon classes to make your Java applications easier to write, debug, and maintain.

THE *APPLICATION* CLASS

The *Application* class is used to create "an applet within an application." Of course, a simple class such as *Application* cannot duplicate all of the intricacies of a browser, so there are some things that an *Application*-based application cannot do—most notably, it cannot load images. However, the majority of applets execute as an application just fine by using the *Application* class.

The following code fragment demonstrates the *Application* class in use:

```
import Application;
public class AppletName extends AwtUIApplet
{
    AppletName()
    {
        super(new MyApplet());
    }

    public static void main(String[] arg)
    {
        new Application(new MyApplet());
    }
}


class MyApplet extends UIApplet
{
    // showStatus - If MyApplet is being invoked as an
    //                applet, output message in status
    //                bar; otherwise, just output.
    public void showStatus(String s)
    {
        if (getApplet() != null)
        {
            super.showStatus(s);
        }
        else
        {
            System.out.println(s);
        }
    }

    // init - This is where your applet picks up.
    public void init()
    {
        // Remaining applet code...
    }
}
```

The starting class for the program is *AppletName*. Although the application programmer must create this class, the class always follows the same pattern. *AppletName* extends *AwtUIApplet* as it would any other AFC applet and consists of two functions: a default constructor and *main*.

The *AppletName* constructor is invoked by the browser when the program is executed as an applet. This constructor creates an object of class *MyApplet* and passes it to the constructor for the base class *AwtUIApplet*. The *MyApplet* class contains the actual program code. AFC automatically attaches the *My-Applet* applet object to the *AppletName* object. When the browser invokes a standard method such as *init*, AFC passes this on to *MyApplet*'s corresponding method. This is the normal way in which AFC applets are created.

AppletName includes the method *public static void main* that is invoked when the program is executed as an application. The *main* method also creates an object of class *MyApplet* to represent the actual program code. Instead of pass-ing this to AFC, however, *main* passes this object to the class *Application*. *Application* builds a reasonable simulation of a browser environment for the *MyApplet* object. In this way, *MyApplet* thinks it is executing as an applet under a browser when it is actually being executed as an application.

The code for the *Application* class is shown here:

```
// Application - Allows a UIApplet object to be
//               executed by an application
import java.awt.*;
import com.ms.ui.*;

public class Application extends UIFrame
{
    // The applet within the frame
    UIApplet uiapplet = null;

    // small constructor - Default the name,
    //                     width, and height.
    Application(UIApplet uiapplet)
    {
        this(uiapplet,
            "AFC Application",
            300,
            200);
    }

    // full constructor - Specify the name and size
    //                    of the applet frame along
    //                    with the applet.
    Application(UIApplet uiapplet,
                String sName,
                int nWidth,
                int nHeight)
```

>>

>>

```
    {
        // Open a frame with the specified name,
        // width, and height.
        super(sName);
        setSize(nWidth, nHeight);

        // Save the child applet.
        this.uiapplet = uiapplet;

        // Now add the applet to the frame.
        setLayout(new UIBorderLayout());
        add(uiapplet, "Center");

        // Invoke the applet's init and start functions.
        // (If the applet hadn't been running as an application,
        // the browser would have invoked these functions
        // when the applet was loaded and entered, respectively.)
        uiapplet.init();
        uiapplet.start();

        // Display the results.
        setVisible(true);
        repaint();
    }


    // handleEvent - When the user clicks the Close button
    //               in the upper right corner of the window,
    //               exit the application.
    public boolean handleEvent(Event e)
    {
        if (e.id == Event.WINDOW_DESTROY)
        {
            // Invoke the stop and destroy methods
            // as the browser would.
            uiapplet.stop();
            uiapplet.destroy();

            // Now exit.
            System.exit(0);
        }

        // Handle all other events in the default
        // fashion.
        return super.handleEvent(e);
    }
}
```

Application extends *UIFrame* in order to provide the application with a window in which to execute. *Application* actually provides two constructors. The full, more involved constructor allows the programmer to provide the name to be affixed to the frame heading and the initial size of the frame. The simpler constructor assigns default values to these two settings and then calls the full constructor.

The *Application* full constructor starts by invoking *super(sName)* (the *UIFrame(String)* constructor) to name the frame and by calling *setSize* to establish the frame size. It continues by adding the *UIApplet* object to the center of this frame for display. *Application* then invokes the *UIApplet* object's *init* and *start* methods to mimic the operations of a browser. Last *Application* makes its frame visible to the user and calls *repaint* just to be sure that everything is updated.

The *handleEvent* method of *Application* is invoked when an event occurs within the frame window. The only event that the *Application* object is interested in is the WINDOW_DESTROY event, which occurs when the user clicks the Close button in the upper right corner of the frame. When this event occurs, *Application* calls the *UIApplet* object's *stop* and *destroy* methods, just as the browser would do when the user exits the window containing the applet. The *handleEvent* method then terminates the application by calling *System.exit*.

THE *IMAGES* CLASS

The *Images* class is extremely useful for loading image files into an applet. *Images* can handle either a single filename or an array of filenames. *Images* also provides the capability to monitor the progress of the load operation.

The following code fragment demonstrates the *Images* class in use:

```
class MyApplet
{
    // The names of the GIF files
    String[] sNames = new String[2] {"File1.gif", "File2.gif"};

    public void init()
    {
        // Create an Images object with the filenames.
        Images images = new Images(this, sNames);

        // Now load the images.
        images.load();
```

>>

>>

```
        // Fetch a particular image by index.
        Image file1 = images.getImage(0);
    }
}
```

Here the applet defines an array of *String* objects containing the names of the image files to load. (These image files are understood to be in a subdirectory named Images from the code's base URL.)

When the applet starts, the *init* function creates an object of class *Images* to hold the names of these files. The next call, to the *load* method, actually causes the images to be loaded from disk. Once the images have been loaded, the *getImage* method gives the applet access to the individual images by index, where *0* is the index of the first image.

The code for the *Images* class is shown here:

```
// Images - Utility class designed to load and manage images.
//          A single object of class Images acts like an
//          array of images.
//          The images are assumed to be in a subdirectory
//          named Images under the directory containing the
//          HTML file.
import java.applet.*;
import java.awt.*;
import java.awt.image.*;
import java.net.URL;

import com.ms.ui.*;

public class Images
{
    Image[]  img = null;        // Array of images
    String[] sName = null;      // Their names

    UIApplet applet = null;     // Base UIApplet
    boolean  bLoaded = false;   // True if images are loaded
    boolean  bLoadFailed = false; // True if the load operation
                                // failed

    MediaTracker tracker = null;  // Used to track image load

    // Images - Load multiple images.
    //          imNames is an array containing the names
    //          of the images; these images are
    //          assumed to be in the subdirectory Images.
    public Images(UIApplet applet, String imNames[])
```

```
{
    // Assign initial values.
    this.applet = applet;      // Parent applet

    // Create Image objects.
    URL url = applet.getCodeBase();
    int numimages = imNames.length;
    img = new Image[numimages]; // Allocate room for arrays.
    sName = new String[numimages];

    for (int i = 0; i < numimages; i++)
    {
        sName[i] = imNames[i];
        img[i] = applet.getImage(url,
                                 "Images/" + imNames[i]);
    }
}


// Images - This version loads a single image.
//          (Create an array of one object with
//          [0] equal to imName, and pass this
//          array to the full constructor for
//          processing.)
public Images(UIApplet applet, String imName)
{
    this(applet, new String[1] {imName});
}


// Access methods
// getImage - Return the first image; this method
//            is most useful when the user created
//            the Images object using a single image.
public Image getImage()
{
    return getImage(0);
}


// getImage - Return the specified image.
public Image getImage(int nIndex)
{
    if (bLoaded)
    {
        return img[nIndex];
    }
    return null;
}
```

>>

```
// getImageName - Return the name of the image.
public String getImageName()
{
    return getImageName(0);
}
public String getImageName(int nIndex)
{
    return sName[nIndex];
}


// getIndex - The next two functions return the
//            index of an image by reference or
//            by name; the reference and the name
//            can be combined using getImage and
//            getImageName.
public int getIndex(String sN)
{
    // Loop through the names.
    for (int i = 0; i < img.length; i++)
    {
        // When we find one that matches,...
        if (sName[i].compareTo(sN) == 0)
        {
            // ...return the corresponding image.
            return i;
        }
    }

    // Didn't find a match; return illegal index.
    return -1;
}
public int getImage(Image myimg)
{
    for (int i = 0; i < img.length; i++)
    {
        if (img[i] == myimg)
        {
            return i;
        }
    }
    return -1;
}

// loaded - Return indication of whether images are
//          loaded. (If we have yet to load the images, go
//          ahead and attempt to do so.)
public boolean loaded(boolean bLoad)
```

```java
{
    if (!bLoaded && bLoad)
    {
        load();
    }
    return bLoaded;
}

// getChildCount - Return the number of images.
public int getChildCount()
{
    return sName.length;
}

// load - Load the images;
//        return true if load operation is successful.
public boolean load()
{
    // Don't bother if the images are already loaded...
    if (bLoaded)
    {
        return true;
    }

    // ...or if we've already tried and failed to load them.
    if (bLoadFailed)
    {
        return false;
    }

    // Assign a MediaTracker object to all images.
    tracker = new MediaTracker(applet.getApplet());

    // Now attach the images to the MediaTracker.
    for (int i = 0; i < img.length; i++)
    {
        tracker.addImage(img[i], i);
    }

    // Finally, wait for the images to load and
    // then get the error return status.
    try
    {
        tracker.waitForAll();
        bLoadFailed = tracker.isErrorAny();
        bLoaded = !bLoadFailed;
    }
```

```
      catch(InterruptedException e)
      {
          bLoadFailed = true;
      }

      // Return the success/failure indication.
      return bLoaded;
  }


  // Load progress functions:
  // getTargetProgress - Returns the maximum load
  //                     progress score
  public int getTargetProgress()
  {
      return getChildCount();
  }


  // getLoadProgress - Returns the current load progress score
  public int getLoadProgress()
  {
      int nScore = 0;

      // If there is no tracker,...
      if (tracker == null)
      {
          //...we haven't started yet.
          return 0;
      }

      // Loop through each image added to the MediaTracker.
      for (int i = 0; i < img.length; i++)
      {
          // Get the status.
          int nStatus = tracker.statusID(i, false);

          // If the status is COMPLETE,...
          if (nStatus == MediaTracker.COMPLETE)
          {
              // ...score a point.
              nScore += 1;
          }
      }

      // Return the accumulated score.
      return nScore;
  }
}
```

The full constructor for the *Images* object accepts the parent *UIApplet* object and an array of *String* objects containing the names of the image files as arguments. This constructor prefixes the directory name Images to the image name provided and creates an *Image* object from the result by calling *getImage*. This *Image* object and the local name are stored in the *Images* object.

A second constructor for *Images* is provided. This constructor accepts a single *String* filename instead of an array of names. This function simply creates an array of one object with the given filename and passes this array to the full constructor for processing.

The *load* method is called to actually load the images from disk. After checking to see whether the image has already been loaded, this method begins by creating a *MediaTracker* object. The *MediaTracker* class is used to monitor the loading of image and audio files. The *load* method adds all of its images to the *MediaTracker* object by calling *addImage* for each *Image* object. Last the *load* method signals the *MediaTracker* object to load the images by calling *waitForAll*. Once this function returns, *load* records the results locally in the *bLoadFailed* and *bLoaded* flags.

The *Images* object provides a number of access methods for fetching *Image* objects by index or by name and for returning the index of a given *Image* object. The *getLoadProgress* method returns a count of the number of image files that have already been loaded by iterating through the *Image* objects attached to the *MediaTracker* object and incrementing a counter for each object marked COMPLETE. This information can be used to update a *UIProgress* indicator. (See Chapter 13, "Resource Files.")

THE *FILEDESCR* CLASS

The *FileDescr* class is used by those applets and applications that display file and file directory information. The following code fragment demonstrates the *FileDescr* class in use:

```
class MyApplet
{
    public void init()
    {
        // Create a sorted list of files.
        FileDescr fileList = new FileDescr("c:/temp");
        fileList.sort(true);
```

⟩⟩

```
        // Now add the elements from the file list to
        // a list of choices.
        int nLength = fileList.getChildCount();
        UIChoice choice = new UIChoice();
        for (int i = 0; i < nLength; i++)
        {
            choice.addString(fileList.getChild(i));
        }

        // Start with the first element selected.
        choice.sctSelectedIndex(0);
    }
}
```

Here *init* begins by creating a *FileDescr* object for the C:\temp directory. Since C:\temp is a directory, *FileDescr* creates a listing of the contents of this directory. The *init* method then sorts this list by calling *FileDescr.sort*. Passing a value of *true* to *sort* tells it to perform a case-insensitive sort. Last *init* creates a file selection box of class *UIChoice* to which it adds the contents of the directory. The call *getChild(i)* returns the *i*'th filename in the directory.

The code for the *FileDescr* class is shown here:

```
// FileDescr - Creates a file descriptor. The file
//             descriptor can be queried to find
//             information about the file.
//             If the current descriptor is really a
//             directory, its contents can be
//             queried as well.

import java.io.File;

// The following package is defined only in the Microsoft
// environment; remove for non-Microsoft implementations
// of AFC.
import com.ms.security.*;

public class FileDescr
{
    String   sName;          // Name of the file
    String   sFullPath;      // Full pathname
    File     file;           // File handle
    String[] contents = null; // If a directory, the names
                             // of the files in this directory
    int      length;         // If not a directory,
                             // length of the file
```

```java
// constructor - Open the specified file. If the
//                file is a directory, create a
//                list of its contents.
// single constructor
FileDescr(String sName)
{
    this(null, sName);
}


// Open the filename specified under the path
// specified in root.
FileDescr(FileDescr root, String sName)
{
    // For the Microsoft Java VM, it is necessary to set
    // the permissions to allow file I/O; however, this
    // call will throw an exception from non-Microsoft
    // VMs because the call is not defined.
    try
    {
        PolicyEngine.assertPermission(PermissionID.FILEIO);
    }
    catch(Throwable e)
    {
    }

    // Save the name of the file.
    this.sName = sName;

    // Now create the full pathname.
    sFullPath ="";
    if (root != null)
    {
        sFullPath = root.sFullPath + "/";
    }
    sFullPath += sName;

    // Open the file/directory.
    length = 0;
    try
    {
        file = new File(sFullPath);
```

>>

```
                // If this is a directory,...
                if (file.isDirectory())
                {
                    // ...get a list of the files
                    // contained in the directory; otherwise,...
                    contents = file.list();
                }
                else
                {
                    // ...just store some information.
                    length = (int)file.length();
                }
            }
            catch (Exception e)
            {
            }

            // If we couldn't open the file,...
            if (contents == null)
            {
                // ...just create a string with
                // one entry and specify "<empty>".
                contents = new String[1];
                contents[0] = "<empty>";
            }
        }

// getName - Return the name of the file.
String getName()
{
    return sName;
}

// getFullPath - Return the path.
String getFullPath()
{
    return sFullPath;
}

// isDirectory - Return true if the current fileDescr
//               refers to a directory.
boolean isDirectory()
{
    // Set file I/O permission.
    try
```

```
    {
        PolicyEngine.assertPermission(
                            PermissionID.FILEIO);
    }
    catch(Throwable e)
    {
    }

    // Return the isDirectory indicator.
    return file.isDirectory();
}

// getChildCount - Return the number of files in the
//                 directory referenced by this fileDescr;
//                 if this is not a directory, return
//                 the length of the file.
int getChildCount()
{
    if (!isDirectory())
    {
        return length;
    }
    return contents.length;
}

// getChild - Return the nth name in the directory.
String getChild(int nIndex)
{
    return contents[nIndex];
}

// sort - Sort the list of children in ascending order.
//        If bIgnoreCase is true, ignore the
//        case of the strings. Note that this sort
//        algorithm is extremely inefficient, but
//        for a reasonable number of objects, it
//        should work fine.
void sort(boolean bIgnoreCase)
{
    // Use a bubble sort - it's the easiest.
    // Keep looping until the list is sorted.
    String sTemp;
    boolean bSwap;
    do
    {
        bSwap = false;
```

>>

```
                // Loop through the list, comparing each item
                // to its neighbors.
                for (int i = 0; i < contents.length - 1; i++)
                {
                    // Fetch the first and second items.
                    String sFirst = contents[i];
                    String sSecond= contents[i + 1];

                    // If we are to ignore their case,...
                    if (bIgnoreCase)
                    {
                        // ...convert both items to lowercase.
                        sFirst  =  sFirst.toLowerCase();
                        sSecond = sSecond.toLowerCase();
                    }

                    // If one item is greater than its neighbor,...
                    if (sFirst.compareTo(sSecond) > 0)
                    {
                        // ...swap the items.
                        sTemp             = contents[i];
                        contents[i]       = contents[i + 1];
                        contents[i + 1] = sTemp;

                        // Note that a swap occurred.
                        bSwap = true;
                    }
                }
            } while (bSwap);
    }
}
```

The *FileDescr* class provides two constructors. The first constructor expects the name of a file. A second, full constructor is provided that accepts both the name of a file and a reference to another *FileDescr* object. This other *FileDescr* object is assumed to refer to a directory in which the filename provided is a member.

The full *FileDescr* constructor begins by asserting file I/O permission. This step is necessary in order for the Microsoft Java Virtual Machine (VM) to allow the parent applet to access the disk. (This step can be performed only from either a trusted applet or an applet being executed under the debugger.) If the *assertPermission* method is not defined, the applet is probably being executed on some other Java VM—in which case, *FileDescr* catches the exception thrown and ignores it.

The constructor then continues by saving both the local filename and the extended filename, the extended filename being the filename prefixed with the name of the root *FileDescr* object.

Using the resulting full pathname, *FileDescr* creates a *File* object. If the *File* object created turns out to be a directory, *FileDescr* saves the contents (that is, the names of the files that make up that directory) in the local member *contents*. If the *File* object is not a directory, *FileDescr* saves some information that the application program can display (in this case, the length of the file, although other parameters are available as well). If the attempt to create the *File* object results in an exception being thrown, *FileDescr* creates an array with the single member "*<empty>*".

FileDescr provides an assortment of access methods, including a *getChild* method that returns the name of a member file by index.

The *sort* method arranges the filenames contained in *contents* in ascending order. The *sort* method uses a bubble sort. It begins by setting the flag *bSwap* to *false* and then makes its way through the list, comparing each member to its neighbor. This comparison is either case sensitive or case insensitive, depending on the value of the argument *bIgnoreCase*. If the two entries are found to be out of order, *sort* swaps them and sets the *bSwap* flag to *true*. Once it gets to the end of the list, if *bSwap* is still *false*, the *sort* method knows that the list is now in order and exits. Otherwise, it returns to the top and starts all over again.

INDEX

Page numbers in italics refer to figures, graphics, or program listings.

W

Z

ABOUT THE AUTHOR

Stephen R. "Randy" Davis is a programmer and writer who specializes in object-oriented languages such as C++ and Java. He counts eight books and numerous technical articles to his credit. Randy works as a software process specialist for E-Systems in Greenville, Texas, where he lives with his wife, Jenny; one son, Kinsey; two dogs; three cats; and a pot-bellied pig. He can be contacted at srdavis@ACM.org.

The manuscript for this book was prepared and submitted to Microsoft Press in electronic form. Text files were prepared using Microsoft Word 97. Pages were composed by Microsoft Press using Adobe PageMaker 6.51 for Windows, with text in Melior and display type in Imago Extra Bold. Composed pages were delivered to the printer as electronic prepress files.

COVER GRAPHIC DESIGNER
Tim Girvin Design

COVER ILLUSTRATOR
Glenn Mitsui

INTERIOR GRAPHIC DESIGNER
Kim Eggleston

INTERIOR GRAPHIC ARTIST
Travis Beaven

PRINCIPAL COMPOSITOR
Jeffrey Brendecke

PRINCIPAL PROOFREADER/COPY EDITOR
Roger LeBlanc

INDEXER
Richard Shrout

Maximum *Java!*

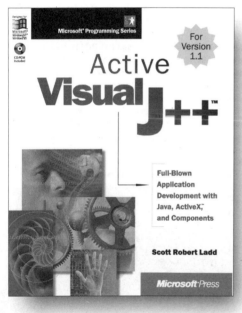

Active Visual J++
Microsoft® Programming Series

For Version 1.1

Full-Blown Application Development with Java, ActiveX, and Components

Scott Robert Ladd

Microsoft Press

U.S.A.	**$39.99**
U.K.	£37.49 [V.A.T. included]
Canada	$53.99
ISBN 1-57231-609-8	

Visual J++™ is Microsoft's powerhouse implementation of Java—the one that offers pure Java compatibility and is optimized for Windows® programming. And for intermediate programmers who know the basics of Java, there's no better guide to Visual J++ than ACTIVE VISUAL J++. It gives you an overview of the strengths of Visual J++, version 1.1, and how to put them to best use. It shows you how to combine powerful Internet technologies—Application Foundation Classes (AFC), Java, and ActiveX™—to create exciting interactive applications for the Web and intranets. And you can give them the full look and feel of Microsoft® Windows. ACTIVE VISUAL J++ gives you clear guidance on taking Java beyond its Web-based roots, gives you insight into Microsoft's Internet strategy, and lets you work with plenty of valuable code samples on CD-ROM. In short, to build the hottest Web sites and applications, you need Visual J++. And to get the most from it, you need ACTIVE VISUAL J++.

Microsoft Press® products are available worldwide wherever quality computer books are sold. For more information, contact your book or computer retailer, software reseller, or local Microsoft Sales Office, or visit our Web site at mspress.microsoft.com. To locate your nearest source for Microsoft Press products, or to order directly, call 1-800-MSPRESS in the U.S. (in Canada, call 1-800-268-2222).

Prices and availability dates are subject to change.

Microsoft Press

DATE DE RETOUR L.-Brault

L.-Brault

IMPORTANT—READ CAREFULLY BEFORE OPENING SOFTWARE PACKET(S). By opening the sealed packet(s) containing
the software, you indicate your acceptance of the following Microsoft License Agr

MICROSOFT LICENSE A

(Book Companion CD)

This is a legal agreement between you (either an individual or an entity) and M
packet(s) you are agreeing to be bound by the terms of this agreement. If you do not
unopened software packet(s) and any accompanying written materials to the place

MICROSOFT SOFTWARE LI

1. GRANT OF LICENSE. Microsoft grants to you the right to use one copy of the
"SOFTWARE") on a single terminal connected to a single computer. The SOFTW
temporary memory (i.e., RAM) or installed into the permanent memory (e.g., har
puter. You may not network the SOFTWARE or otherwise use it on more than one

2. COPYRIGHT. The SOFTWARE is owned by Microsoft or its suppliers and is
tional treaty provisions. Therefore, you must treat the SOFTWARE like any other
except that you may either (a) make one copy of the SOFTWARE solely for backup
a single hard disk provided you keep the original solely for backup or archival purp
nying the SOFTWARE.

3. OTHER RESTRICTIONS. You may not rent or lease the SOFTWARE, but you
ten materials on a permanent basis provided you retain no copies and the recipient
verse engineer, decompile, or disassemble the SOFTWARE. If the SOFTWARE is
the most recent update and all prior versions.

4. DUAL MEDIA SOFTWARE. If the SOFTWARE package contains more than
may use only the disks appropriate for your single-user computer. You may not use
or transfer them to another user except as part of the permanent transfer (as provide

5. SAMPLE CODE. If the SOFTWARE includes Sample Code, then Microsoft gr
the sample code of the SOFTWARE provided that you: (a) distribute the sample cod
product; (b) do not use Microsoft's or its authors' names, logos, or trademarks to
notice that appears on the SOFTWARE on your product label and as a part of the si
to indemnify, hold harmless, and defend Microsoft and its authors from and agains
arise or result from the use or distribution of your software product.

DISCLAIMER OF WARRAN

Bibliofiche 297B

The SOFTWARE (including instructions for its use) is provided "AS IS" WITH
FURTHER DISCLAIMS ALL IMPLIED WARRANTIES INCLUDING WITHOUT LIMITATION ANY IMPLIED WARRAN-
TIES OF MERCHANTABILITY OR OF FITNESS FOR A PARTICULAR PURPOSE. THE ENTIRE RISK ARISING OUT OF
THE USE OR PERFORMANCE OF THE SOFTWARE AND DOCUMENTATION REMAINS WITH YOU.

IN NO EVENT SHALL MICROSOFT, ITS AUTHORS, OR ANYONE ELSE INVOLVED IN THE CREATION, PRODUCTION,
OR DELIVERY OF THE SOFTWARE BE LIABLE FOR ANY DAMAGES WHATSOEVER (INCLUDING, WITHOUT LIMI-
TATION, DAMAGES FOR LOSS OF BUSINESS PROFITS, BUSINESS INTERRUPTION, LOSS OF BUSINESS INFORMA-
TION, OR OTHER PECUNIARY LOSS) ARISING OUT OF THE USE OF OR INABILITY TO USE THE SOFTWARE OR
DOCUMENTATION, EVEN IF MICROSOFT HAS BEEN ADVISED OF THE POSSIBILITY OF SUCH DAMAGES. BECAUSE
SOME STATES/COUNTRIES DO NOT ALLOW THE EXCLUSION OR LIMITATION OF LIABILITY FOR CONSEQUEN-
TIAL OR INCIDENTAL DAMAGES, THE ABOVE LIMITATION MAY NOT APPLY TO YOU.

U.S. GOVERNMENT RESTRICTED RIGHTS

The SOFTWARE and documentation are provided with RESTRICTED RIGHTS. Use, duplication, or disclosure by the Government is subject to restrictions as set forth in subparagraph (c)(1)(ii) of The Rights in Technical Data and Computer Software clause at DFARS 252.227-
7013 or subparagraphs (c)(1) and (2) of the Commercial Computer Software — Restricted Rights 48 CFR 52.227-19, as applicable.
Manufacturer is Microsoft Corporation, One Microsoft Way, Redmond, WA 98052-6399.

If you acquired this product in the United States, this Agreement is governed by the laws of the State of Washington.

Should you have any questions concerning this Agreement, or if you desire to contact Microsoft Press for any reason, please write:
Microsoft Press, One Microsoft Way, Redmond, WA 98052-6399.

Register Today!

Return this
AFC Programmer's Guide
registration card for
a Microsoft Press® catalog

U.S. and Canada addresses only. Fill in information below and mail postage-free. Please mail only the bottom half of this page.

1-57231-732-9   *AFC PROGRAMMER'S GUIDE*   *Owner Registration Card*

_____

NAME

_____

INSTITUTION OR COMPANY NAME

_____

ADDRESS

_____

_____

CITY   STATE   ZIP

Microsoft®*Press*
Quality Computer Books

**For a free catalog of
Microsoft Press® products, call
1-800-MSPRESS**

BUSINESS REPLY MAIL
FIRST-CLASS MAIL   PERMIT NO. 53   BOTHELL, WA

POSTAGE WILL BE PAID BY ADDRESSEE

MICROSOFT PRESS REGISTRATION
AFC PROGRAMMER'S GUIDE
PO BOX 3019
BOTHELL   WA   98041-9946

NO POSTAGE
NECESSARY
IF MAILED
IN THE
UNITED STATES